# Culture, Subject, Psyche
Dialogues in Psychoanalysis and Anthropology

# Culture
# Subject
# Psyche

## Dialogues in Psychoanalysis and Anthropology

Edited with an Introduction by
ANTHONY MOLINO PHD

W
WHURR PUBLISHERS
LONDON AND PHILADELPHIA

© 2004 Anthony Molino and the Contributors
First published 2004
by Whurr Publishers Ltd
19b Compton Terrace
London N1 2UN England and
325 Chestnut Street, Philadelphia PA 19106 USA

All rights reserved. No part of this publication may be
reproduced, stored in a retrieval system, or transmitted in any form
or by any means, electronic, mechanical,
photocopying, recording or otherwise, without the prior
permission of Whurr Publishers Limited.

This publication is sold subject to the conditions that it shall not, by
way of trade or otherwise, be lent, resold, hired out, or otherwise
circulated without the publisher's prior consent in any form of
binding or cover other than that in which it is published and
without a similar condition including this condition being imposed
upon any subsequent purchaser.

**British Library Cataloguing in Publication Data**

A catalogue record for this book
is available from the British Library.

ISBN 1 86156 445 7

Typeset by Adrian McLaughlin, a@microguides.net
Printed and bound in the UK by Athenæum Press Ltd, Gateshead, Tyne & Wear.

# Contents

About the editor     vii
Contributors     ix
Editor's note     xi

## Part I    The Contexts of Dialogue     1

### Prologue     3

Shadow dialogues: on the (early) history of anthropology and psychoanalysis
*Wesley Shumar*

### Introduction     20

Rethinking relations between psychoanalysis and anthropology
*Anthony Molino*

## Part II    Dialogues in Psychoanalysis and Anthropology     43

Anthony Molino in conversation with:

1. Gananath Obeyesekere     45
2. Vincent Crapanzano     63
3. Katherine Ewing     80
4. Paul Williams     98
5. Michael Rustin     116
6. Kathleen Stewart     137
7. Marc Augé     156

**Part III  Afterword** 173

**Chapter 8** 175

Between desire and culture: conversations between psychoanalysis and anthropology
*Waud Kracke and Lucia Villela*

Index 211

# About the editor

**Anthony Molino** is a psychoanalyst and award-winning translator of Italian literature, as well as general editor of *Disseminations: Psychoanalysis in Contexts*, a series co-published by Wesleyan University Press (USA) and Continuum International (UK). He received his PhD in Anthropology from Temple University in Philadelphia in 1997. Based in Italy, he is best known for the books *Freely Associated: Encounters in Psychoanalysis* (FAB, 1997) and *The Couch and the Tree: Dialogues in Psychoanalysis and Buddhism* (FSG, 1998; Open Gate, 2001), for which he won a Gradiva Award from the National Association for the Advancement of Psychoanalysis in 1999. A member of the Site for Contemporary Psychoanalysis (London) and of the National Association for the Advancement of Psychoanalysis (New York), Dr Molino has also compiled the two-volume *Squiggles & Spaces: Revisiting the Work of D.W. Winnicott* (Whurr, 2001) and, with Christine Ware, edited *Where Id Was: Challenging Normalization in Psychoanalysis* (Continuum/Wesleyan, 2001).

# Contributors

**Wesley Shumar** holds a Master's degree in Cinema Studies and a PhD in Cultural Anthropology. Assistant Professor of Anthropology in the Department of Culture and Communication at Drexel University in Philadelphia, Dr Shumar is the author of *College for Sale: A Critique of the Commodification of Higher Education* (Falmer Press, 1997) and co-editor of *Building Virtual Communities: Learning and Change in Cyberspace* (Cambridge University Press, 2002). His research interests include psychoanalysis, higher education, virtual community, the semiotics of mass culture, and the articulation of selfhood as it relates today to personal and political issues of identity and globalization.

**Waud H. Kracke**, PhD, is Professor of Anthropology at the University of Illinois in Chicago, a research graduate of the Chicago Institute for Psychoanalysis, and a founding and faculty member of the Chicago Circle Association, affiliated with the 'Ecole Freudienne du Québec'. He is a member of the American Anthropological Association, of the International Federation for Psychoanalytic Education (IFPE), and of the Comité Scientifique of the journal *Savoir*. His publications include *Force and Persuasion: Leadership in an Amazonian Society* (a psychoanalytic-anthropological study of leadership among the Parintintin Indians of Brazil), and a number of articles, from a psychoanalytic perspective, on dreaming and culture shock in other cultures. The most recent of these include: 'Dreams of an Amazonian Insomniac' (*International Journal of Psychoanalysis*, 1999); 'Dream: Ghost of a Tiger, a System of Human Words' (in *Dreams and the Self*, edited by Jeannette Mageo, SUNY Press) and the 'Afterword' to *Dreamtravelers of the Western Pacific* (edited by Roger Lohmann, Palgrave).

**Lucia Villela**, PhD, was born in Taquaritinga, São Paulo, Brazil, and now practises psychoanalysis in Chicago. She is a founding and core faculty member of the Chicago Circle Association (affiliated with the 'Ecole Freudienne du Québec'), and a member of the 'Comité de Redaction' of the Journal *Savoir*. She has taught and published extensively on psychoanalytic theory, dreaming, culture and psychoanalysis, and cinema and psychoanalysis. Her many articles include: 'The Said and Unsaid of Self Psychology: The Question of Language' (*Psychoanalytic Psychology*, 1991, 24–42); 'The Fatal Attraction of Nostalgia' (*American Journal of Semiotics*, 1993, 13–26); 'The Return of the Repressed in Brazil' (*Journal for the Psychoanalysis of Culture and Society*, 1998); 'From Film as Case Study to Film as Myth' (*The Annual of Psychoanalysis*, 1999); 'Executors of an Ancient Pact', in Malone and Friedlander (eds), *The Subject of Lacan* (SUNY, 2000); and 'Western Perspective on a Film from the East: *Not One Less* (*Psychoanalytic Review*, 2003).

# Editor's note

My intent in compiling this book has been to reflect on issues of theory and practice within anthropology as they relate to and engage contemporary psychoanalysis – particularly on matters concerning subjectivity, the 'status' of the unconscious as an instrument of research, and contemporary conceptions of the self. In doing so, I've worked from an underlying assumption that synchronous developments are under way in both fields that warrant a renewal of the kind of cross-fertilization efforts that had, in the past, for many years characterized interdisciplinary research in anthropology and psychoanalysis. In the course of my research, I have sought to deploy a particular expertise doubly informed by my clinical experience as well as by an idiomatic sensibility akin to the ethnographer's. I refer, specifically, to a mode of interviewing which has, as one of its aims – above and beyond the mere collection of 'data' – the production of a text, of an 'object' at the crossroads of psychoanalysis and ethnography. It is, in fact, through my appropriation and transposition to anthropology of the *genre* of the interview – a literary and self-reflexive device to which psychoanalysts often resort, as a way of breaking their proverbial, confining professional silences – that I hope to have enhanced the interview's intrinsic value. For all of their field conversations and shop talk, anthropologists have traditionally been rather reticent to discuss their work – let alone their lives – in the context of in-depth interviews. Paradoxically, where the analyst committed to anonymity has frequently been known to indulge in the pleasures of self-revelation, the chatty ethnographer with the trusty tape-recorder rarely opens up. The relative novelty of such an exercise is, then, quite intriguing, as a representative group of notable fieldworkers is here engaged in a study which places the anthropologist in a peculiar role, one not unlike that of 'informant'.

From a methodological standpoint, I have invariably needed to work through my interlocutors' lenses – of their writings, scholarly interests, and personal sensibilities – to flesh out themes of particular concern to my research. It is in this sense that the interviews, or dialogues, all unfolded in a way that blended and made room – in varying degrees – for the intellectual and personal history of my interlocutors as well as for my own queries, imaginings and aesthetic experience. In this way I was greatly aided by my training as a psychoanalyst. While I obviously had a research 'agenda', and only a limited amount of time within which to collect the data I sought, I knew from experience that the very nature and quality of the encounter would be such as to invite the vagaries of memory, the rightful narcissistic pleasures of narrative, and my informants' own unspoken (and perhaps unconscious) agendas. In fact, the more successful and fluid the encounter, the more I could expect my counterpart to be emotionally engaged in the exercise. Thus inspired by a comparatist's mood and, dare I say, 'optimism', I was always aware of the need to be open to the vicissitudes of the dialogue. Time and again the trick was to strike a balance, allowing, in a way, for the 'space' created at the interstices of my request and the gift of my host's time, to expand and make room for both the pleasures of speech and the restrictions of work. In retrospect, I would argue that this very welcome but potentially distracting element of open-endedness – or, if you will, of 'ambiguity' – conferred something of an ethnographic dimension to my research.

Some explanation, at this point, is probably in order for my selection of the featured interviewees. In any work of this kind the people excluded are likely to outnumber those ultimately hosted. Where *Culture, Subject, Psyche* is concerned, moreover, among those not interviewed are researchers of exceptional stature: the names of Melford Spiro, Nancy Chodorow, Paul Assoun, Robert Paul, Gilbert Herdt, Sudhir Kakar, Alan Roland are among the first to come to mind. Except for Assoun and Kakar, however, the other names are of Americans, and it was my intention from the very conception of this project to reach beyond the confines of the United States, to the extent that resources allowed. This primary consideration, however, speaks more to my criteria for exclusion rather than inclusion. So let me begin by saying that I just as readily determined, from the start, that there were at least two figures in psychological anthropology whom I *could not* afford to neglect: namely, Vincent Crapanzano and Gananath Obeyesekere. Their work, in the field as in the academy, has in many ways set the standard for the generation or two of psychological anthropologists who've followed, and their publications are by and large recognized as contemporary classics destined to endure. I'm thinking, of course, of their landmark ethnographical studies, Obeyesekere's *Medusa's Hair: An Essay on Personal Symbols and Religious Experience* and Crapanzano's *Tuhami: Portrait of a Moroccan*, as well as of the corpus of essays both have produced: primarily, *The Work of Culture: Symbolic Transformations in Psychoanalysis and Anthropology*, which collects Obeyesekere's 1982 'Lewis Henry Morgan' lectures; and Crapanzano's *Hermes' Dilemma and Hamlet's Desire: On the Epistemology of Interpretation*, which among other pearls contains, as Waud Kracke evidences in the Afterword to this volume, one of the finer contributions that an anthropologist has made to psychoanalysis – the essay 'Text, Transference, and Indexicality'.

My other interlocutors were chosen for different reasons. Katherine Ewing arrived on the scene in the wake of Crapanzano and Obeyesekere, was deeply influenced by their work and, unlike her predecessors, actually underwent in-depth psychoanalytic training. This aspect is not to be neglected, as it is a rare choice among anthropologists who concern themselves with psychoanalysis. Ewing's many essays and long-standing research on psychoanalysis and anthropology, epitomized in *Arguing Sainthood: Modernity, Psychoanalysis, and Islam* (published in 1997, just as I was fine-tuning my own research), made me want to interview her. From outside the US, Marc Augé, I think, was an especially felicitous choice, especially when I think back at how I didn't know his work until I read an interview of his in the Italian edition of the *New York Review of Books* some years ago. Augé, arguably, sounds the territory of our problematic contemporary universe as perhaps no other anthropologist has, or can. His awareness of the intricacies of what I'll call, for lack of a less overused and abused term, our 'postmodern' predicament, bridges the intrapsychic and the communal in ways I find truly astounding. Books like *Non-Places*, or *The War of Dreams*, seem both years ahead of their time and as if they've been around forever. Working in that richest of recent anthropological, literary and philosophical traditions, the French, with Bachelard and Foucault, Barthes and Baudrillard, De Certeau and Girard (not to mention Lacan) among his nearest of kin, Augé offers us ways to rethink and image our inner and social worlds, our dreamscapes and cityscapes, that are crucial to a work like *Culture, Subject, Psyche*.

Where Paul Williams is concerned, I chose him because I believed it important to speak to at least one practising psychoanalyst who had trained in anthropology. Moreover, whereas my other interlocutors practically covered the corners of the globe with their fieldwork (Augé in Africa and Paris, Crapanzano in Morocco, Obeyesekere in Sri Lanka, Ewing in Pakistan, Stewart in Appalachia), Williams's own, with psychiatric patients in London's famed Maudsley Hospital, allowed for a privileged view into the workings of psychosis and the human mind that made for a dramatically different kind of conversation concerning psychoanalysis and anthropology. It is a conversation which points, in my estimation, to a potentially radical enrichment of contemporary anthropological theory.

The non-specialist may not know that the people discussed so far bring to their understandings of psychoanalysis different theoretical influences. Crapanzano's debt, aside from Freud, is by and large to Lacan, who also lurks around Augé. (Personally, I also sense Jung's presence in Augé's work, especially around his notion of the collective imaginary, but Augé himself disavowed any such link in our conversation.) Ewing and Obeyesekere, albeit in different ways (owing also to the decades that separate them age-wise), echo a world of American ego-psychology even as they fathom other sensibilities, like the Lacanian in Ewing's case. Williams is out of the British Psychoanalytical Society's Independent Group, a disciple of D.W. Winnicott and Nina Coltart. With him we enter the tradition of the object relationists, prefigured by Melanie Klein, whose own work was most significantly furthered by Wilfred Bion. With Michael Rustin, one of Europe's foremost social theorists (who also oversaw Paul Williams's doctoral research), we are treated to a unique appraisal of the applications of Klein and Bion's work, and of their largely ignored relevance to anthropology. I like to think that this fact alone, aside from Rustin's undisputed stature as one of Europe's finest and most respected social *scientists*, vouches for his presence here. Indeed, one of Rustin's more compelling and far-reaching arguments is the one made on behalf of psychoanalysis as a science in its own right, with no concessions made to those who would dismiss or demean it as pseudo-science.

Finally, a few words on my choice of Kathleen Stewart. At the time of our conversation in 1995, Kathleen was an especially young anthropologist just publishing her first book, *A Space on the Side of the Road: Cultural Poetics in an 'Other' America*. There is nothing *overtly* psychoanalytic about her work, no evident analytic influence, no reference even to Freud or his followers. But the intriguing aspect of Stewart's writing is her relentlessly creative struggle with the problematic notion of the self. Working to reproduce, throughout the pages of her ethnography, the self's performative dimensions, Stewart epitomizes *for me* the anthropologist whose striking theoretical elaborations (consider, for example, her idea of 'contamination') and literary representations of informants' lives lead invariably to the discoveries and intuitions of today's psychoanalysis. This may well sound presumptuous, but is a presumption which, as the author of *Culture, Subject, Psyche*, I'd like to think I can be afforded. It is a presumption, moreover, more than justified by the degree of enthusiasm, intelligence, and genuine dialogue with which Kathleen enriched our interview and opens new horizons for interdisciplinary discourse.

The idea for *Culture, Subject, Psyche* derives from my 1997 doctoral dissertation in Anthropology at Temple University in Philadelphia. The dissertation, and the book, could not have been completed without the support and dedication of a group of truly extraordinary people. Special thanks go to Professor Thomas Patterson, in his role at the time of Chairperson of the Anthropology Department's Graduate Committee. A particular debt of gratitude goes to my doctoral committee members, Professors Samuel Laeuchli, Denise O'Brien, and Wesley Shumar, and to the late Peter Rigby, all of whom contributed to specific aspects of my work and professional development. The collaboration with Wes, through ups and downs, has continued fruitfully to this day, and finds new and significant expression here in his Prologue.

# Editor's note

My fondest thanks go to my dissertation advisor, Professor Elmer Miller, to whom I dedicate *Culture, Subject, Psyche*. It was Elmer's own experimentation in his book *Nurturing Doubt*, where he tracks the ethnographer's pilgrimage across the interstices of personal history and motivation, of enduring memory and transformative field encounters, that inspired my original study. More importantly, it was Elmer who first suggested that I interview a group of anthropologists as part of my research, bringing to his advisor role two critical but often-neglected complementary attributes: the ability to identify and maximize a person's talents and skills, as well as a fundamental respect for his personal shortcomings. Needless to say, he has remained a constant and remarkable source of support in the long years following completion of the dissertation and its transformation into a book. For this I am doubly, triply grateful.

I also take this opportunity to acknowledge the essential and generous participation in the project of Gananath Obeyesekere, Kathleen Stewart, Vincent Crapanzano, Katherine Ewing, Michael Rustin, Marc Augé and Paul Williams. It is their work that is at the heart of this book, and enucleates a vision – as Lucia Villela and Waud Kracke suggest in their Afterword – for what may well be the future of the dialogue between psychoanalysis and anthropology. Lucia and Waud have themselves been the most precious of collaborators, whose wedded, daily dialogue as analyst and anthropologist is incarnated in their remarkable essay. Without their passionate contribution of interest, time and intellectual energy, over the course of a long and demanding year, this book could never have materialized.

Wesleyan's Tom Radko stood by this singular project through thick and thin for the better part of five years, while Colin Whurr helped rescue it when its publishing fate appeared seriously compromised. Joyce McDougall, Corinne Raclin and Marisa Roncato in Paris; Mike Eigen and Alan Roland in New York; Christopher and Suzanne Bollas, Pina Antinucci, Emily Rustin, Robin Baird-Smith and the late Nina Coltart in London; Joseph Finio, Christine Ware, and Susan Larkin in Philadelphia; and Fabio Gambaro, Luigi Billi, Laura Pampallona and my wife Marina closer to home here in Italy, have all been instrumental in helping me complete this book: some in the most practical of ways (translating, transcribing, offering hospitality), others in more emotionally demanding capacities. I thank them all for their invaluable assistance.

Finally, readers should note that the interview with Paul Williams was first published in *The International Journey of Psychotherapy* 4(1), 1999. My thanks to the journal's editors for permission to reprint our conversation.

Anthony Molino<br>
Vasto, Italy<br>
June 2004

# PART I
# THE CONTEXTS OF DIALOGUE

PROLOGUE
# Shadow dialogues: on the (early) history of anthropology and psychoanalysis

WESLEY SHUMAR

Vincent Crapanzano has suggested that anthropology and psychoanalysis are both dialogic practices involving 'shadow dialogues' whose absent interlocutors – in the field as in the treatment setting – are subject to what he calls 'the complex play of desire and power' (Crapanzano, 1992: 215). One of the aims of *Culture, Subject, Psyche* is to suggest that each discipline is, in turn, an absent interlocutor of the other – to the extent that both have been, in recent years at least, somewhat neglectful of the richness of each other's researches, and dismissive of the potential applications of each other's expertise. While the complex plays of desire and power operating in each direction may not always be immediately ascertainable (outside of the universalizing tendencies of psychoanalysis, or the territorial angst of anthropology in its unchecked diffusion across the territory of the human sciences), the respective foreclosures of each discipline vis-à-vis the other are, I would argue, unequivocal.

Regarding the foreclosure of psychoanalysis to anthropology, I cite from a book entitled *In Search of Self in India and Japan*, by the American psychoanalyst Alan Roland, throughout which the author laments 'the overwhelming orientation of Freudian psychoanalysis to intrapsychic phenomena' as it generally ignores 'how historical, social, and cultural patterns shape the inner world' (Roland, 1988: xvii). Referring to the earlier discoveries of Copernicus and Darwin, and their displacing effects on a self-centred orientation to the cosmos, Roland has this to say about Freud's own intuitions: 'Perhaps we should now add a further blow to the self esteem of Western man: the realization that the prevailing psychological maps and norms assumed to be universal are in fact Western-centric' (ibid.).

Conversely, from the point of view of anthropology, the discipline's historical bias against psychoanalysis is outlined in a fine article by Katherine P. Ewing entitled 'Is psychoanalysis relevant for anthropology?' (Ewing,

1992). Here the representational insufficiency of psychoanalysis as a tool of anthropological enquiry is seen to derive historically from two determining factors: (1) the foreclosure operated against psychoanalysis by the interpretivism of Clifford Geertz (in light of Geertz's emphasis on 'public' and 'shared' phenomena as the lone appropriate objects of ethnographic investigation);[1] and (2) the purported unacknowledged debt accrued with psychoanalysis by the likes of Claude Lévi-Strauss and Victor Turner.[2] In the essays and interviews here collected, Anthony Molino builds on Ewing's analysis to explore the 'absent interlocutor' that psychoanalysis is for anthropology. The premise for such an exercise is that, given the preoccupation in anthropology and other disciplines with issues of subjectivity and the construction of the self, the time is ripe for a new wave of interdisciplinary work between psychoanalysis and anthropology that can counter both the reductionist applications of a long-outdated psychoanalysis as well as anthropology's somewhat ossified understanding of what psychoanalysis is all about. Indeed, as there is a general tendency for intellectual work to be insular, ideas are often not shared across disciplines, which has made it difficult for anthropology to be alerted to new trends and developments in psychoanalytic theory and technique. It is against this insularity that an approach is outlined which can make room, if not for distinctly psychoanalytic 'applications', for a psychoanalytic sensibility that might be brought to bear on ethnographic understandings of the self and its representations. An aim, then, of this book, is to engage more fully the very shadow dialogues that inhabit the spaces between the two disciplines, in an attempt to revive and sustain between them the kind of agonistic relationship that Vincent Crapanzano (1992) envisions in his essay entitled 'Talking (about) psychoanalysis'. In the words of Crapanzano:

> Relationships between individuals, institutions, or disciplines that surrender the agonistic approach to facile affirmations of harmony and accord are in danger of losing the vigour, critical reflection and creativity that come with the disquieting knowledge that the world may indeed appear differently to those with whom we engage. Even more disquieting is the knowledge that there is no knowledge complete in and of itself, but only a thinking that aspires to a knowing. Such, I like to think, was Freud's project; and such is the project of any psychoanalysis; and such is the project of an anthropology that has the courage to accept its own mission. It is in terms of this thinking that any meaningful engagement between disciplines or people has to occur. (Crapanzano, 1992: 153–4)

In these pages, I look to chart the genuinely agonistic origins of these 'shadow dialogues', discussing some of the early twentieth-century historical relationships between anthropology and psychoanalysis. From the work of Bronislaw Malinowski and Alfred Kroeber, two of the most influential anthropologists of the early twentieth century, through the development of the culture-and-personality school, there has been a rich tradition of work in anthropology drawing on psychoanalysis. But while this chapter will not provide anything like a comprehensive history of the relationship between anthropology and psychoanalysis,[3] it will suggest that two central processes set the stage for future relations between the two fields. First, the attacks on psychoanalysis and particularly on Freud's anthropology by Kroeber and, in much more detail, Malinowski (Kroeber, 1979a; Malinowski, 1924, 1927; Stocking, 1986). Secondly, the significant developments of Kardiner's psychoanalytic model of the self in conjunction with his work with anthropologists (LeVine, 1982; Manson, 1986). My contention is that a particular process of memory-and-forgetting concerning these historical events has long set the stage for the current, prevailing view of psychoanalysis among anthropologists.

## The early history of anthropology and psychoanalysis

Jacques LeGoff (1992) has suggested that memory and forgetting are central to the process of history. These processes are both individual and collective and are themselves another bridge between the psychoanalytic and the social. I would argue that the vast majority of American cultural anthropologists, like the dominant intellectual culture in the United States, sees psychoanalysis in a particular and often negative way. That view is itself a construct of a sort of logical argument that exists in the culture, and that argument depends on some specific processes of memory and forgetting.

The first component of this argument is that Freud is synonymous with psychoanalysis. This idea exists in a kind of 'double think' because while many intellectuals are very aware of Jung and Adler and may even know of some other psychoanalytic thinkers, when they critique psychoanalysis they critique Freud. In anthropology this would be similar to equating Franz Boas with anthropology.[4] While it is certainly true that Boas, who founded the anthropology department at Columbia University, was the key figure in establishing an 'American School' of anthropology and helped form the mindset of the country's first anthropologists (Stocking, 1974), it is also true that many anthropologists have long since moved through and beyond the Boasian framework. Likewise, Freud is one moment – albeit the founding one – in the development of psychoanalysis that many psychoanalysts have also moved beyond. The second component to the argument is that Freud engaged in armchair research and did not take the existing data about human societies into consideration. He was more concerned with propounding his universal theories than with the actual data he encountered. And, finally, the last step of this logical argument is that psychoanalysis is, consequently, really an ideology and not a legitimate field of enquiry precisely because it is synonymous with the failings of Freud.

Specifically in anthropology we have the moments of Malinowski's encounter and later rejection of Freud's ideas, and Kroeber's critique of Freud's *Totem and Taboo* and *Moses and Monotheism*. The complex history of Malinowski's encounter with Freud is not well known, even though most contemporary anthropologists are familiar with Malinowski's critique of Freud in *Sex and Repression in Savage Society*. Kroeber's work, instead, is better known, and his critiques of Freud's anthropology are both very concise and often used to introduce students to the dangers of universalism and armchair anthropology. They stand as a sign of the classic relationship of anthropology to psychoanalysis.

It is certainly true that Freud and the early analysts he 'fathered' contributed to this view of psychoanalysis. They are part of what is remembered. But what is often forgotten is the ways in which Freudian analysis was, in point of fact, sometimes based on very careful observation yielding many important insights.[5] Further, what is forgotten is that psychoanalysts of later generations have moved beyond Freud and opened up new theoretical vistas. One instance of such a new direction occurred directly in an encounter with anthropology, through the groundbreaking seminars Abram Kardiner held at the New York Psychoanalytic Institute in 1936 and 1937.[6] While Malinowski and Kroeber's critiques are well known, Kardiner's work is all but forgotten. I propose looking here at each of these stories, of Kroeber, Malinowski, and Kardiner, to see just how this process of memory and forgetting got instituted.

Alfred Kroeber (1876–1960) was Boas's first student in anthropology, at a time when anthropology as a profession was just beginning. In fact, he earned only the second PhD to be awarded in anthropology in the United States, and went on to help establish the department of anthropology at the University of California at Berkeley, where he became Full Professor in 1919. Kroeber's critique of psychoanalysis came at the same time that he was deeply interested in psychoanalysis (Manson, 1986: 75). There are two central articles Kroeber wrote. In 1920 he first published a critique of Freud's *Totem and Taboo*; later, in 1939, he published another critique of Freud's anthropological ideas (Kroeber, 1979a, 1979b). In Kroeber's analysis there are essentially three levels of critique. First, he argues that what Freud suggests is not necessarily logically consistent. His second point is a supposed lack in Freud of ethnographic evidence to support his theorizing. (For instance, Kroeber questions the idea that there would be logical connections between the father and the totemic animal, of the expulsion of the sons from an original society, or of connections between blood sacrifice and totemism, etc.) Finally Kroeber notes that the persistence of these originary ideas into modern society would require some sort of model to explain how that happened.

Kroeber is particularly careful to show that there is little ethnographic support for the Oedipal story put forth in *Totem and Taboo*, arguing instead that much ethnographic work exists to challenge the idea. This critique is, of course, consistent with modern-day ideas that deny the historical precedence of patrilineal and patriarchal systems over matrilineal kinship systems. Kroeber is vehement about Freud's failure to look at the research data and about his attachment to the theory irrespective of the data. It should be noted here that at the time of Kroeber's second critique, psychoanalysis was particularly strong in the US. It is clear that Kroeber conceives of psychoanalysis as being a part of the social sciences. And it is equally clear that he saw value in a science that could explain some of the psychic mechanisms of the individual and how these might intersect with the social. There is no doubt, then, that psychoanalysis for Kroeber was important, but needed to be transformed. It needed to adjust its theories to the extant data and develop as a science. This is something he saw Freud resisting, but nevertheless assumed would happen. It is worth remembering, as a result, that when we read Kroeber's critique today it is not in a context where psychoanalysis strongly appeals to anthropology, but in a context that forcefully criticizes it as a pseudo-science.

Polish-born Bronislaw Malinowski (1884–1942) earned a PhD at the University of Krakow and a second doctorate at the London School of Economics. Often credited with being the father of modern-day participant observation, Malinowski spent several years (1915–18) in the Trobriand Islands doing fieldwork. Out of that research he published in 1922 *Argonauts of the Western Pacific*, to this day considered a classic of ethnographic writing. One of the best treatments of his relationship to psychoanalysis is that of George Stocking (1986). Stocking points out that several factors shape Malinowski's interest in psychoanalysis. Theoretically, Malinowski was very interested in both reason and the passions (Stocking, 1986: 17). Stocking shows how Malinowski is pulled as a young scholar by both positivism and romanticism, a dual pull that nicely sets the stage for Malinowski's interests in a psychoanalytic model of the self that is constructed out of reason and emotion. Stocking further shows how Malinowski rejects the models of collective subjectivity put forward by Emile Durkheim.[7] According to Malinowski, Durkheim basically cheated in his model of the collective and the individual. He did this by attributing social phenomena to collective processes, but when explaining these processes he resorted often to notions of individual subjectivity. For Malinowski, all social phenomena must ultimately come out of 'individual psychic processes' (Stocking, 1986: 21). Finally, Stocking points out that Malinowski was a 'highly eroticized' individual whose libidinal energies and contradictions fuelled a good part of his theoretical thinking and creativity, as well as some of the contradictions in his personal life. It was for these reasons, Stocking argues, that Malinowski's interest in Freud's libido theory was so marked.

The libido theory was very important to Malinowski because it allowed him to think about the connection between individual consciousness and social institutions in a way that he believed Durkheim had failed to do. Malinowski took Freud's Oedipus complex and made it relative to the social formation and family structure in which desiring individuals exist. It was along these lines that Malinowski made the famous observation that in the matrilineal structure of Trobriand society one did not find the classic European Oedipus complex. Rather, what presented was a situation where the intrapsychic developmental process was not in conflict with the external family structure, thus allowing libidinal development to continue in an unrestricted fashion. He further argued that unimpeded sexual development was the main reason why Trobriand society remained backward and less developed as a whole. There is no contradictory mechanism pushing individuals to sublimate their desires into the social and cultural arenas of life (Stocking, 1986: 35–8).

Malinowski's reconstruction of libido theory met with a good bit of resistance. It was resisted by the Freudian orthodoxy which saw the Oedipus complex as not something that could be influenced by external familial structures, but as something internal to the individual and universal. Stocking (1986: 38) points out that in 1924, when Malinowski is presenting his revisions of Freudian theory, there were internal divisions that were creating tensions in the psychoanalytic ranks. This moment, then, was one when psychoanalysts were not particularly open to change, and Malinowski's theory could only be rejected outright. We see then how Malinowski developed his critique of the orthodox Freudian position along lines similar to Kroeber. While there was certainly in Kroeber, and perhaps in others, anthropological support for Malinowski's critique of Freudian theory, there is however also a psychoanalytic critique of Malinowski in the anthropological ranks later articulated by Melford Spiro (1982). Spiro will return to the Trobriand Islands and suggest that the Trobriand denial of paternity was in fact not a reality. Malinowski had missed important aspects of Trobriand social life that led him to take the native denial of the knowledge of paternity at face value.

It is at this moment that psychoanalysis begins to slip away from the anthropological interest in England. Stocking is interested in this fading from view and so offers a few ideas about why this forgetting originates. He points out that Malinowski is now better known for his critique of the Freudian orthodoxy than for his development of a revisionist libido theory. The main reason for this, in Stocking's (1986: 42) view, is that Malinowski never systematically developed his new theory. He spoke out against the Oedipus complex but did not produce a work that systematically developed his own theoretical position. This is unfortunate, because Malinowski was perhaps one of the earliest anthropologists to recognize that a model for understanding the self and subjectivity is very important in understanding the relationship of structure to agency, and how one can move from the level of individuals to the level of social institutions. There can be no question, along these lines, that Malinowski today is remembered more as a writer and ethnographer than as a theorist.

While interest in psychoanalysis never developed very much beyond Malinowski among British anthropologists,[8] American anthropologists were very interested in psychoanalysis. In passing, suffice it to say that Margaret Mead and Ruth Benedict, both students of Boas, had developed an early interest in psychoanalysis and Freud's libido theory. Mead was particularly interested in child-rearing practices and their influence on adult personality and the culture at-large. Edward Sapir, also heavily influenced by Boas (he received his PhD at Columbia in 1909), first at Chicago and then at Yale developed a strong interest in psychoanalysis. But where psychoanalysis and American anthropology are concerned, I limit my focus here to Abram Kardiner's seminar on culture and personality. It is my impression, in fact, that Kardiner, among the Americans and particularly in his collaboration with Linton and DuBois, did the most to advance the use of psychoanalytic models in anthropology.[9]

More systematically than Malinowski, Abram Kardiner provided an important revision to Freudian libido theory with his ideas of the basic personality type (LeVine, 1982; Manson, 1986). Kardiner briefly trained as an anthropologist under Boas before returning to medical school and his psychiatric training (Manson, 1986: 74). From the beginning it appeared that he was sensitive to the dynamic interplay between the individual and the cultural spheres. Manson points out that a cluster of historical events paved the way for a kind of development of a 'critical mass' between what he calls the 'culturalist' (e.g. Horney, Sullivan, Fromm) psychoanalysts and anthropology (Manson, 1986: 78). Critical to this development was, on the one hand, the culturalist rejection of drive theory and any universal biological basis of human development in favour of a greater influence attributed to the environment.[10] The culturalist movement, as a result, made it possible for psychoanalysts to begin to think about other forms, or modes, of personality development. On the other hand, it was the interest in psychoanalytic models of Mead, Benedict, Sapir, DuBois,

Linton and others – core figures of a dynamic group of Columbia anthropologists – that helped generate this novel, albeit diversified, interdisciplinary approach. Indeed, Manson points out that the anthropologists were not necessarily all in agreement in their appreciation of psychoanalysis, with Mead and Benedict[11] being more influenced by orthodox drive theory and Linton and DuBois more partial to the ideas of revisionists like Horney. Nonetheless, it was the activities of this group that eventually led to Kardiner's culture and personality seminars at the New York Psychoanalytic Institute. While overall interest in psychoanalysis remained fairly low, in this context a group of noteworthy anthropologists and psychoanalysts – including Benedict, Sapir, Horney, and Brill – came together to explore questions and themes concerning the relationship between personality and culture. In 1936, Cora DuBois joined Kardiner's seminar as a post-doctoral research fellow, and was instrumental in advancing Kardiner's work (Manson, 1986: 79).

It was during this time, in fact, that Kardiner, along with other revisionist psychoanalysts, begins to reject the universality of libido theory and to replace it with a theory of 'adaptational psychodynamics', a model whereby the ego adapts to both internal and external pressures (Manson, 1986: 80). This model, in part through the fruitful collaboration of Ralph Linton, was to develop into the 'basic personality structure' for which Kardiner is known. Linton, who unlike Boas was very interested in psychoanalysis, encouraged the work of Kardiner's seminar and presented data on his own fieldwork there. Manson (1986: 81) points out that Linton's arrival at Columbia and his chairmanship of the Anthropology department was quite significant, insofar as it was his support for Kardiner that made the latter's seminars possible. (In time, Linton's presence also overshadowed that of Benedict, who then pulled out of Kardiner's seminar.) Ultimately, it was Linton's own participation in the seminar and presentation of his fieldwork on the Marquessans that would inspire Kardiner to formulate his theory of the basic personality structure.

Kardiner's argument runs something like this. It is inevitable that out of the contradictions that inhere in primary institutions, or in the sociocultural contexts in which infants are raised, certain traumas will occur. In this model, the focus is not on universal drives, but on the budding but tested ego's response to the limitations of maternal and environmental provision. These early childhood traumas will later be projected upon what Kardiner calls 'secondary institutions', in such a way that religion and belief systems in general will come to reflect the deprivations of childhood and give birth to gods with ambivalent features (i.e. features that reflect the intermittent nature of early maternal care).

Kardiner argued that primary institutions were those to which the individual was required to adapt socially. They create the basic problems confronting the ego, generating forces that produce widespread individual patterns like the Oedipus complex (Kardiner, 1939; LeVine, 1982; Manson, 1986: 84). The personalities produced by these primary institutions then play a major role in the production of secondary institutions, as unconscious projective systems both define and help individuals identify with social movements, religious institutions, etc.[12] Cora DuBois elaborated Kardiner's approach with her fieldwork from Alor. She developed a statistical construct for what she called a 'modal personality type' in contrast to Kardiner's basic personality. This allowed her to escape the difficulties of the idea that the same basic personality is produced in all individuals (DuBois, 1944).

Kardiner's work was extremely significant. As LeVine (1982) and others point out, his approach helped develop one of the strongest non-reductive approaches to culture and personality studies. At the same time, this approach provided a critique and major revision of the Freudian orthodoxy from an anthropologically informed psychoanalytic perspective. The model Kardiner develops is an important first effort in understanding the construction of the self and the impact of the unconscious on culture in a psychoanalytic framework. This work will later be developed by Whiting and Child (1953) and their colleagues. Kardiner's framework will remain one of the important models in modern psychological anthropology.[13]

Over time, the psychoanalytic ideas of figures like Malinowski, Kardiner and DuBois begin to slip from centre stage into relative obscurity, except to be salvaged by a few specialists in psychological anthropology who continue to work with them. This particular instance of historical forgetting, however, is somewhat difficult to understand in the case of Kardiner, who unlike Malinowski had carefully worked out a theory of personality and its relationship to culture. Manson gives us several clues about this fading from public view. First, Linton left Columbia and with him went a lot of support for Kardiner's seminar. Mead and Benedict were more interested in libido theory and went on to develop their interests elsewhere. With the advent of World War II, anthropologists began studying culture from a distance, paying greater attention as a result to more reductive approaches like Benedict's psychology of culture. Perhaps it is also the case that as anthropology moved into the second half of the century, like many other disciplines it too became increasingly specialized. The ideas of Kardiner, important as they may be for understanding the relationship of individuals to culture (and for what today is referred to as structure and agency), became the ideas of specialists in psychological anthropology and less well-known to the community of anthropologists at-large.

Early in the twentieth century the researches of anthropology and psychoanalysis were very much bound up with each other. As Melford Spiro says in the introduction to *Oedipus among the Trobrianders*, both disciplines were trying to understand incest prohibitions, totemism and the question of the Oedipus complex. These shared concerns, along with a concern to understand how one moves from individual behaviour to collective representations, led many anthropologists and psychoanalysts to work together. But as interests and concerns became more specialized and divergent, a particular history was reinvented.

The reinvented history is not shared by all and is certainly not the official history. Sometimes very important folk models held by anthropologists persist because they cannot be held up to public scrutiny but represent some important aspects of a current ideological configuration (Rosaldo, 1989). This particular unofficial history, as I've already suggested, has also come to mirror the wave of Freud-bashing that has become very popular in the last few years, especially in the United States.[14] It is a version of history that makes Kroeber and Malinowski into early cultural relativists who critiqued the irrationality of the Freudian universalist view and hence were among the first to foretell the death of psychoanalysis. Instead, the efforts of Kardiner and DuBois, as well as of other psychoanalytically oriented anthropologists, to push Freudian theory in new directions is completely forgotten by the general anthropological community. The end-result is that while the anthropological consciousness is obviously aware of its own development as a field in the course of more than a century, its images of psychoanalysis remain linked to the century-old ideas of Freud and the limitations of the orthodox Freudians. Thus, the anthropological view of psychoanalysis arguably derives from processes not dissimilar from those that Fabian (1983) suggests anthropologists use routinely to reify the 'other' in a denial of a shared coevalness. Fabian's notion is that in the process of moving from fieldwork to ethnographic writing, anthropology constructs an Other who is made to live in a separate time and place. This denial of a shared world, of a shared time and space, makes for a breach of ethics, as it moves the ethnographer to ignore the common humanity of his informants and the obligations that might inhere in his relationship with them. In a similar way, I am suggesting that anthropology has 'othered' psychoanalysis, relegating it to a mythical time and space. Indeed, for many anthropologists, psychoanalysis is a field that has not changed since the days of Kroeber, Malinowski and Kardiner.

There is one exception to this pattern and that is Lacan. If one looks at references in the current anthropological literature, amidst a dearth of psychoanalytic works cited the name of Lacan stands out, along with but a few others also in the French tradition (i.e. Kristeva, Irigaray, key figures in feminist discourse). To some extent this may well reflect the profound impact of French structuralism and poststructuralism on anthropological thinking. But it may also represent the need for a model of the psyche in anthropological research.[15]

In the pages that follow, one of Anthony Molino's claims is that anthropological research is attempting to understand the globalizing forces of capitalism as they impact peoples and cultures around the world. The processes of social change are complex, taking place on a scale unimaginable until only recently. One reaction to these problems has been for anthropologists to retreat into questions of representation and into the uncertainty of any research that attempts to draw a picture of what is going on in the world. This is certainly understandable as a reaction, and perhaps even important as long as it does not become too solipsistic an exercise. Another reaction is to try and trace the lines of force and the ways in which power relations constitute subjects and objects in the new world order. This is why the work of Foucault has been so important to so many contemporary anthropologists. But at the same time there is a need to understand the ways in which those power relations get interiorized in the process of constituting subjects.[16] While produced in a social context, desire only comes into problematic existence when mediated by the human psyche (Butler, 1993). A model of the psyche, it follows, is necessary if we are to understand the complex interactions between inner and outer, between personal and public spheres, and the ways these interactions are currently shaped. A first step in this process, as I've tried to illustrate here, is for anthropology to rethink its own past and realize that its ideas about psychoanalysis are to a significant extent shaped by a discursive process that has reduced psychoanalysis to a reified 'other'. A second step is one this book takes, in Anthony Molino's conversations with Gananath Obeyeskere, Vincent Crapanzano, Katherine Ewing, Paul Williams, Kathleen Stewart, Michael Rustin, and Marc Augé. In these conversations, we witness a vital, engaging attempt to move the dialogue between anthropology and psychoanalysis out of the shadows and into the fragmented but dazzling light of our bewildered times: into non-places (Augé) and marginal places (Stewart's Appalachia) alike, into the unfamiliar spaces of Islam (Ewing) and psychosis (Williams). In doing so, Molino not only rescues aspects of the history of that dialogue (particularly through the evocations of Obeyeskere and Crapanzano, and of Rustin where the UK is concerned), but maps out new and fruitful areas of interdisciplinary work that may well constellate and mark the future of any dialogue between the two disciplines. Indeed, the blueprint for such work is here.

In point of fact, each of Molino's interviews highlights aspects of contemporary psychoanalytic thought that are critical for anthropology, sociology and cultural theory to consider. Where Bradd Shore (1996) suggests that basic anthropological questions concerning the psychic unity of mankind, the location of culture, and the relationship of individual to culture now need to take into account the revolution in the cognitive sciences, I would argue that there has been a parallel failure in anthropology to deal with the affective spheres of social life and social interaction. It is Molino's awareness of this failure that leads him, in his conversations with Obeyesekere, Ewing, Williams and Crapanzano, to elicit reflections on the distinct need to take the emotional and mental life of informants into consideration. Along these lines, Obeyesekere and Ewing remind us that if we fail to understand how a person's emotional life, unconscious motivations and social contexts all interrelate, we fail to see how new culture is produced and how that very production in turn relates to the culture from and within which it was generated.

From another angle, Crapanzano and Williams show us how the tools of psychoanalysis and attention to the emotional life of informants are important to fathom the powerful kinds of emotions that the ethnographic encounter releases and the forms of cathexis that occur between informant and ethnographer. Michael Rustin elaborates these insights on something of a different plane, pinpointing as he does the ways in which psychoanalysis can contribute to the development of a 'realist science', in an attempt to model the structures underlying social situations and contexts. It is a short step for Rustin, from this kind of groundwork, to emphasize then the value of psychoanalysis in understanding the significant ways in which individuals relate to institutions. Where Augé and Stewart are concerned, both engage psychoanalysis to understand how desire works in contemporary societies and is ubiquitously deployed in relations of power.

These themes, in my estimation, cannot be disregarded by contemporary cultural theory, ethnography and anthropology, especially given their implications for many of the major theoretical issues being debated. Suffice it here to list: the relationship between public and private realms; structure versus agency; issues of voice, power and representational authority; post-positivist critiques of science; and the very status of the concept of 'culture'. When social scientists turn to psychoanalysis to address these issues it is either to critique an old and outmoded version of psychoanalysis and its inability to speak to contemporary issues, or to turn to Lacan. Of course, Lacan's work is certainly important here and is a major influence in the work of Augé and Stewart. But what Molino's book will show, and this is one of its distinctive contributions, is that Lacan's work itself needs to be contextualized in the broader discourse of contemporary psychoanalysis. For instance, the recent social theorizing of Slavoj Žižek (1989, 1997) has looked to the work of Lacan in order to establish a 'real' or a ground upon which social constructions are imagined and built. And he further looks to Lacan to define a process by which we can understand those social constructions. But Lacan's work, in the Freudian tradition, looks primarily to the post-Oedipal construction of subjectivity, and therefore presupposes the formation of a linguistic and discursive self. What *Culture, Subject, Psyche* explores, above and beyond the discourse and applications of what is admittedly an ever-rich Lacanian hermeneutic,[17] are the potential infusions of other psychoanalytic traditions. Among these, first and foremost, is the object relations tradition, which has sounded the pre-Oedipal world and devised new models for understanding unconscious communication and the ways in which desire impacts and shapes our universes of meaning. But this is just one of the schools of thought, just one of the branches of a vigorous psychoanalytic tree, that Molino's book investigates. Indeed, there is a tremendous range of unrecognized material in contemporary psychoanalysis, and it is one of the merits of *Culture, Subject, Psyche* to bring some of it out of the shadows and to the attention of anthropologists and cultural theorists working today. In so doing, the dialogues in this book provide us, as social scientists, with an invaluable resource to make better sense of the complex relationships between individuals and the social contexts in which we all live, work, and love.

## Notes

1. Clifford Geertz's interpretivism marks a watershed in the study of culture. By locating cultural symbols outside the private sphere, the Geertzian tradition separated psychic process from the cultural realm, and altogether ignored any appreciation of the unconscious. Such was the power of this tradition that even psychoanalytically oriented anthropologists participated in the Geertzian transformation. In anthropology, the later development of structuralism (Lévi-Strauss, Leach, Turner, etc.) led to a brief rapprochement between psychoanalysis and anthropology as scholars began to think about the unconscious in culture. But this trend quickly shifted towards Marxist and post-Marxist approaches which, like the work of Geertz, externalized all cultural symbols and limited the role of psychic processes in culture. On the subject of Geertz's influence, see Anthony Molino's 'Rethinking relations between psychoanalysis and anthropology' in this volume.
2. Where Turner is concerned, his paper 'Encounter with Freud: the making of a comparative symbologist', appeared rather late in his career (1978). It may be of interest here to note how two Italian psychoanalysts are now pursuing aspects of Turner's work, particularly in an exercise comparing and contrasting his notion of liminality (and its original conception in Van Gennep (1960), with D.W. Winnicott's theorization of transitional spaces – all this in the context of a major study on termination in psychoanalysis. See Ferraro and Garella (2001).
3. For something of a comprehensive overview of the history of relations between the two disciplines, see Chodorow (1999).

4. Franz Boas (1858–1942) became professor of anthropology at Columbia in 1899. As an aside, it may be of some interest to note that Boas attended Freud's lectures at Clark University in September 1909. Donn (1988) writes: 'Dr. Franz Boas, the renowned anthropologist, had given up one of his hours to speak so that Freud might lecture [and was] "enthusiastic over the sacrifice"' (p. 104).
5. See Anthony Molino's interview with Michael Rustin in this volume. Calling on the work of Bruno Latour, Rustin argues quite cogently that the careful clinical practice of psychoanalysis strongly resembles a scientist's laboratory where data are yielded and collected. Rustin's argument is rooted in a far-reaching critique of empiricism more broadly articulated in his book *The Good Society and the Inner World* (Rustin, 1991; see especially chapter 5, titled 'Psychoanalysis, philosophical realism, and the new sociology of science') and finds its clearest statement in his recent *Reason and Unreason: Psychoanalysis, Science, and Politics* (Rustin, 2001; see especially chapter 2, 'Give me a consulting room: the generation of psychoanalytic knowledge').
6. See pp. 9–12 of this essay, and especially Barnouw (1973: 148–9), concerning Ralph Linton's years at Columbia University and his influence on Kardiner's seminar there.
7. Emile Durkheim (1858–1917) put forth one of the first social theories to suggest that individual behaviour and thinking are influenced by larger social forces. The question for Durkheim was the location of these social structures that influence behaviour. With the notion of 'collective representations' he suggested that collectively held ideas about the world, magical powers, the nature of life, and so on, influenced the attitudes and behaviours of groups of people. But while Durkheim understood that real material pressures, such as food shortage or power relations, might create these collective representations, he did not clearly articulate the relationship of these representations to the individual psyche. On the idea of collective representations, see Durkheim (1926, 1965, 1967).
8. On this score, see Anthony Molino's interviews with Paul Williams and Michael Rustin in this volume.
9. Kardiner was himself in analysis with Freud in 1921. See Kardiner (1977).
10. Seen essentially as developers of Alfred Adler's individual psychology, Karen Horney, Harry Stack Sullivan and Erich Fromm have also been referred to as 'neo-psychoanalysts'. In his monumental study *The Discovery of the Unconscious*, Henri Ellenberger has this to say of the movement: 'The role of instinct is played down and emphasis is laid on the role of the environment, particularly of interpersonal relationships. Man is no longer conceived as a naturally anxious and destructive being. Instead of analysing the conflicts between the id, ego, and superego, current patterns of behaviour are analysed in the form of neurotic styles' (Ellenberger, 1970: 638). Ellenberger goes on, of course, to detail distinctions between this group and the more loyal followers of Freud, but here we already intuit a sensibility akin to that of Kardiner.
11. Margaret Mead (1901–78) did fieldwork in New Guinea and Bali during the 1930s. She published several important works on childhood, most notably *Growing Up in New Guinea* (Mead, 1930). She also collaborated with Gregory Bateson both on several photographic essays, as well as on series of films on child-rearing. Ruth Benedict (1887–1948) studied under Boas and later taught at Columbia from 1923 to 1948. Margaret Mead was a student of hers before they became friends. See Benedict (1934, 1946).

12. Kardiner argues that a given culture would produce among its members somewhat typical traumas and forms of reactive personality.
13. Barnouw (1973: 176) points out that Whiting and Child (1953) saw child-rearing practices as influenced by the social, economic and political structures of society. These practices produce personality characteristics that lead to particular projective systems. He further points out this is very similar to Kardiner's model. Manson (1986: 89), citing LeVine (1982: 56), makes a similar point about Whiting and Child.
14. On the recent wave of Freud-bashing, see Williams (2001).
15. A very recent ethnography that tries to develop a model capable of not only situating a group of people historically, structurally and culturally, but that can make sense of the subjective experiences of actors and fieldworker alike is Katherine Ewing's *Arguing Sainthood: Modernity, Psychoanalysis and Islam* (1997). In this book, informed by the work of Lacan, Ewing shows how the Sufi Pir is not only a construct of colonialism and the post-colonial state, but how the Islam articulated through this figure structures the fears, desires, and longings of the people in the local community.

    Interestingly, while Ewing's is one of the few efforts to take up the challenge of using psychoanalysis to analyse the forms of consciousness produced by external historical conditions, she too does not go much beyond a Lacanian analysis – even though she would like to (see Ewing (1997: 270), for her take on Lacan). Rejecting, for example, Lacan's premise that the symbolic order constitutes the speaking subject, she argues that 'access to the world unmediated by language is not only possible but constitutive of many aspects of subjective experience . . .': a conviction that would find much sympathy, say, in the British tradition of psychoanalysis stemming from D.W. Winnicott. But as Ewing herself points out, anthropology had long reduced the psychoanalytic tradition to Freud while largely ignoring, until recently, even Lacan. A goal of hers was to bring Lacan into the discourse. An invigorated dialogue requires that anthropologists now go a step further and look to include the work of a new generation of heretofore neglected psychoanalysts. To this end, see Anthony Molino's Introduction ('Rethinking relations between psychoanalysis and anthropology', Chapter 1, below) and the interviews collected in this volume.
16. A most important work in this direction is Anthony Elliott's *Subject to Ourselves: Social Theory, Psychoanalysis and Postmodernity* (1996). In this work, the psychoanalysis that Elliott privileges – that of the British School, primarily, together with the contributions of Lacan and Kristeva even more notably – is one that challenges dominant notions and approaches to the study of subjectivity by insisting on the vital force of *fantasy* as a crucial if not defining element of what it means to be human. This very element is then seen to be 'subjected' to – even as it engages, reinterprets, and individually refashions – the convulsive and kaleidoscopic interplay of social forces that are the hallmark of postmodernity. Not content with constructing an elaborate but self-sufficient theoretical edifice, Elliott also aims to bring his theorizations to bear on the wounded flesh of our globalized postmodern era, as he looks to filter, through those same ideas, instances of the tragic bloodletting (i.e. Bosnia) of our times.
17. In their Afterword to this book, Waud Kracke and Lucia Villela exemplify the kind of substantial contribution Lacanian thought makes to the dialogue between anthropology and psychoanalysis.

# References

Barnouw V (1973) Culture and Personality. Rev. edn. Homewood, IL: The Dorsey Press.
Benedict R (1934) Patterns of Culture. New York: Houghton & Mifflin.
Benedict R (1946) The Chrysanthemum and the Sword. New York: Houghton & Mifflin.
Butler J (1993) Bodies that Matter. New York, London: Routledge.
Chodorow N (1999) The Power of Feelings. New Haven, CT: Yale University Press.
Crapanzano V (1992) Hermes' Dilemma and Hamlet's Desire: On the Epistemology of Interpretation. Cambridge, MA: Harvard University Press.
Donn L (1988) Freud and Jung: Years of Friendship, Years of Loss. New York: C. Scribner & Sons.
DuBois C (1944) The People of Alor: A Social Psychological Study of an East Indian Island (analyses by A Kardiner, E Oberholzer). Minneapolis, MN: The University of Minnesota Press.
Durkheim E (1926) The Elementary Forms of the Religious Life. London: Macmillan [c. 1915].
Durkheim E (1965) The Division of Labor in Society. New York: Free Press [c. 1933].
Durkheim E (1967) Primitive Classification (with M Mauss). Chicago: University of Chicago Press [c. 1963].
Ellenberger HF (1970) The Discovery of the Unconscious: The History and Evolution of Dynamic Psychiatry. New York: Basic Books.
Elliott A (1996) Subject to Ourselves: Social Theory, Psychoanalysis and Postmodernity. London: Polity Press.
Ewing KP (1992) Is psychoanalysis relevant for anthropology? In: T Schwartz et al. (eds), New Directions in Psychological Anthropology. Cambridge: Cambridge University Press, pp. 251–68.
Ewing KP (1997) Arguing Sainthood: Modernity, Psychoanalysis, and Islam. Durham, NC: Duke University Press.
Fabian J (1983) Time and the Other: How Anthropology Makes its Object. New York: Columbia University Press.
Ferraro F, Garella A (2001) In-Fine. Milan: Franco Angeli Editore.
Kardiner A (1939) The Individual and His Society: The Psychodynamics of Primitive Social Organization (foreword and two ethnological reports by R Linton). New York: Columbia University Press.
Kardiner A (1945) The Psychological Frontiers of Society (with collaboration of R Linton, C DuBois, J West [pseud.]) New York: Columbia University Press.
Kardiner A (1977) My Analysis with Freud: Reminiscences. New York: W.W. Norton.
Kroeber AL (1979a, 1920) Totem and Taboo: An Ethnologic Psychoanalysis. Reprinted in: WA Lessa, EZ Vogt (eds), Reader in Comparative Religion: An Anthropological Approach. New York: Harper Collins.
Kroeber AL (1979b, 1939) Totem and Taboo in retrospect. Reprinted in: WA Lessa, EZ Vogt (eds), Reader in Comparative Religion: An Anthropological Approach. New York: Harper Collins.
LeGoff J (1992) History and Memory. New York: Columbia University Press.

LeVine RA (1982) Culture, Behavior, Personality, 2nd edn. Chicago: Aldine Publishing Co.

Malinowski B (1922) Argonauts of the Western Pacific: An Account of Native Enterprise and Adventure in the Archipelagos of Melanesian New Guinea (Preface by JG Frazer). London: Routledge; New York: E. P. Dutton.

Malinowski B (1924) Psychoanalysis and anthropology. Psyche 4: 293–332.

Malinowski B (1927) Sex and Repression in Savage Society. Cleveland, OH: The World Press.

Manson WC (1986) Abram Kardiner and the neo-Freudian alternative in culture and personality. In: GW Stocking, Jr (ed.), Malinowski, Rivers, Benedict, and Others : Essays on Culture and Personality. Madison, WI: University of Wisconsin Press.

Mead M (1930) Growing Up in New Guinea: A Comparative Study of Primitive Education. New York: W. Morrow & Co.

Mead M (1942) Balinese Character: A Photographic Analysis (in collaboration with G Bateson). New York: New York Academy of Sciences.

Mead M (1951) Growth and Culture: A Photographic Study of Balinese Childhood (in collaboration with F Cooke Macgregor, based on photos by G Bateson). New York: Putnam.

Mead M (1988) Bathing Babies in Three Cultures. Videorecording by G Bateson, ed. J Bohmer. Text written and narrated by Mead. University Park, PA: Audio-Visual Services, Pennsylvania State University.

Roland A (1988) In Search of Self in India and Japan. Princeton, NJ: Princeton University Press.

Rosaldo R (1989) Culture and Truth: The Remaking of Social Analysis. Boston, MA: Beacon Press.

Rustin M (1991) The Good Society and the Inner World. London & New York: Verso.

Rustin M (2001) Reason and Unreason: Psychoanalysis, Science, and Politics. Middletown, CT: Wesleyan University Press.

Shore B (1996) Culture in Mind: Cognition, Culture, and the Problem of Meaning. New York: Oxford University Press.

Spiro ME (1982) Oedipus in the Trobriands. Chicago: University of Chicago Press.

Stocking GW Jr (ed.) (1974) The Shaping of American Anthropology, 1883–1911: A Franz Boas Reader. New York: Basic Books.

Stocking GW Jr (1986) Malinowski, Rivers, Benedict, and Others: Essays on Culture and Personality. Madison, WI: University of Wisconsin Press.

Turner V (1978) Encounter with Freud: the making of a comparative symbologist. In: G Spindler, L Spindler (eds), The Making of Psychological Anthropology. Berkeley, CA: University of California Press, pp. 556–83.

Van Gennep A (1960) The Rites of Passage. Chicago: University of Chicago Press (first published, 1909).

Whiting JWM, Child IL (1953) Child Training and Personality. New Haven, CT: Yale University Press.

Williams P (2001) Freud-baiting. In A Molino, C Ware (eds), Where Id Was: Challenging Normalization in Psychoanalysis. Middletown, CT: Wesleyan University Press.

Žižek S (1989) The Sublime Object of Ideology. London and New York: Verso.

Žižek S (1997) The Plague of Fantasy. London and New York: Verso.

INTRODUCTION
# Rethinking relations between psychoanalysis and anthropology[1]

ANTHONY MOLINO

> Consciousness nourishes itself by recentering itself around its Other: cosmos, bios, or psyche. It finds itself by losing itself. It finds itself instructed and clarified after losing itself and its narcissism . . . This is why we must admit that the meaning of psychoanalysis as an event within modern culture remains in suspense and its place undetermined. (P. Ricoeur)

In an article entitled 'Psychoanalysis and the movement of contemporary culture', Paul Ricoeur (1974) makes the point that the human sciences remain far from achieving an integrated hermeneutical model – or what he calls a 'philosophical anthropology' – that can account for the discoveries and insights of Marx, Nietzsche and Freud. But while Marxist and Marxian applications have always found fertile ground in anthropology, the deconstructionist spirit of Freud remains for the most part on the margins of mainstream ethnographic practice.[2] In fact, to say that the place of psychoanalysis as a model for anthropological research is undetermined is more than an understatement. To risk claiming as much, in some quarters, is tantamount to heresy. There is, I believe, with regards to psychoanalysis, a form of narcissism that shapes and informs certain strands of modern-day ethnography. It is a form of 'narcissism', if you will, that derives in part from anthropology's 'othering' of psychoanalysis and its repudiated object of study, the unconscious. It is a narcissism highlighted by Katherine Ewing when she suggests that a primary reason for anthropology's 'almost visceral rejection' (Ewing, 1992: 251) of psychoanalysis has been its inability to move beyond Freud's early drive model and the metaphor of depth on which it relied.

As that which is recondite and removed from the surface of observable cultural data cannot, a priori, constitute or be framed within the anthropologist's object of study, the psychological dimension of human experience came to be equated with the private sphere, and thus excluded from ethnographic consideration. Banished, according to Ewing, were issues related to symbolization processes, personal motivation, and the generative dynamics of the ethnographer's field encounters and relationships. Culture became abstracted, as communications between people became, in Ewing's words, 'only cultural (acts) revealing nothing of psychological or idiosyncratic processes. [Clifford] Geertz relied on this image of the (deep and private) psyche to construct a firm barrier dividing anthropology from psychology, the study of culture from the study of the individual and the mind' (Ewing, 1992: 254). Before looking to advance in the direction of the kind of integrated hermeneutical model advocated by Ricoeur, it would be appropriate, I think, to look more closely at the origins and consolidation of this very barrier.

> In a way, most cultural anthropologists still operate very much within a Geertzian paradigm. (Dorinne Kondo, personal communication)

While models of the self are important to social science and social theorists, there has been little development within anthropology of psychoanalytic models of subjectivity and the self outside, perhaps, of the attention reserved to the insights of Jacques Lacan – a symptom, one might say, of what Henrietta Moore calls anthropology's problem of 'under-theorization' in its reluctance to 'get inside the heads of actors' (Moore, 1994: 142).[3] In essential agreement with Ewing, Moore too notes how the supposed representational insufficiency of psychoanalysis is still defined, to a great extent, by the near-doctrinal foreclosure operated against it by Geertz's interpretivism. The force of the Geertzian bias is perhaps nowhere more evident than in Geertz's award-winning *Works and Lives*, in particular the chapter entitled 'I-witnessing: Malinowski's children' (Geertz, 1988). Consider the following excerpt:

> there is a lot more than native life to plunge into if one is to attempt this total immersion approach into ethnography. There is the landscape. There is the isolation. There is the local European population. There is the memory of home and what one has left. There is the sense of vocation and where one is going. And most shakingly, there is the capriciousness of one's passions, the weakness of one's constitution, and the vagrancies of one's thoughts: *that nigrescent thing, the self*. It is not a question of going native ... It is a question of living a multiplex life: sailing at once in several seas (Geertz, 1988: 77, my italics)

In a single breath, we have an inkling of what I'd dare call Geertz's awkward contempt of that 'thing' that grows black (and, arguably, is one with the 'darkness' out which it grows – making it unobservable, and hence not subject, presumably, to the rigors of scientific scrutiny), as well as a timid, *au courant* accommodation of the language of postmodernism ('a multiplex life').

Referring to the paragraph just cited, Geertz continues:

> It is, again, essential to see that, despite the vocabulary in which I have just now cast it (and in which, largely because of Malinowski's apotheosis of empathetic fieldwork, it is usually cast), this issue, negotiating the passage from what one has been through 'out there' to what one says 'back here' *is not psychological in character*. It is literary . . . (ibid., p. 78, my italics)

Or, as he writes further on:

> The problem, to rephrase it in as prosaic terms as I can manage, is to represent the research process in the research product; to write ethnography in such a way as to bring one's interpretations of some society, culture, or way of life, or whatever, and one's encounters with some of its members, carriers, representatives, or whomever, into an intelligible relationship. Or quickly, to refigure it again, *before psychologism can set in*, it is how to get an I-witnessing author into a they-picturing story . . . (ibid., p. 84, my italics)

'. . . before psychologism can set in'. We have here an unequivocal restatement of a foundational position which now harkens back at least thirty years (Geertz's *The Interpretation of Cultures* was published in 1973). As Geertz is all too quick to echo: 'this issue . . . *is not psychological in character*. It is literary.'

To highlight the persistent force, *over time*, of the Geertzian foreclosure I'd like to cite two examples which are almost two decades removed from one another. First, I suggest looking at Michelle Rosaldo's ethnography, *Knowledge and Passion: Ilongot Notions of Self and Social Life* (1980). For starters, Rosaldo's debt to Geertz is openly stated. Citing his 'Person, time, and conduct in Bali' (in Geertz, 1973) as 'an exemplary discussion of the mutual bearing of styles of action, temporal orientation, and the classification of persons among the Balinese' (p. 26), Rosaldo goes on to write:

> For [Geertz], social and ritual practice is interpreted from the point of view of self-conceptions – accounts of how and why to act – that must inform the social lives of actors. For [Geertz], the intelligible, compelling, and significant nature of such 'symbols' as the Dinka cow, or perhaps, American marriage, *has less to do with their ability to play on hidden psychic chords* than with commonplace assumptions that are bound up with daily use. (Rosaldo, 1980: 26, my italics)

As a psychoanalyst concerned with those very psychic chords, it is striking for me to note the author's relentless attack, throughout the book, against anything suggestive of 'the depths' of psychic life. Clearly, the depth metaphor is not a welcome one. What follow are but a few more revealing excerpts from the book. (Unless noted, all italics are mine for emphasis.)

> Thus, talk of the heart is, much as we would expect, talk of 'interior experience', but it is also talk of social life and public situations, *describing not unconscious process* but such qualities of consciousness as inform the ways that people act. (Rosaldo, 1980: 38)

> the heart's emotional gymnastics, although providing a vivid way of talking about feelings, *are not the stuff of memories, excuses, accounts of motives, or the explanations of one's plans* . . . Through talk of hearts, Ilongots characterize the relation between the self and its situation . . . *Their talk of hearts has less to do with histories that give reasons* than with the fact that hearts that stand apart, are moved, itch, etc. (Rosaldo, 1980: 42–3)

> *their talk is less concerned with introspection and the 'inner life'* than with the affective quality of a world where social bonds themselves depend upon potentially divisive founts of 'energy' or 'anger' . . . (Rosaldo, 1980: 44)

And, finally, on page 225: '*Ilongots do not speak of personalities forged in childhood years*, or of enduring differences in "moral" character', and so on.

These quotes by no means exhaust the expressions of what I can only reckon to be an extraordinary 'defence' against the rival claims of a form of ethnography potentially inspired by depth psychology. It is not my concern here to ascertain what motivates such a systematic defence against an alternative theory. But it may, perhaps, suffice at this point simply to quote Rosaldo one more time, on the acknowledged limits of her own understanding, and on the telling implications of these limits for the 'narcissism' that informs ethnographies like *Knowledge and Passion*. Again the italics are mine.

> *Perhaps because I could not fathom the psychological or moral implications of their acts* . . ., I found that in both fieldwork and in writing this account my interests focused less on *liget* as a psychic state realized in crazed and frightening acts (of headhunting) than on its social and collective meaning. (Rosaldo, 1980: 226)

I take as my second example a more recent essay by George Marcus, in Debbora Battaglia's *Rhetorics of Self-Making* (Marcus, 1995). In a paper entitled 'On eccentricity', Marcus explores identity formation and the construction of selfhood in contemporary American financial dynasties. It is perhaps one of the more telling, and somewhat fumbling, examples of the kind of effort that seeks to circumvent the so-called 'inner' sphere. Here are some examples.

After stating from the outset that eccentricity, as a 'fully viable form of life in society', is not to be confused with 'mental illness', Marcus goes on to establish what for him is the defining character of eccentricity. After further distancing himself from any possibility of having eccentricity confused with madness (note the escalation in terminology masked as synonymy: mental illness = madness, where the latter is equated with a form of hyper self-awareness characteristic of high modernism), Marcus writes:

> Eccentrics, in contrast, exhibit very little self-awareness or self-consciousness in the sense of introspection. Rather, they are hyper-aware that their selves are being constructed elsewhere by other agencies, that they are keenly aware of their selves being multiply authored. Thus, eccentricity arises not so much from an extreme awareness of self, but from an extreme awareness of how one's self is being constructed by other agencies. (Marcus, 1995: 48)

Such a statement poses quite a few problems: since consciousness is more than implied, 'who' occupies this seat of 'hyper-awareness'? what difference is being posited between a self whose hyper-awareness is introspective, and one whose awareness is lived in the direction of being elsewhere authored? Such selves, it seems, are disembodied; they need to be located 'nowhere', as it were; as if this quality of hyper-awareness, in either direction, is not intrapsychically experienced and, more than likely, suffered. And yet, while obliquely acknowledging 'psychological theories about obsession and fetishism' that could contribute to the personality formation of such subjects, Marcus continues: 'I prefer to focus on the specifically microsocial conditions that might give a context to eccentric obsession' (Marcus, 1995: 50).

Clearly, such an attitude is typical of the inability/unwillingness of the social sciences to integrate psychological/psychoanalytic understandings within the province of the cultural. Such a disavowal is pervasive – even as it perpetuates the culture/psyche boundary which, as a parallel to the outer/inner one so widely questioned, is firmly maintained. And yet, as with Marcus, the language of psychology, broadly speaking, continues to be employed. (I'll refrain here from reviewing the further and many shortcomings of his case study of Howard Hughes, set against the backdrop of Pirandello's *Six Characters in Search of an Author* and the 'naming', defining function of the Father in the play. It is lamentable that even a basic application of such a crucial Lacanian tenet is eschewed in such a context.)

---

To limit one's understanding of psychoanalysis to but a single one of Freud's own multiple models (or to simply limit an update of the tradition to Lacan's school) is the equivalent, roughly, of restricting one's study of physics to the day an apocryphal apple chanced upon Newton's head. For anthropology to have remained focused on the early drive model has meant the neglect of Freud's entire lifework which, however flawed as an expression of the dominant ideological discourses of his time (of nineteenth-century enlightenment 'science' and the vestiges of an ancestral Judaeo-Christian patriarchy), was nevertheless to spawn the rich and often competing traditions of the Kleinian school, ego psychology, object relations and the British Independents, Lacan's 'return', self-psychology, neo-Freudians and French feminists – not to mention the similarly rich and rebel traditions of Jung and Adler. And yet the specifics of many, if not all, of these influences have remained largely extraneous to mainstream anthropology, which has ignored the multiple visions and theoretical sophistication of the new generation of today's psychoanalysts.

In these postmodern times, when the fieldworker's subjectivity is known to infiltrate every stage of the creative process, right up to and through publication of the ethnographic text, ethnography cannot help but be challenged and engaged by today's psychoanalysis in a way that subverts the tendency that has traditionally characterized interdisciplinary work between the two disciplines. Whereas much of the literature bringing together psychoanalysis and the social sciences has, in the past, used a reductionist psychoanalysis to analyse aspects of culture (or to identify 'syndromes' found in other cultures but foreign to the West), rarely has a more sophisticated effort been engaged to assess the parallel development of models in psychoanalysis and the social sciences, and the impact of these models for social theory.[4]

Not unlike anthropology, psychoanalysis is itself in the concurrent throes of a 'self-reflexive' moment of its own; and, not unlike anthropology, psychoanalysis too is burdened by its past, as it suffers and problematizes the sins of its Father, in the hope of delivering on the promise of what Adam Phillips (1995) calls a 'post-Freudian Freud'. The critique produced from within psychoanalysis points, in fact, to a model of investigation into human life and relationships that is increasingly less invested in the preservation of psychoanalysis as a master discourse than in problematizing its own tools and traditional strategies. It is, in fact, through the deployment of new strategies concerned with reflexivity, representation, narrativity, and literary and feminist discourses, that psychoanalysis now situates its basic insights about the nature of consciousness and the construction of the self within a world that is increasingly multiple and fragmented.

In this light, psychoanalysis can itself be seen in the throes of a fertile crisis of 'identity' and redefinition that parallels the reconceptualization of the ethnographic project and context. In psychoanalysis, for example, not only is the authority of the analyst's interpretations increasingly questioned, but the very therapeutic efficacy of any interpretation is generally assumed to be but one factor in a more complex relational 'cure'. Similarly, no longer viewed as a catalogue of the exotic serving to authoritatively categorize a collection of 'objective' data, ethnography nowadays concerns itself increasingly with texts and innovative modes of representation (personal, poetic and dialogic). In point of fact, the 'postmodern turn' in ethnography moves towards a reconfiguration of the ethnographic Other (the object) within an intersubjective matrix that invariably involves a questioning of the status of the fieldworker/author (the subject). Ethnographer and social theorist Kathleen Stewart's idea of 'contamination' points most clearly in this direction, in a way that converges strikingly with developments in psychoanalytic thought.[5] In both contexts, the supposed neutrality of the subject/analyst is exploded, as the messy indeterminacy of subject and object transposes the struggle over power and meaning into a relational encounter in which two actors are potentially transformed.

This turn in anthropology is also evidenced by the marked concern with issues of reflexivity, as is attested by the shifts in ethnographic writing towards personal and 'confessional' styles.[6] Hence, it is concerned with the dispersion of the self into texts where truth (including one's own) is not pre-given but interrogated in the process of a literary construction. In an essay entitled 'Ethnicity and the post-modern arts of memory' (1986), Michael Fischer illustrates a singular aspect of this turn, while also pointing to new ways in which the contemporary ethnographic project can draw on psychoanalysis. Starting out from the premise of a 'pluralist, multidimensional, or multi-faceted concept of self', Fischer sees the relationship between identity and ethnicity as one being fruitfully explored, in a series of ethnic autobiographies, through 'processes analogous to the dreaming and transference of psychoanalytic encounters' (Fischer, 1986: 196). In his review of the genre, Fischer identifies what he calls 'transference-like techniques of repetition, indirection, and reworking' that are also deployed as textual strategies in works more generally regarded as ethnographic. Citing Gananath Obeyesekere's *Medusa's Hair* (1981) and Vincent Crapanzano's *Tuhami* (1980) among his cross-referencing examples, Fischer advocates

> reading ethnographies as the juxtaposition of two or more cultural traditions, and paying attention both in reading and in constructing ethnographies to the ways in which the juxtaposition of cultural traditions works on both the conscious and the unconscious level (Fischer, 1986: 199–200).

In his essay, Fischer thus returns us to the problem that is the unconscious for anthropology. Over the years, the discipline's unfortunate reliance on a metaphor of 'depth' for its critique of psychoanalysis has had as one of its corollaries what might be called a positivist/functionalist understanding of the unconscious. The unconscious, in fact, has posed a problem for anthropology to the extent that it not only lay 'beneath' the surface of the privileged, observable 'data' of culture, but precisely because of its supposed 'location', it could not be unequivocally situated or 'identified'. An assumed material quality, a quality of 'thing-ness', seemed to colour prevailing understandings of the unconscious which, combined with its encased and sedimented interiority, made it not only mysterious but impermeable to the research methods of a positivist science. Thus, it was easier – and understandable – for the unconscious to be disavowed, especially since anthropology had for the most part already disavowed the study of subjectivity.[7]

Nowadays, however, it is interesting to note how the very depth/surface metaphor that informed yesterday's critical positions has yielded to a more pervasive concern with the so-called 'inner/outer' boundary.[8] At one level, this transposition – from a vertical to a horizontal metaphor – readily denotes the assumption, on the part of anthropology, of a discourse of subjectivity. The boundary in question, in fact, is to some extent (if not altogether) clearly inspired by an evocation, or prefiguration, of the body of the human person: that is to say, of the human 'subject' in his/her materiality, as a (semi-) permeable membrane of sorts (and not only as an abstract discursive production) presumed to exist in an intersubjective context. It is through this light that we can begin to see how the residue of an outdated understanding of the unconscious can still mark the discipline's present-day foreclosures to psychoanalysis. But think of the radical change in conceptualizations of the unconscious from the time, say, of culture-and-personality studies in anthropology. Think of how anthropology might orient itself differently towards psychoanalysis today if understandings of the unconscious, and of the self, like those put forth by Christopher Bollas, were more widespread throughout the anthropological community.

For Bollas, the self is a process of becoming that involves the selection and use of objects and others in our world, and the ways those objects and others work upon us. The selection process itself is a product of our idiom: an inherited disposition, or orientation, towards life and the world that is shaped and first articulated through contact with the mother, and enhanced as we grow and become transformed by this meaning-invested world of objects. Like Lacan's, Bollas's model of the unconscious avoids the essentializing and ontologizing that for so many years met with anthropology's rightful criticism. Again, the unconscious is not a thing: it is not a bag full of symbols, or a receptacle of repressed mental contents. Rather, it is perhaps best conceptualized as a generative locus of 'disseminations',[9] of dialectical operations between self and world which, were we to witness them, would unfold like 'an aesthetic movement which articulates and elaborates the idiom of the self' (Bollas, 1995:64) Along these lines, Bollas (1992) also uses the notion of the waking life as a dream, in which each moment leading us to the next is determined by the past but also reshapes and reinterprets that past. Transposed into interpersonal contexts, such 'dis/located' visions of the unconscious dovetail with and lend themselves to many of the contemporary representational devices deployed by a postmodern ethnography, roughly summarized by Fischer as 'transference, dream-translation, talk-story, multiple voices and perspectives, the highlighting of humorous inversions and dialectical juxtaposition of identities/traditions, cultures, and the critique of hegemonic discourses' (Fischer, 1986: 202). In this context, however, it is especially important to recognize that when experimental ethnographers turn their attention to the implications for social research and cross-cultural understanding of an unproblematized inner/outer boundary, what they are also performing is a critique of the traditional, disciplinary boundaries of anthropological knowledge. It seems to me near-sighted, in fact, to look to challenge traditional, objectifying understandings of the ethnographic Other, as well as the established rhetorics of anthropological representation, while insisting to exclude psychoanalysis as a viable methodological instrument. It would be regrettable, in fact, if the so-called 'crisis' in anthropology, concomitant with the general breakdown of boundaries across the territory of the human sciences, for some reason necessitated that a line of demarcation and exclusion, an inner/outer boundary of sorts, be drawn at the 'site' of psychoanalysis.

---

How might a Geertzian anthropology benefit from an opening to psychoanalysis? Katharine Ewing, less conservative than Geertz in her broader recognition of the inescapable impact of postmodern and deconstructionist sensibilities, writes that modern-day ethnographers 'often take the nihilistic stance that since participation is unavoidable, observation is, therefore, not possible' (Ewing, 1992: 262). As a counter-measure, she suggests that today's ethnographer might look to psychoanalysis – albeit with a critical eye – for new strategies to ethically manage field issues of involvement and power. For starters, Ewing maintains that anthropologists might benefit from an exposure to psychoanalytic technique – what she identifies as 'the process of observing one's own participation in dialogue with another' (Ewing, 1992: 264). While remaining mindful of the differences that inhere between psychoanalysis and fieldwork (especially with regards to the peculiarities of their respective power imbalances, as well as to the fundamental therapeutic dimension of psychoanalysis), Ewing does not shy away from insisting that 'anthropologists still have much to learn about how to use their reactions as an observational tool'. And if it is true, as she maintains, that while meta-narratives and interpretative frames remain in crisis, 'the anthropological project shifts to one of examining informants' interpretative strategies in a social world of conflict and inconsistencies' (Ewing, 1992: 265), then recommendations like hers may well point the way towards expanding the terms of what constitutes an 'authentic account of an alien way of life'.

As a means of investigation into the history and emotional life of a person, the technical (or 'clinical') tools of psychoanalysis are, arguably, unsurpassable. Among these, first and foremost, is a strategy and sensibility in interviewing that has remained, for the most part, foreign to ethnographic practice.[10] And it is this very sensibility – enhanced by an essential familiarity with and respect for the transference/countertransference matrix – that lies at the heart of calls from within the ranks of anthropology for a 'clinically-based ethnographic perspective' (Chodorow, 1995), or for the more comprehensive project that Gilbert Herdt and Robert J. Stoller term a 'clinical ethnography' (Herdt and Stoller, 1990).

The product of a collaborative effort between an anthropologist (Herdt) and a psychoanalyst (Stoller), *Intimate Communications: Erotics and the Study of Culture* is, in one sense, an ethnographic study of gender and identity among the Sambia of Papua New Guinea. In another sense, however, it is also a postmodern text that defies traditional categorization: part manual and part manifesto, the book is a multivocal exploration of the possible field applications of psychoanalysis. It is a work that attempts to translate into ethnographic practice the intuitions of researchers like Chodorow and Ewing: intuitions which, through the authors' elaborations, are transformed into a comprehensive model for the study of subjectivity.

Striving to make room, real room, for the voices of their field interpreters,[11] the authors criticize what they see as the positivist ideology of fieldwork (Herdt and Stoller, 1990: 352). In a fierce critique of Geertz's 'philosophic behaviourism', the authors insist that 'the failure of contemporary anthropology to enlighten her sister disciplines' (on the subject matter of erotics) is the fateful result of the disregard of the individual that Geertz's brand of interpretivism helped codify. Sounding a note similar to Chodorow's,[12] the call here is to reclaim 'the whole person – as a source of intrapsychic and interpersonal meanings' (Herdt and Stoller, 1990: 361). Invoking a capacity for a 'bifocal vision' (Sapir) that can image simultaneously the realities of person and group, of both psyche and culture, Herdt and Stoller are not so much concerned with questions like the 'nature' of self as they are with the processes whereby ethnographic observation (of the illusory, if not delusional, 'detached' kind) edits out human subjectivity. Like physicists who are keenly aware of the effects of their observing on the object under study, Herdt and Stoller are ever-sensitive, at least in their theorizing,[13] to the nuanced reconfigurations of the interpersonal field – potentially, if not invariably altered, by any single aspect or expression of their human presence, including their very discourse.

Decrying anthropology's withdrawal from the study of subjectivity – defined as 'one's private experience of experiencing, the awareness of one's awareness' – the authors propose adopting the two-person psychoanalytic model in an attempt to refocus ethnography on the fieldworker's 'communications with real people: people creating and exchanging meanings within interpersonal relationships' (p. 29). Or, as they continue:

> To understand meaning systems and the more private motivations and fantasies of people, we need accounts of the natives as individuals, not just as presumed spokesmen for their cultures . . . The cross-cultural study of subjectivity – a major aim of clinical ethnography – describes, interprets and compares the ways people express feelings, beliefs, and motives. 'Clinical' is meant to represent our interest in these processes – intimate communication, subjective meanings of self, others, cultural ideas and institutions, identity and culturally patterned states of awareness. (Herdt and Stoller, 1990: 30)

Claiming that psychoanalysis is, in effect, a form of 'microethnography' (echoing Bollas (1989), who speaks of the analyst's efforts to access the patient's 'private culture'), Herdt and Stoller look to transpose the basic structure of the psychoanalytic interview – the 'depth interview', as they call it – to the very centre of ethnographic practice. In doing so, the authors' intention, amid the blurred boundaries of objective and subjective, inner and outer, is to make authentic the case for a person-centred ethnography.

How the depth interview facilitates this project is through its tested efficacy as part of the psychoanalytic process: namely, 'by showing how psychodynamic processes such as projection, fantasy, and transference occur across cultural boundaries' (Herdt and Stoller, 1990: 5). Ultimately, for Herdt and Stoller, ethnography is a matter of trust and transference, unfolding in a sea of countless, sometimes imperceptible currents ebbing-and-flowing at multiple depths. Until recently, as I've more than implied, the currents could be ignored and the depths disavowed. Nowadays, however, in a climate that is clearly more receptive to and concerned with the researcher's idiomatic expertise and experience, perhaps anthropology can again make room for the talents and techniques of the psychoanalyst – especially since, as Stoller correctly notes, 'psychoanalysts have been more concerned with the distortions introduced by subjective factors [of observation] than any other investigators of human behavior' (Herdt and Stoller, 1990: 5).[14]

There are two other important aspects of Herdt and Stoller's project which warrant attention. One is the rescuing of desire. Or, as Maurice

Blanchot implies, in an article entitled 'The speech of analysis', of the unconscious itself:

> The negation that is not simply a wanting, but a relation to what is wanting – desire. A desire whose essence is eternally to be desire: a desire for what is impossible to attain, and even to be desire.[15] (Blanchot, 1993: 230)

Focusing on Sambia sexuality, and in particular on the transitional, ritualized forms of adolescent male homosexuality in Sambia culture, Herdt and Stoller manage to elicit – albeit not without an awkward quality of intrusiveness, and an occasional disregard for both their interpreter's sensibilities as well as their own theory – precious communications regarding the most intimate sphere of human activity. In doing so, they become privileged interlocutors in the singular process of both documenting and generating a form of discourse that opens onto the ensconced arenas and playgrounds of human desire, where culture becomes most exquisitely operative, 'in and through human beings' (Kroeber). Or, as Herdt and Stoller emphasize: 'Between the social facts of culture and the psychologic events of someone's fantasies and scripts lie desires' (Herdt and Stoller, 1990: 356).

This, I believe, is the other achievement, or at least the other fundamental insight, of Herdt and Stoller's work. As I've suggested earlier, the authors are not concerned with using psychoanalysis to postulate either an essentialist self or a self that is a cultural construct. Rather, in what Pauline Roseneau (1992) terms the 'affirmative' spirit of postmodernism, a spirit differentially embodied, where ethnography is concerned, by the likes of Crapanzano, Stewart, and a host of others,[16] Herdt and Stoller are willing to remain fruitfully engaged in the pursuit and pleasure not of answers, but of questions. In fact, where the 'nature' of self and self experience is concerned, the questions are countless. (See, for example, *Intimate Communications*, pp. 356–61.) Where the authors most convincingly make their case, however, is on the matter of method that informs the questions: 'We agree that each culture provides for a self and that the experience of the I/me can be charted in its details, through clinical ethnography' (Herdt and Stoller 1990: 361). Throughout this book, a similar principle has informed my interviews, through which I hope to have pointed to new possibilities for the self-reflexive explorations of the fieldworker: that is to say, for new ways to map out the I/me 'moves,' both conscious and unconscious, that inform the ethnographer's journey.

---

To prefigure some of the potential benefits of a psychoanalytic sensibility capable of exploring just how the horizontal axis of cultural meaning intersects with the vertical axis of personal history,[17] I'd like now to use the work of Bollas to examine two noteworthy, modern-day ethnographic studies – Michael Taussig's *The Devil and Commodity Fetishism* and John and Jean Comaroff's 'The madman and the migrant'. These studies, while not distinctly Geertzian, are characterized by a similar neglect of the intrapsychic dimension.

In 1980 anthropologist Michael Taussig's *The Devil and Commodity Fetishism* significantly advanced anthropological thinking about the self and subjectivity. An exploration of magical practices that have grown around colonialist exploitation and the consequent grafting of capitalist economic structures onto subsistence communities, *The Devil and Commodity Fetishism* (Taussig, 1980) moves beyond functionalist thought on the role of belief systems in human society. Through his study of small villages in Colombia and Bolivia where peasants worked on plantations and in tin mines, Taussig developed an alternative explanation to the devil worship cults that emerged in these contexts. Traditional anthropological explanations follow the functionalist notion that magic reduces anxiety; the reason one worships the devil in a tin mine is that an offering to the devil gives the illusion of control over a situation in which one is powerless. Taussig suggests, however, that such practices are not just attempts at gaining control over circumstances; they are also ways to make sense of the world.

Using Marx's notion of commodity fetish, Taussig suggests that the world the mine owners bring – a world of private property, wage-labour, money, interest, etc. – represents a reified set of ideological categories that we in the West take for granted. For example, we understand the metaphorical meaning of 'your money works harder at such-and-such bank'. But for people not socialized into what Taussig calls the 'commoditized apprehension of reality', the expression is gobbledegook. Everyday business-as-usual practices turn the world upside down for people reared in a pre-industrial subsistence culture: no longer are social goods distributed fairly, and those who work hard get poorer while those who own the means of production get richer. The devil, in this context, is a reasonable explanation for what is going on.

While Taussig has at his disposal a language to talk about the social aspects of the above interpretation, he does not have available a language of subjective process. Such a language could contribute useful insights into the ways symbols are motivated and mobilized in particular cultural contexts. For example, when Taussig points out that many of the images of the devil are traditional and indigenous (i.e. as when miners report a reverie or an image of the devil walking around the mine), these are often unknowingly described as one of the European owners. Aware of this paradoxical imagery, Taussig wonders if there are unconscious processes operating in the production of the Bolivians' way of understanding their experience as exploited workers. It is our contention that it is precisely in such situations that a model like Bollas's can be fruitfully appropriated by anthropology, with tremendous implications for research that attempts to link the object world and the subjective states of individuals.

Bollas talks about how objects get infused with personal meaning, and how an idiom grows out of infantile experiences, forming a way of relating to self and world. Attributing to objects an inherent vitality that makes of them elements of transformation, Bollas theorizes the conception of multiple relationships capable of being generated by any object (be this a person, a piece of music, a toy or a pitchfork), and the dialectical interplay between the object and the way it is used and reinterpreted by an individual. The individual, in turn, is herself 'used' by the object – that is to say, her existence is aesthetically shaped and emotionally impacted by the object's material, evocative quality. While Bollas's theory is quite complex and cannot be done justice here, there are some implications that can be drawn from his work and have potential impact for efforts like Taussig's. For instance, devil worship, essentially a repetitive magical practice, could be compared to the psychoanalyst's discussion of trauma, in that it involves symbolic repetition rather than symbolic elaboration (Bollas, 1992: 69–70). Thus, while magic – as a creative response to a situation of oppression – gives meaning to a heretofore meaningless capitalist world, like trauma it has limited or no liberatory potential. (This is significantly different than the application of a reductionist psychoanalysis that sees magic and ritual as expressions or features of obsessional neurosis in the culture.)

In an article entitled 'The madman and the migrant', Jean and John Comaroff (1992) have developed ideas similar to those of Taussig. In their work on the Tshidi of South Africa, the authors observe that official local history, written by those in positions of power and constructed in linear narrative, is more likely to be the story of the oppressor than of the oppressed. In order to understand the peoples and cultures of Southern Africa, it is necessary to combine political and economic analysis with what might be called the poetics of everyday life. The Comaroffs' madman is one who expresses such a poetic, as his clothing and accessory symbols merge the world of wage-labour in the mines with the social life of Tshidi villages. This poetic merging is an articulation of the horror of oppression and death at the hands of Western colonial powers. To the white doctors in the hospital, the madman's behaviour was psychotic nonsense. To black African patients, he was a healer.

Through the story of this unlikely prophet, the Comaroffs illustrate how the Tshidi have symbolized the contact of their world with colonialism by constructing different categories. The world of work in the village is contrasted by the Tshidi with the world of labour in the mines; the first is seen as life-affirming, while the second is associated with death, both literal and symbolic. The Comaroffs' major point is that human actors strive together in specific cultural and historical contexts to represent themselves and their worlds. Further, the poetic expression of one's existence is no less compelling or important than a 'realistic' account of the local history; on the contrary, it might capture lived experience in a way impossible to achieve otherwise.

This concern with everyday poetics and how the mind articulates experience calls for the strengths of clinicians and researchers like Bollas, who shares with any number of contemporary analysts an attitude towards psychoanalysis that is at an infinite remove from the understandings many anthropologists have about psychoanalysis. When American Michael Eigen, for example, claims that 'nowadays I think of psychoanalysis as an aesthetic, as a form of poetry' (in Molino, 1997: 104), or when Londoner Adam Phillips writes that for him psychoanalysis 'is a kind of practical poetry' (Phillips, 1994: xi), both are expressing an altogether new psychoanalytic sensibility, with implications and possible applications for researchers like the Comaroffs, whose own poetics necessarily neglect conscious/unconscious process in the context of how subjects come to interpret their world. Like Taussig, the Comaroffs do make a political point about the poetics of everyday life and how this is a viable lens through which to view the world. They point out that while we have a tendency to see official history as the truth, the truth of people's lives is often missed or deleted by official history. Employing the poetic, the Tshidi find in the madman a voice that brings some comfort and helps make sense of their lives. The madman's own redeeming effort to find a voice, moreover, occurs in a world where the Tshidi have not only lost culture, life and family, but the very ability to represent themselves to themselves. It is against this background that an applied psychoanalytic sensibility, like that of Bollas or Phillips or Eigen, can only enrich the perceptual tools of the ethnographer. Imagine, for example, a 'reading' of the madman's self-representation inspired by the following reflections of Bollas:

> I think that 'character' is an aesthetic. If our way of being refers to our very precise means of forming our world, both internal and intersubjective, then each of us is a kind of artist with his or her own creative sensibility. We know that the distinctiveness of that creation is the particular form we have brought to it . . . It is a pleasure to express and articulate the self: there's an erotic dimension to that kind of representation . . . My own view is that in the formation of character we similarly have a pure arc of the pleasure of representation . . . (Bollas, in Molino, 1997: 9)[18]

Clearly the madman and the patients in the mental hospital are not experiencing any ordinary sense of pleasure. And yet, there is an unequivocal 'erotic' quality to the madman's idiosyncrasies. He is a healer and a prophet for his ability to bring together the contradictory symbols of oppressor and oppressed, and there is an odd sensuality in his presentation of self. In the words of the Comaroffs:

> Famous for an ingenious costume he would never remove, the man was, literally, a prophet in polythene robes. His crazy clothes spoke the language of his obsession. His boots, standard issue for mineworkers, were topped by intricately knitted leggings, the painstaking product of many unravelled orange sacks. He wore a cloak and a bishop's mitre, fashioned from black plastic garbage bags. Across his chest stretched a brilliantly striped sash, on which were stitched three letters: SAR.[19] (Comaroff and Comaroff, 1992: 155)

While the language of the Comaroffs betrays the madman's sensuality, it cannot help but fall short in any attempt to fathom or convey how the particular objects that inform and constellate the madman's 'idiom' work to foster both subjective and shared meanings. For in the intersubjective context of the Tshidi, the madman does help patients to experience a healing pleasure – a therapeutic outcome which also reflects, if you will, an unconscious 'grammar' of relationship. Clearly, while the local miners resonate with the madman's objects and idiomatic expressions, the doctor's estrangement from and devaluation of those same expressions is what leads to a very different apprehension of (and response to) the madman's and his patients' reality.

To conclude this overview, I would like to mention a critical article by Kathleen Stewart, 'On the politics of cultural theory: a case for contaminated critique' (1991). In this article, Stewart also draws upon a poetics of everyday life, 'picturing' articulations of self through processes of narrative and dialogue. One image she offers is of an Appalachian man expressing the loss of culture and habitat in his critique of the strip mining practices in the area. The man's discourse is a fertile poetic reverie, in which self and community are imaginatively constructed in the space left barren by the mining companies; it is also, however, a denunciation completely misunderstood by the city slicker/social worker to whom the story is told. As in this instance, such benevolent outsiders, with no sense of the way 'place' and 'talk' work together to construct what Kirkpatrick Sale (1991) calls dwellers (people who are part of the landscape and belong to a place), often presumptuously fill in the spaces and gaps in the local discourse with their own self-righteous sense of what needs to be done about the loss. By interpreting the local rhetorical style as one of helplessness, the outsider attempts to fill in the meaning he sees 'missing' in the discourse by redefining the local in cosmopolitan terms.[20]

The resulting image of the redefined local is one Stewart uses to express her concern for an anthropology that constructs a barrier between ethnographer and informant, and then makes a virtue of the barrier. Stewart, drawing upon the work of Mikhail Bakhtin, suggests that a contaminated critique is preferable; an attitude that recognizes that interpretation is not a neat scientific process but one where ethnographer and informant struggle together to define and understand each other in a polysemic and dialogic process. This process will yield no seamless results but will rather be one in-filled with uncertainties, gaps and misrecognitions.

The struggle that Stewart describes is about power and who has power over meaning; but it is also one where important questions about truth and knowledge are recognized in all their ambiguity. This is very similar to the interpretative struggle engaging many post-Freudian analysts. For instance, Stewart's use of the word 'contaminated' reflects the relatively recent turn in psychoanalysis that places increasing emphasis on the dynamics of the so-called 'countertransference'. In a move away from Freud's ideal of the analyst's supposed neutrality and blank-screen function (akin to the fiction of the ethnographer's 'decontaminated' distance from his/her object of analysis), focus on the countertransference can well be understood in terms of 'making the analyst more vulnerable to something that someone like Bakhtin would call trans-subjective relations' (see my interview with Stewart in this volume, Chapter 6, below). It is in this sense that the transference/countertransference dynamic, as it unfolds in a mutually constitutive space (thus lessening the patient's 'responsibility' for the quality of the emotional engagement and experience) also forms a relational, trans-subjective field.

---

In *The War of Dreams*, French anthropologist Marc Augé suggests that contemporary societies are being overrun by the mass-produced images of our consumer culture, in the context of a global phenomenon he refers to as 'supermodernity'. In Augé's view, this poses a threat to our species' timeless sources of the social imaginary: to the very functions that dreams, myth and ritual, and fiction, have always served in helping us to imagine our relationship to the Other and think through identity and alterity. Nowadays, instead, within modern cultures, the mass-production of images is rendering the Other more and more abstract. And with that abstraction comes increased difficulties for thinking about relationships of identity and alterity (Augé, 1999: 14). So when anthropologists think about any culture in the world, the effect of 'supermodernity' must be taken into account.

Psychoanalysis and semiotics, according to Augé, are natural allies of anthropology in the effort to understand images, their sources and effects on human societies. To simplify Augé's complex and important argument somewhat, mass-produced images are seriously threatening the creative capacities of humankind's ancestral sources of images. To this extent, the relationship to other cultures and the ideas that exist within contemporary societies about other cultures are very different than they were earlier in the twentieth century. In a similar way, the media critic Herbert Schiller (1985) argued that mass media were now dominating the entire perimeter of human consciousness and fuelling our fantasies and imagination for us in unprecedented ways. This new phenomenon requires that we rethink the relationship of the individual to the sources of social imagination. It requires, moreover, that we rethink the relationship between object representations and contemporary subjects – for whom we also require a new and viable theory of subjectivity. To this end, in a dizzying global economy that operates through vast and dense semiotic systems (in ways that acritically promote and develop our desires in every possible direction), the insights of psychoanalysis can only contribute to prevailing models for understanding contemporary articulations of the self, desire, multiplicity and our relationship to the objects in our worlds.

It is for these reasons as well, then, that a new dialogue between psychoanalysis and anthropology is an important project for future work in anthropology. To promote this dialogue I have, in recent years, conducted a series of interviews with seven prominent anthropologists and social theorists from around the world. Obviously enough, I could not bring together all the important anthropologists who have used psychoanalytic models in their work. Indeed, some of the most significant voices in the field are not here. Instead, in talking to Paul Williams, Vincent Crapanzano, Michael Rustin, Katherine Ewing, Kathleen Stewart, Gananath Obeyesekere, and Marc Augé, what I sought to do was elicit a far-reaching and diversified set of views about psychoanalysis and its value for anthropological research today, particularly on issues concerning the field encounter, fantasy, social change, identity and experience.

While the scholars cited are likely to be known to readers of this volume, a few words of introduction are nonetheless in order. (Detailed biographical sketches are otherwise provided at the start of each interview.) Williams bridges both worlds, insofar as he is a practicing psychoanalyst who has looked anthropologically at the clinic in light of his long-standing investigation into the workings of psychosis. Crapanzano, Ewing and Obeysekere are all anthropologists who have used psychoanalysis in their fieldwork, pushing and reworking the boundaries of psychoanalytic theory while contributing, often in radical and profound ways, to anthropological thinking about the self in contexts as diverse as Morocco (Crapanzano), Sri Lanka (Obeyesekere), and Pakistan (Ewing). Stewart is an anthropologist concerned with a dialogical approach to notions of subjectivity. She is interested in narrative, ethnopoetics, post-structuralism, US popular culture, and Appalachia. And while psychoanalysis does not play a big part in her work, Stewart's research does represent one of the more compelling intersections where anthropology's interest in subjectivity can be fruitfully contrasted and compared with psychoanalysis. Finally, Augé and Rustin, in different ways, are the voices of distinctive theoretical interest. While the other anthropologists interviewed also provide valuable theoretical insights, it is Rustin and Augé who specifically address what psychoanalysis can do for social theory. It is my sense that their work typifies some of the best comparative research being done, in transnational contexts, both micro and macro, which are ever-changing and defy most traditional categories of experience and constructs of identity. Contexts where to risk knowing 'the other' increasingly requires that we remain open to the potential wisdom that everywhere ferments in disorienting ambiguities. Or, as Augé claims to end our conversation, in a discussion on identity and alterity (hinting as well at the value of certain psychoanalytic understandings):

> Let us bear in mind that individual and collective identities, as well as individual and collective cultures, get constructed through confrontation and negotiation with alterity – this being, by the way, the meaning of ritual activity. If we were to insist only on the exterior of symbolic meaning, any understanding of the complexity of the identity/alterity nexus gets necessarily limited. And by limiting such understanding, we further weaken or rupture the nexus, and thus end up threatening both forms of existence. (p. 159)

## Notes

1. Parts of this essay previously appeared in a shorter article of mine (co-authored with Wesley Shumar) entitled 'Returns of the repressed: some new applications of psychoanalysis to ethnography', in *The Vitality of Objects: Exploring the Work of Christopher Bollas* (J. Scalia, ed., Wesleyan/Continuum, 2002). The excerpts are here reprinted by permission of Sage Publications Ltd.
2. Nancy Chodorow, in her noteworthy book *The Power of Feelings* (Yale, 1999), argues somewhat differently, claiming that anthropology 'is now the only contemporary social science with a flourishing psychoanalytic subfield' (p. 132). While this may well be true, it is precisely the marginal status of that *subfield* that concerns me, and has prompted me to interview for this collection researchers not otherwise identified with the specific subfield of 'psychoanalytic anthropology'.
3. Together with Chodorow's above-cited *The Power of Feelings*, another book that vigorously and incisively makes this case is Anthony Elliott's *Subjects to Ourselves* (Polity Press, 1996). Elliott's aim, in focusing on the relationship between fantasy and the existing social order, 'is to develop a novel account of the implications of internal conflict and psychic division for the current debate over modernity and postmodernity . . . The book proposes that without a psychoanalytical concept of fantasy – of the representational expression of desires and passions – we are unable to grasp the inseparability of society and subjectivity in the late modern age' (p. 2).
4. Chodorow (1999) significantly advances this comparative exercise. See especially ch. 5 and pp. 204–6.

5. See p. 35–36 of this Introduction, as well as my interview with Stewart (Chapter 6, below).
6. According to Geertz, it is with Malinowski that 'diary disease' is born, and with it the 'pretensions' of its modern-day offshoots, 'confessionalism' and 'authorial self-inspection' – his term, I assume, for what is more commonly referred to as 'reflexivity'. See Ch. 4 of Geertz's *Works and Lives*.
7. I would like to emphasize this crucial point. Even psychoanalytically inspired researchers such as Ewing, Herdt and Stoller, and Chodorow herself do not always extend their studies to include consideration of unconscious processes. Rather, they often fall back onto the more distinctly technical, or clinical, applications of psychoanalysis.
8. On the matter of the 'inner/outer' boundary, see my interview with Dorinne Kondo in Molino and Ware (2001).
9. 'Dissemination refers to a kind of dialectic: as person A encounters object B, A splits into separate ideational parts each with its own logical valorization. B has inspired A's split. But the outcome is not a synthesis between A and B or a compromise formation between the integrity of B and integrity of A. Alternately, however, the splits that occurred in A could not have occurred without confrontation with B – or should one say except through B? So A's encounter with B is rather like a moment of conception' (Bollas, 1995: 61–2). If we think of the fieldwork situation, we can imagine a movement of mutually infusing disseminations, a matrix of the kind that is perhaps best evidenced by Vincent Crapanzano in his landmark book, *Tuhami* (Crapanzo, 1980).
10. See Marcus and Fischer (1986) for a discussion of the psychoanalytically inspired interviewing strategies of Waud Kracke (*Force and Persuasion: Leadership in an Amazonian Society*, Chicago, 1978), Robert Levy (*The Tahitians: Mind and Experience in the Society Islands*, Chicago, 1973), and G. Obeyesekere (in the cited *Medusa's Hair*, 1981).
11. Herdt and Stoller prefer the term 'interpreter', or cultural translator, to the standard *informant*. This is but one aspect of the authors' detailed, threefold critique of a positivist ideology that extends to the concepts of participant observation and culture shock as well.
12. I refer here to an unpublished paper by Chodorow, entitled 'Reflections on cultural meaning and personal meaning', where she specifically calls for a 'person-centred ethnography'. I take this to mean a kind of fieldwork that involves the anthropologist in an holistic project that both recognizes the irreducibility of psychological experience and, in problematizing the notion of culture, is sensitive to the co-creation of psychological and cultural meanings. See also note 17, below.
13. I say 'at least in their theorizing' because of the gap sometimes evidenced in *Intimate Communications* between theory and practice. Indeed, for all of the rigorous consistency of their theory and the richness of their clinical insights, Herdt and Stoller at times fail, I believe, in the application of a clinical ethnography to the arena of fieldwork. The authors fall short especially when it comes to creating a field-specific interview setting that can transpose – without necessarily replicating – the essentials of a psychoanalytic setting that might honor the person of the interpreter (or 'informant') while inviting the most intimate of communications.

For the sake of brevity, I refer the reader to chapter 6 of *Intimate Communications*, entitled 'Portrait of a woman' (Herdt and Stoler, 1990: 152–201). Note here how the researchers speak for their female interpreter,

Penjukwi, in a manner that not only generates the data they seem to be seeking but suggests a fundamental disrespect for the person interviewed. Consider how, from the very start, Penjukwi is not allowed to answer for herself. Whereas it would have sufficed – and been methodologically appropriate – to ask the initial question, Herdt reveals in the excerpt that follows a penchant for the very framing devices – or 'centering plays' – to which critics like Crapanzano alert us. (See Crapanzano's essay 'Centering' in his collection titled *Hermes' Dilemma and Hamlet's Desire*.)

'Session' participants (Herdt and Penjukwi) are discussing 'screwing':

H: Um hm. What do you feel inside? Happy? Afraid?
P: Just happy. (*Pause*) Then—
H: When do you picture this? Only when screwing?
P: At that time.
H: When you see (your lover's) face?
P: No, when I see his cock. Only then.
H: First he himself removes his trousers or grass sporran—?
P: (*Cuts in.*) He does that.
H: And when you see his penis, you recall the fantasy of you and the boy playing around.
P: Right.
H: Now I want to look closer at the fantasy. The boy says, 'Look at my cock.' You like that.
P: Yeah.
H: Then what? Is he then forceful? Removes your grass skirt? Or what?
P: He may be forceful and . . . removes my grass skirt. . . and then we don't have . . . (*mumbles*).
H: What?
P: We do it, just play at it [screwing]. (*Smiles*.)
H: Do you see his cock in the image? His boy's cock . . . What do you feel?
P: Happy.
H: Happy? You're not afraid of his cock? (Herdt and Stoller, 1990: 174–5)

And so on. What, if anything, of Penjukwi's account is not framed by the interest of the researcher? How is this exercise at all construed in the service of a person-centred ethnography? Is there any true sense that Penjukwi and a story from her life are what are being elicited here, and invited to unfold? What does it say about the directionality of the exchange, to be given a textual indication that the interpreter, at one point, 'cuts in' on the researcher?!? To make room for the subjectivity of the researcher is not to usurp the rightful, fundamental and co-creative presence of the interpreter in the ethnographic process. But I will not belabour the point.

14. On this score, and along the lines already suggested by Ewing and Chodorow, as well as by Crapanzano in works like *Tuhami* (1980) and 'The self, the third, and desire' (in Crapanzano, 1992), the ubiquitous, relational dynamics of the transference and countertransference define the singularity of this interpretative framework.
15. In Bollas' words: 'The unconscious breaks up its own desire' (Bollas, 1995: 63).
16. Among these I include, to name just a few, fieldworker-authors like Jean Briggs (*Never in Anger*, Harvard, 1970), Michele Stephen (*A'aisha's Gift*, California, 1995), and Carol Laderman (*Taming the Winds of Desire*, California, 1993).

17. In *The Power of Feelings*, Chodorow (1999: 173) specifies: '[W]e need to cross what might be called the horizontal view of cultural meaning – thick description, multiplicity, polysemy, webs of meaning, forests of symbols – with a vertical view, in which each individual's internal history is its own emotionally polysemic web of continually created unconscious and conscious personal meaning, animated by fantasies, projections, and introjections. This psychobiographical personal meaning calls on, intersects with, and itself helps shape the complex web of culture.' This position echoes what Gananath Obeyesekere, in *Medusa's Hair* calls 'subjective imagery': namely, the process whereby 'cultural patterns and symbol systems are put back into the melting pot of consciousness and refashioned to create a culturally tolerated set of images' (Obeyesekere, 1981: 169). His is a feedback system of sorts which grants ontological, creative status to the individual unconscious, whose products are 'mediated by culture before being transformed by our conscious, rational and cognitive faculties' (Obeyesekere, 1981: 9).
18. These words of Bollas are also illustrative, albeit in a near-imperceptible way, of the kinds of theoretical breaks there have been in psychoanalysis from the time of Freud and his early drive model.
19. The initials 'SAR' stand for South African Railway, an object that for the Tshidi mediates between the world of their villages (that the people symbolically associate with life) and the world of the mines (which evokes death). The Comaroffs themselves make this point, in a way that is consistent with Object Relations theory.
20. Consider the tragically arrogant determination of the US-led coalition in Iraq to 'export' democracy there as an example of this kind of 'benevolence'.

# References

Augé M (1999) The War of Dreams. London: Pluto Press.

Blanchot M (1993) The Infinite Conversation. Minneapolis, MN: University of Minnesota Press.

Bollas C (1989) Forces of Destiny: Psychoanalysis and Human Idiom. Northvale, NJ: Aronson.

Bollas C (1992) Being a Character: Psychoanalysis and Self Experience. New York: Hill & Wang.

Bollas C (1995) Cracking Up: The Work of Unconscious Experience. New York: Hill & Wang.

Chodorow NJ (1995) Reflections on cultural meaning and personal meaning. Unpublished paper, delivered at the Annual Meetings of the American Anthropological Association, 1995.

Chodorow NJ (1999) The Power of Feelings. New Haven, CT: Yale University Press.

Comaroff John, Comaroff Jean (1992) The madman and the migrant. In Ethnography and the Historical Imagination. Boulder, CO: Westview Press, pp. 155–178.

Crapanzano V (1980) Tuhami: Portrait of a Moroccan. Chicago: University of Chicago Press.

Crapanzano V (1992) Hermes' Dilemma and Hamlet's Desire: On the Epistemology of Interpretation. Cambridge, MA: Harvard University Press.

Elliott A (1996) Subjects to Ourselves. Cambridge: Polity Press.
Ewing KP (1992) Is psychoanalysis relevant for anthropology? In: T Schwartz et al. (eds), New Directions in Psychological Anthropology. Cambridge: Cambridge University Press.
Fischer M (1986) Ethnicity and the post-modern arts of memory. In: J Clifford, G Marcus (eds), Writing Culture: The Poetics and Politics of Ethnography. Berkeley, CA: University of California Press.
Geertz C (1973) The Interpretation of Cultures. New York: Basic Books.
Geertz C (1988) Works and Lives: The Anthropologist as Author. Stanford, CA: Stanford University Press.
Herdt G, Stoller RJ (1990) Intimate Communications: Erotics and the Study of Culture. New York: Columbia University Press.
Marcus GE (1995) On eccentricity. In: D Battaglia (ed.), Rhetorics of Self-Making. Berkeley, CA: University of California Press.
Marcus GE, Fischer MMJ (1986) Anthropology as Cultural Critique: An Experimental Moment in the Human Sciences. Chicago: University of Chicago Press.
Molino A (ed.) (1997) Freely Associated: Encounters in Psychoanalysis, with Christopher Bollas, Joyce McDougall, Michael Eigen, Adam Phillips and Nina Coltart. London: Free Association Books.
Molino A (2001) Interview with Dorinne Kondo. In Molino A, Ware C (eds) Where Id Was: Challenging Normalization in Psychoanalysis. Middletown, CT: Wesleyan University Press.
Moore H (1994) Gendered persons: dialogues between anthropology and psychoanalysis. In: S Heald et al. (eds), Anthropology and Psychoanalysis: An Encounter through Culture. London and New York: Routledge.
Obeyesekere G (1981) Medusa's Hair: An Essay on Personal Symbols and Religious Experience. Chicago: University of Chicago Press.
Phillips A (1994) On Flirtation: Psychoanalytic Essays on the Uncommitted Life. Cambridge: Harvard University Press.
Phillips A (1995) Terrors and Experts. London: Faber & Faber.
Ricoeur P (1974) Psychoanalysis and the movement of contemporary culture. In: The Conflict of Interpretations. Evanston, IL: Northwestern University Press.
Rosaldo MZ (1980) Knowledge and Passion: Ilongot Notions of Self and Social Life. Cambridge: Cambridge University Press.
Roseneau P (1992) Post-Modernism and the Social Sciences. Princeton, NJ: Princeton University Press.
Sale K (1991) Dwellers in the Land: The Bioregional Vision. Philadelphia, PA: New Society Publishers.
Schiller HI (1985) Culture, Inc.: The Corporate Takeover of Public Expression. New York: Oxford University Press.
Stewart K (1991) On the politics of cultural theory: a case for 'contaminated' cultural critique. Social Research 58(2): 395–412.
Taussig MT (1980) The Devil and Commodity Fetishism in South America. Chapel Hill, NC: University of North Carolina Press.

# PART II
# DIALOGUES IN PSYCHOANALYSIS AND ANTHROPOLOGY

CHAPTER 1
# Gananath Obeyesekere

Gananath Obeyesekere was born and raised in Sri Lanka (then Ceylon), where he entered the local State University in 1951, originally to study English literature. After years spent collecting folk songs across Sri Lanka, his decision to become an anthropologist matured in the course of subsequent fieldwork on mother goddess cults, published years later as *The Cult of the Goddess Pattini* (Chicago, 1984). In time, influenced by the likes of Melford Spiro, Edmund Leach, Weber and Freud, Obeyesekere turned his attention to the larger historical and cultural-cum-psychological forces that were being played out in different political and social arenas. These newer concerns found expression in two works primarily: in *Medusa's Hair: An Essay in Personal Symbols and Religious Experience* (Chicago, 1984), and (with Richard Gombrich) *Buddhism Transformed* (Princeton, 1981). There followed a culmination of the Weber–Freud enterprise (plus Ricoeur) in *The Work of Culture: Symbolic Transformation in Psychoanalysis and Anthropology* (Chicago, 1990), a reformulation of the *Lewis Henry Morgan Lectures* Obeyesekere delivered in 1982 at the University of Rochester.

In the last decade or so, Obeyesekere's interest in the colonial transformation of Buddhism and a scepticism about so-called 'emic' approaches have resulted in *The Apotheosis of Captain Cook: European Mythmaking in the Pacific* (Princeton, 1992) and *Cannibal Talk: Dialogical Misunderstandings in the South Seas* (California, 2004), a book that combines postcolonial criticism with Freudian and other theories. During this same time, Obeyesekere has also renewed his attention to Weber and proposed a structural reformulation of the ideal type via Braudel and Lévi-Strauss: this research, combined with methodological considerations of Freud, Wittgenstein and Nietzsche, yielded the recent *Imagining Karma: Ethical Transformation in Amerindian, Buddhist and Greek Rebirth* (California, 2002). His present research, hinted at in our conversation, involves what he calls 'a Nietzschean and psychoanalytic interpretation of the visionary experience'. In 2003, Obeyesekere was awarded the Royal Anthropological Institute's highest honour, the Huxley Medal, for his contributions to Anthropology. In that same year he also gave the Huxley Memorial Lecture, based on his work on cannibalism.

The following interview with Gananath Obeyesekere took place on the campus of Princeton University on 25 May, 2000 shortly after his retirement from a long and prestigious teaching career there. Indeed, we met just as he was clearing out his office to return to his native Sri Lanka. At the time the interview was the first he'd ever granted, and remains to date the only one in which Professor Obeyesekere discusses issues related to psychoanalytic anthropology.

Anthony Molino: Let me begin with a simple question: How did psychoanalysis come to appeal to you, and how did it develop into a core research interest of yours?

Gananath Obeyesekere: I came to psychoanalysis via English Literature, generally reading some Freud, more or less in diluted form. However, I was fascinated by the whole idea of unconscious motivation, sexual conflicts, especially the Oedipal one, because such conflicts were endemic in Sri Lankan families. English literary critics in the fifties – like F.R. Leavis and his followers – idealized the English 'organic' community prior to the inroads of modernity. This romanticized version of peasant society had little appeal to me, from my insider knowledge of Sri Lankan life. Freud (and later Weber and Marx) provided me a way of grasping conflicts endemic in the families I was acquainted with. The communities in which I grew up seem benign in relation to the nation's contemporary addiction to violence; yet aggression and intrafamilial hostilities were easily visible even then. Psychoanalysis also seemed to make sense of my own Oedipal conflicts – though the detailed discussion of this will have to wait for my memoirs!

I should like to say here that my interest in anthropology also developed out of my undergraduate studies in English literature in Sri Lanka. Critics like Leavis at the time, both in England and in the States, were dealing with the artist as mythmaker in such figures as W.B. Yeats, T.S. Eliot and James Joyce. It was inevitable that my introduction to anthropology was through such figures; consequently, my anthropology was Frazerian. My undergraduate days provided me with an introduction to village life also. It was then with the folly of youth that I embarked on a study of a communal thanksgiving ritual for the goddess Pattini, the major Sri Lankan female deity. I was introduced to a priest of the Pattini cult who lived near my mother's village. Soon for a period of over a year I witnessed virtually every ritual performed by this group and tape recorded them.

I later obtained a Fullbright award in 1956 to the University of Washington in Seattle where I studied social anthropology. This was the time that Radcliffe-Brown's influence was being felt in the US, displacing the earlier Boasian culture history as 'old-fashioned'. But while I was excited with this new movement, I was always somewhat sceptical of its scientistic pretensions. While at Washington I attended lectures from a charismatic teacher in the medical school, Gert Heilbrunn who was an expatriot psychoanalyst – from Vienna, I think. In anthropology I took a class on Culture and Personality from Melville Jacobs, one of Boas's students. Mel Jacobs wrote extensively on Northwest Coast Amerindian folklore from a psychoanalytic perspective, and he is truly one of the neglected figures in our field. Melford E. Spiro also joined the faculty when I was a student at Washington, and we developed a strong friendship which persists to this day. Naturally, our Buddhist interests coincided, though Mel had not yet decided on his Buddhist fieldwork venue. Thus my early interests were reinforced by contact with Mel Spiro, and while I now have questions about his methodological stance and his strong commitment to a 'scientific model', I owe a great intellectual debt to him.

AM: I'd like to use this occasion of your 'retirement', so to speak, of your imminent departure from Princeton and the United States to return to Sri Lanka, to ask you about your own sense of place within a certain anthropological tradition. Might you provide both an overview of your lifework and, in the process, assess it critically, especially in light of your crucial efforts to bridge psychoanalysis and anthropology?

GO: The best way to answer, I believe, is for me to proceed chronologically. In Seattle I learned the *sine qua non* of ethnography: that one has to work in a village or small community for at least a year and know its culture and community from the inside. I used a small sequence from my Pattini material for my Master's degree and then went to teach in the University of Sri Lanka, where I also did fieldwork in the classic mode, in the Eastern part of the hill country and then in another village in the South of Sri Lanka, close to the Sinharaja tropical forest . While I was in the field I read Edmund Leach's book, *Pul Eliya: A Village in Ceylon*, based on his work in the North Central province. This influenced my fieldwork, as I saw in the South a pattern similar yet different from Leach's. The upshot of this experience was that I put aside temporarily the study of religion and the uses of Freud in the field for a work that later became my PhD dissertation, entitled *The Natural History of a Land Tenure System*. Weber, rather than Radcliffe Brown, was a strong influence here, and I used the village study to move from the single village to the nation at large. (It's no accident, you see, that Weber and Freud link up in my later work!) I showed the drastic changes that occurred in the village system and then isolated those 'factors of change' as something exogenous to the village. I located those changes in colonial policy; their disastrous impact on the village helped me to understand parallel consequences in the national context. This period, by the way, also forged the strategy that I would employ in later work: I like to argue with a major thinker in great detail and formulate my own position in the process. In my landtenure book, it was Leach I was having an argument with. Some of my later work, especially *Medusa's Hair* and *The Work of Culture*, was similarly refined and took form as a result of arguments with another brilliant thinker like Mel Spiro. So you see, this 'Oedipal model' of argumentation is endemic in my work, and I hope creatively so.

As you've probably gathered, my PhD dissertation was not on psychological anthropology at all. The reason is simple: I had no intention of narrowly specializing in psychoanalytic anthropology; and though that subdiscipline still excites me I am also excited by other things, even though in my sociological and historical work I still use psychoanalytic insights. At that time I also wanted to prove something else: that I could use the dominant paradigm of kinship analysis and Radcliffe-Brownian structuralism as anyone else. In fact, it wasn't until 1963 that I published my first paper in psychological anthropology, 'Pregnancy cravings in relation to social stucture and personality in a Sinhalese village'. After I had obtained my PhD, in 1964, I went to Cambridge for six months on an invitation from Leach, who had already become a very important intellectual influence in my life. I liked his unorthodox positions and his penchant for irreverence, his lack of petty mindedness, and his refusal to allow intellectual debate to descend into personal vendetta. I participated in his seminar at King's College, where I presented a paper titled 'Theodicy, salvation and rebirth in a sociology of Buddhism'. This paper, published in 1968, contained in germ the ideas that I have now developed, after many years, in my recent *Imagining Karma*. It was also at Cambridge, under Leach's encouragement, that I revised my PhD dissertation for publication.

After my stint in Cambridge I worked primarily in the Sociology Department in the University of Sri Lanka, where I became chair in 1968. A few years later, in 1971, Sri Lanka experienced the first of a continuing series of violent political movements that has plagued the nation. Led by disenfranchised Sinhalese Buddhist youth, this Maoist-inspired movement brought the country to a virtual halt. Though the insurrection itself was crushed (only to resurface sixteen years later), it spelled the end of academic freedom in the universities. The government view was that the leadership and much of the fighting cadre came from the campuses and this provided an excuse for the government control of the once free academy. At this point I resigned from the University and joined the University of California, San Diego, where Mel Spiro had in the meantime built a department with a strong psychoanalytic orientation.

AM: I guess what I'm most interested in, apropos of 'a certain anthropological tradition', is your own sense of place in the history of psychoanalytic anthropology. Would you consider discussing your 'heritage' from that angle, and perhaps even comment on the work of figures like Malinowski, Mead, Roheim, Kardiner, and Spiro himself?

GO: Let me state that in general I am reluctant to talk about my place in the history of psychoanalytic anthropology. I find that kind of thing difficult to do and rather pretentious, and have refused similar requests before. I've also written on the matter, on the tradition that is, in a chapter of *The Work of Culture* titled 'Freud and anthropology'. But I will agree here to comment, if only briefly.

If you read Milton Singer's essay on that subject, published a long time ago in Bert Kaplan's book *Studying Personality Cross-Culturally*, you will note that the tradition of psychoanalytic anthropology is dominated by a positivist model. And I don't mean just Kardiner. Take Devereux, a wonderfully creative thinker; he also cannot escape methodological objectivism in most of his work. Or another creative thinker, Erik Erikson: I find *Childhood and Society* not too useful, and the structural scheme Erikson employs in that work to designate the stages of psychosexual development is wrought with binary thinking. It is not just Lévi-Strauss's structuralism that was given to such dichotomies; such binary thinking was in the air at the time, and you see it in Talcott Parsons's 'pattern variables'. By contrast, I was very much excited by Erikson's work on 'psychohistory' (though it has been put to such shallow uses by others). The first article of mine strongly influenced by his work was called 'Personal identity and cultural crisis: the case of Anagarika Dharmapala' which appeared in 1976 in *The Biographical Process*, edited by Frank Reynolds and Donald Capps. Implicitly, Erikson's influence appears in *The Work of Culture*, where I deal with parricide in Buddhist history.

You ask about Malinowski: I use him primarily in *The Work of Culture* to relativize the Oedipus complex and show that there are various forms of life that can be subsumed under that generic term and one must recognize the possibility that some societies may simply ignore that complex. Malinowski also plays a major role in my newest work, *Imagining Karma*.

Again, you must keep in mind, in this context, that around the time I was at San Diego the use of psychoanalysis was strongly influenced by Kardiner and the positivist paradigm, though I myself was already beginning to question both. *Medusa's Hair* was a later reaction to that kind of thinking and a movement to a more dialogical and hermeneutical model, though my own vision of such a model came only with *The Work of Culture*. In fact, as I may have suggested, the movement against positivism was already burgeoning and I was one of the first, together with Vincent Crapanzano, to question this model as far as psychoanalysis and anthropology was concerned.

Where my work is concerned, it is in *The Cult of the Goddess Pattini* that you can still see the impact of the Kardiner paradigm. The book, while completed in 1978, was published only in 1984, and only after the publication of *Medusa's Hair*, which was in fact completed later. It can be seen as a kind of hermeneutical enterprise. I had translated the texts of the cult in its diverse settings, both Buddhist and Hindu, and described their ritual contexts. I then asked: what are the worlds of meaning that are opened up for us by the reading of these texts? This meant rendering the texts intelligible on a variety of levels: the psychoanalytic significance of the central theme of the 'mater dolorosa' and the dead god; the historical development of the ritual in Sri Lanka; its diffusion from Kerala through waves of migration; the stratification of the various myths that constituted the cult and the analysis of the different strata; the medical meaning of the rites as healing rituals, and so forth. I can say without hesitation that it was at that time the most detailed examination of any religious system for anywhere in South Asia . . .

AM: You've mentioned in passing the two books on which, arguably, your reputation as a psychoanalytic anthropologist rests: *Medusa's Hair* and *The Work of Culture*. I wonder if you'd say more about these two seminal contributions.

GO: In *Medusa's Hair* I planned a different theoretical move than the one operating in the Pattini volume. I have been generally critical of a psychoanalytic ethnography that refused to follow the Freudian model of case history. Thus my focus was on the unconscious motivations of ascetic priests and priestesses as they engage in possession trances and penances. On the theoretical level I tried to link Max Weber's notion of culture with Freud's notion of 'deep motivation', and in the process I dealt with a class of symbols that are both cultural and personal at the same time, abolishing the classic distinction between private and public that had till then kept psychoanalysis separate from the cultural analysis of religious symbolism. By this time, in 1980, I had joined the Princeton faculty and the book was finished there. While it was in press, I was invited to deliver the Lewis Henry Morgan lectures at the University of Rochester in 1982, and I used this as a forum for further developing my thoughts on psychoanalysis and culture. These lectures were radically revised and then produced as *The Work of Culture: Symbolic Transformation in Psychoanalysis and Anthropology*, in 1990.

*The Work of Culture* is my most ambitious theoretical work thus far. The phrase 'work of culture' obviously is indebted to Freud's 'dream work' but now expanded to refer to the processes whereby the stuff of fantasy gets transformed into the stuff of culture, trying to overcome the conventional hiatus between personal and public, between the private fantasy and the public culture. Further, it makes a claim that we take Freud's first topography (the dream book and the great case studies) as the main inspiration for a psychoanalytic anthropology, rather than the second topography of id, ego and superego. This is the move made by Lacan as well, but unlike Lacan I do not advocate a Saussurean reformulation of Freud. I was much more influenced by Paul Ricoeur's *Freud and Philosophy*. Like Ricoeur, I make a case for a hermeneutical reformulation of Freud, but such a reformulation does not entail a rejection of the nomological thrust of Freud's work. Hermeneutics need not result in a kind of *ad hoc* interpretation either, but rather the formulation of 'rules for interpretation', which is how Ricoeur deals with Freud's *The Interpretation of Dreams*. In this work I am critical of some aspects of Wittgenstein's work but suggest that his idea of 'family resemblances' between 'forms of life' can be used to avoid a naive positivism as well as the kind of particularism and relativism entrenched in the work of Geertz and in much of cultural anthropology.

*The Work of Culture* is the culmination of my work on the relevance of psychoanalysis for anthropology. I should note here, perhaps, that two years before its publication, I wrote *Buddhism Transformed* with Richard Gombrich. This book takes a different tack entirely, picking up some themes that I had dealt with consistently in the form of articles and chapters to books: namely, the transformation of Buddhism in the colonial period and its effect on Buddhist thought and consciousness. In this book we show the impact of colonial and Protestant values on Buddhism such that it is possible to label the Buddhism that prevails today as 'Protestant Buddhism'. In the spirit of this work I have also written a series of papers where I show the manner in which European notions of Buddhism as a 'rational religion' *par excellence* was transferred to Sri Lanka (and other Buddhist nations), and was then appropriated by the local intelligentsia as the 'true' or 'pure' Buddhism. This entailed a selective appropriation of Buddhist texts and, on the cultural level, it led to a denigration of village religion and the spirit religion of ordinary people as 'unBuddhist'. These works of mine have been very unpopular with those Buddhist intellectuals who have appropriated colonial values without reflection. I expect a second volume dealing with related topics will appear in the future, which I intend to title *Buddhism, Identity and Nationhood: Sri Lanka and the Colonial Experience*.

AM: Allow me to return to your book *The Work of Culture*, where you highlight a number of concerns that are central to my research. One is the problem that the unconscious poses for anthropology. You seem to summarize in one paragraph the whole problem of the relationship between psychoanalysis and anthropology when you write, on page 224: 'With respect to unconscious materials the anthropologist is in a particular and peculiar dilemma. He must either deny that they exist; or he must adopt a comfortable sociologism that says while they exist they do not manifest themselves in cultural form or social life; or he might ignore them and invoke his lack of training to handle them; or he must adopt a theory that helps him to understand them – whatever the theory might be.' You remind me here of the Geertzian contention that only what is public ought to be the concern of anthropology, a position that contrasts markedly with your work's long-standing focus on deep motivation, overlaps of the public and private spheres, and the crystallization of personal symbols in the interstices of the two . . .

GO: Let me address what I think are the multiple layers of your concern. First, the resistance of ethnographers to unconscious motivation. I am not sure fully why this is the case except that in spite of a strong tradition of psychoanalytic thinking in anthropology, it has never become popular. My guess is that fieldwork in psychoanalytic ethnography is a tough enterprise. One can, I suppose, get dreams easily enough, but without the necessary personal associations, simply because it is difficult to talk about such matters with informants. In several places I've made a plea for a different strategy: namely, following Freud's own example, I've suggested that we focus on specific case studies of individuals in the field situation, but over a long time period. This is what I do in *Medusa's Hair*. But the general strategy of fieldwork, where one goes into the field to study an alien society for one year and tries to understand the language and culture, also makes this approach a very difficult one.

Second, the problem you outline was clearly evident in the positivistic theory and methodology of J.W.M. Whiting and colleagues at Harvard. They employed an elaborate methodology of studying socialization in other cultures, which became embodied in a work known as *The Field Guide to Socialization*. Reading the guide is a Kafkaesque experience, because it is written *in vacuo*, and not from the field. It's armchair anthropology. It would be impossible to implement even a fraction of the information the ethnographer is supposed to garner during fieldwork. The actual fieldwork results were published in a book titled, I believe, *Children of Six Cultures*, where the fieldworkers who did the Indian part of the study fully showed the impossibility of the task – the lack of nuanced knowledge of a language, the inaccessibility of the private arenas where child-rearing takes place, the lack of sympathy of respondents for some of the seemingly silly questions being asked, and so forth. As an aside, I should say here that my attitude to ego psychology, insofar as fieldwork is concerned, and not as a theory (which I can also criticize), is exactly the same. It will simply be impossible to do a study of socialization on that basis. Hence the need to move from socialization to case history. But I'll have more to say about ego psychology later, I'm sure . . .

AM: You've hit on a note here – that of ego psychology – that I'd intended to explore with you in any case, and might as well pursue now. You seem to be at odds with that brand of psychoanalysis, to say the least . . .

GO: My argument entails a second look at Freud's first topography, and at the idea that there is no 'ego' involved there. It is arguably, then, the most radical of Freud's efforts, insofar as it entails a near total rejection of the Cartesian Ego, as in 'I think, I am'. I have made a similar point in *The Work of Culture*, where I suggest the following three points, the first of which I've already anticipated:

One is that all of Freud's major case histories were written before the full development of the second topography of Ego, Id, Superego. This does not mean that the second topography is not anticipated in the case studies, especially the idea of ego. But Freud did not use the second schematic model when it actually came to the *interpretation* of case histories. Secondly, I also made the point that Freud, in his maturer years, placed himself squarely within the Cartesian tradition and in some sense outdoing it by positing *three* domains of the self or ego. I am not sure whether this was a salutary move.

Thirdly, I will now emphasize, if any doubt remains, that I remain unsympathetic to ego psychology. The idea of the Ego receives its fullest development in Europe and the US and, as Nietzsche and others recognized, it comes from prior times in the monotheistic notion of soul (as it is in the Upanishadic idea of *atman*, even though *atman* is a neuter concept, like the *It* – as Nietzsche and Groddeck would call the Id). Additionally, ideas of ego are so important to capitalistic individualism such that one cannot imagine EuroAmericans (but not Japanese, nor the developing Chinese) without Ego. Indeed, Durkheim made the point in *Suicide*, when he talked of the Egoistic suicide that comes from excessive individualism, especially in the West. Thus while forms of Ego psychology are popular and appropriate for the West – witness, for example, the enormous influence of Kohut – it cannot be transferred as easily into cultures where egoism (in Durkheim's sense) is not found. I am not, of course, making the foolish point that other cultures have no individuals, or do not know *individuality* (for individual separatedness is essential for sanity); what I am saying, instead, is that individuality must be distinguished from capitalistic *individualism*. If the ego is historically and culturally constituted, then it does not make sense to use Ego psychology without a radical altering of its premises. This is compounded by the fact that it is impossible, in my opinion, to apply the postulates of ego psychology, whether that of Winnicott or Kohut, owing to the contingencies of fieldwork . . .[1]

AM: . . . especially if it is Geertz that one is challenging . . .

GO: Yes. You were suggesting, if I recall, how the anthropological view of culture as systems of meaning constructed over a long historical period inhibits psychoanalytic probing. And indeed, I find the work of neo-culturologists like Geertz rather limiting on this score. Geertz talks of culture as 'webs of significance' but in my critique of him (in the epilogue of *The Work of Culture*) I make the point that while I see 'webs of significance' everywhere I do not see the spider at work! That is to say, the idea of culture without the notion of agency (people making culture, or 'the work of culture') does not help us understand how cultural ideas as forms of life got started in the first place; and how they change; and why they persist. Of course, agency must also be linked to socioeconomic processes and, depending on our field of research, to ideas of power. And while I must add that agency need not imply that all of us use a psychoanalytic theory of motivation, for me at least it is a powerful tool, especially with regards to what I hold to be the workings of unconscious motivation.

Along these lines, let's not forget that the dominant anthropological view of culture comes immediately from Weber, later popularized at Harvard by Talcott Parsons, who was an important formative influence on Geertz. But Parsons was explicitly sympathetic to psychoanalytic theory and his work *Personality and Social Structure* has some beautiful stuff on such things as the 'father symbol', where he also connects Freud with the understanding of social structure. But while Parsons, with his huge cosmic models, has gone out of vogue, he did borrow the idea of culture from Max Weber. And, as he shows in his introduction to Weber's *The Sociology of Religion*, Weber himself almost seems to postulate a human 'drive for meaning'. Meaning for Weber does not make sense unless it is linked with the motivations of such beings as prophets, charismatic leaders, and so forth, whose motivations in turn are 'determined' by larger socio-economic forces. But Weber was not sympathetic to psychoanalysis – not at least until very late in his life, when apparently he began to read and appreciate Freud. It was in *Medusa's Hair*, I think, that I made a first move to link Freud and Weber, or Weber's theory of culture with Freud's theory of unconscious motivation. That whole book, and especially Part 3, is the exposition of this conjuncture between Freud and Weber.

Finally, it was also in *Medusa's Hair* that I looked to abolish the distinction between public and private symbolism, something entrenched in cultural anthropology even to this day – although nowadays feminist scholars and post-structuralists do not hesitate to abolish that distinction. In my field I think I was one of the first to make the point that the public and the private can be one and the same in respect of what I have called 'personal symbols'. Thus ghosts, demons, and so forth, are part of a public pantheon but they are also, in my estimation, 'demonomorphic' representations of unconscious processes.

AM: You make a very interesting but fleeting point in your work that one of anthropology's primary resistances to psychoanalysis has been the result of somehow confusing psychoanalytic theory with its object of enquiry, or with what for lack of a better term we might call the 'contents' of the unconscious. Is this what you're hinting at?

GO: Yes, and it is not an unusual position. It's in W.H.R. Rivers, one of the pioneers of the discipline, who attempted along with C.G. Seligmann to effect a rapprochement between psychoanalysis and anthropology way back in the late 1920s. And alongside Rivers' classic work *Psychology and Ethnology* is a pioneer effort by Ernest Jones, in an address to the Royal Anthropological Institute titled 'Psychoanalysis and Anthropology'. Among the kind of issues raised were the need to test psychoanalytic theories in the field and try to understand the contents of the unconscious in other cultures. Following this, Rivers wrote the first work on dreams in 'primitive societies'. Unfortunately, this line of enquiry turned out to be unfulfilled in British Anthropology, primarily as a result of the work of Radcliffe-Brown who adopted a Durkheimian sociologism (that Durkheim himself did not subscribe to, by the way) which became a paradigm for British Social Anthropology till recent times. There are now dents in the system; and American Anthropology was left to do the rest of the pioneering.

What we have to remember here, and what motivated me to write *Medusa's Hair*, is that the unconscious refers to and is inhabited by *beings*, and not just drives and wishes. Thus the significance of demons and ghosts in such states as spirit possession. An understanding of this sort is also what makes the work of Melanie Klein and the early Lacan so much more attractive than ego psychology, though the humanization of Klein by Winnicott is important . . .

AM: You talk, in *The Work of Culture*, about how good metatheories combine both generalizing nomological principles with a capacity to address the uniqueness of different life forms. In terms of applying psychoanalysis to anthropology, you invite a reciprocal movement between the disciplines – arguing, it would seem, against, Devereaux's attribution of a certain superiority to the psychoanalytic model . . .

GO: This is a point I develop, albeit briefly, in the Afterword to the second edition of another book of mine, *The Apotheosis of Captain Cook: European Mythmaking in the Pacific*, where I argue that the well-known idea that Cook was treated as a god by Hawaiians was invented in England and not Hawaii, and that it is a myth of 'imperialism, civilization and conquest' having antecedents in previous accounts of apotheoses of European civilizers, such as that of Cortes. I show that European rationality itself is a myth and Europeans, like everyone else, are myth-makers. I use this work as a way of blurring the distinction between the West and the Rest, something that is a widespread implicit or explicit assumption underlying the human sciences.

To get back to your question, however, I also suggest there that though psychoanalysis is a Western implant there is no reason for rejecting its insights *vis-à-vis* other cultures. But it seems to me that the theory simply cannot be put into literal effect, there has to be a creative translation of the theory in terms of postulates from other cultures. This is the problem with Devereux, without denying his creativity and brilliance. But I don't think that his model is going to take us too far in respect of cultures so different from modern Europe. As I say this, I clearly do not mean to subscribe to a simple opposition between the West and the Rest, something I also resist. Let me offer a simple but telling example: I would be laughed out of court in Sri Lanka if I were to literally translate 'castration anxiety' into Sinhala. The whole idea has to be transcreated.

There is, of course, also the interesting historical problem that psychoanalytic insights might well appear in disguise in other cultures, or openly. For example, on the one hand I deal with something like the discovery of the Oedipus Complex by the philosopher Vasubandhu around the sixth century both in *The Work of Culture* and in my most recent work *Imagining Karma: Ethical Transformation in Amerindian, Buddhist and Greek Rebirth*. On the other hand, one can make a good case for the use of concepts from other cultures, be it Africa or India or wherever, to throw light on or interrogate Western epistemological assumptions. A good point is the great Buddhist idea that there is no permanent enduring entity called the Self, either as a transcendental postulate or as an enduring entity within the person. This might force us to reconsider ego psychology, not just in relation to Buddhist societies, but in relation to Western ones also.

AM: This seems to be a way of reiterating your point of needing to move anthropology's idea of itself from that of being a science of man to what you call, in *The Work of Culture*, 'a quest for understanding what it means to be human' . . .

GO: Exactly . . .

AM: Along these lines, I'd like to connect here to your remarks on ego psychology. The emergence of this trend in psychoanalysis in the 1950s seems to coincide with a break in the long-standing historical relation between psychoanalysis and anthropology: indeed, one might argue that it is precisely because of this celebration of the Western ego that anthropology and psychoanalysis part ways . . .

GO: I don't think that the break between the two disciplines had anything to do with the development of Ego psychology, but rather with the British paradigm (which was influential even in the States). In the States itself I would suspect that Ego psychology would be vastly attractive, owing to the preoccupation with self theory, personhood, and identity formation in anthropology itself. But I am not sure what one could do with it in the fieldwork situation. Here the notion of object relations would be relevant but how could that be divorced from the reification of the Ego remains in my opinion problematic.

This reminds me, by the way, of a line by Paul Ricoeur, 'that everybody bears the responsibility for situating psychoanalysis in his own vision of things', which I used as an epigraph for my Introduction to *Medusa's Hair*. One of the things that in my early life attracted me to Freud, and made him congenial in a way, is that I found that some of the things that he mentioned – tensions in the family, Oedipal conflict, the power of sexuality – were real in the society that I grew up in. They were not just something from the West. Perhaps this is why I personally find that Freud makes more ethnographic sense than Lacan – whose early work I like, just as his later arid scienticism puts me off.

AM: In an interview of mine with Kathleen Stewart, we explored the logic and functions of narrative practices in psychoanalysis and ethnography. What do you see as their areas of intersection and reciprocal enrichment? and what is your view, say, of a work like Vincent Crapanzano's *Tuhami*, which arguably broke new ground in such an interdisciplinary context precisely because of its narrative or dialogical experimentation? If I recall, you mentioned earlier that you and Crapanzano were pioneers of sorts . . .

GO: I certainly think that *Tuhami* was a truly innovative ethnography because for once the voice of the informant was given a prime place in a dialogical setting. Thus there was a narrative of the informant which was framed in terms of a minimalist, but nevertheless significant, intervention by the author-interlocutor. I am not sure it is fair to characterize it as an essay in psychoanalytic ethnography because its importance is broader, though those of us interested in the interface between psychoanalysis and anthropology can scarcely ignore it. It also self-consciously recognizes that while the 'methodological objectivism' that held sway in the human sciences is flawed, it is also the case that the authorial voice cannot be stilled because it frames the discourse of the informant. *Tuhami* also remains relevant for our times because while 'ethnographic authority' right now has a bad press, Crapanzano honestly admits there is no way of escaping it. I suspect many of us are decrying 'ethnographic authoritarianism' rather than the voice of the author which cannot be eliminated from the text. *Tuhami* I think appeared a year before *Medusa's Hair*, and hence I was not able to incorporate it into my own thinking; still, it is interesting that both Crapanzano and I adopted a similar methodological stance, even though there is more of Tuhami in Crapanzano's narrative than I have with any one of my informants.

As concerns the areas of 'enrichment', things are still not working. That is, while some of us have used and fused psychoanalytic thinking with the ethnographic idea of culture, there is hardly any mention among psychoanalysts of our work. That is, analysts are unable to escape the narrow confines of the couch into the larger world of another culture, or for that matter their own culture. Not only is this a retreat from Freud and his early disciples but it is also self-defeating to imagine the enclosure of the doctor and patient in a room in a clinic, insulated from the larger culture. I think Lacan is an exception because he does provide tools for us to enter the world of culture (the symbolic order), but he himself does not venture very far. Surely, this is apparent in Winnicott, and even eclectic thinkers like Adam Phillips do not venture into ethnography for insights. Winnicott lived and worked in a world where the 'law of the Father' had gone mad (and still is in my part of the world), yet the Father as part of the symbolic order rarely appears in his text. Freud himself, in *Group Psychology and the Analysis of the Ego*, did provide a model, however imperfect, for linking the father with group leadership. Whereas I think, and as I state in *Medusa's Hair*, it is important to link the theory of deep motivation with that of the Weberian notion of culture. This is not the only path for mutual enrichment but it remains a useful one . . .

This brings us to the distinctive kinds of narratives that one finds in psychoanalytic ethnography. If we think of what is called a 'cure' in a psychoanalytic sense, this process must be more complex when seen from the side of the patient, rather than the analyst's. This insight comes from field interviews with people who, like the women in *Medusa's Hair*, relate their experiences with demonomorphic forces peopling their unconscious through a story or narrative. Though I did not deal with that theme in the book it does come out in my classes on 'Freud and Narrative', where I suggest that there are two kinds of narrative in psychoanalysis: one is the narrative of the analyst, who writes a case history of a patient and tells his colleagues and other readers, usually in formal scientific language, how the cure was effected or not. The other is the narrative of the patient, and of this we hear almost nothing. One beautiful exception to this state of affairs is Marie Cardinal's *The Words to Say It*, where we have a talented novelist writing about her experience with illness, analysis and cure: very simply, I cannot imagine an analyst writing about her in this fashion . . . What I'm implying here, of course, is that narrativization, the very act of telling a story about illness, may itself be part of the cure. Why do I say this?

This takes us back to Weber, and the propensity of human beings to give meaning to experience, often enough cultural meaning. The patient analysed must, it seems to me, articulate the experience of analysis within her own life experience, which might well involve an attempt to incorporate that experience into the frame of her religious/existential experience. This, I imagine, is the success of Jungian analysis, or one strand of its success, as against the extreme rationality of classic psychoanalysis.

In psychoanalytic ethnography we authors employ several narrative forms. One is like the analyst's narrative: the patient is not a partner in the narrative; at least her voice is not heard in the manner stated above. This is the typical form of discourse in psychoanalytic ethnography and exemplified in Kardiner and the culture-and-personality people. I am not wholly opposed to it and I defend a version of this in my book *The Cult of the Goddess Pattini*, because there is little choice but to use this mode. But here is *Tuhami* again; it is awfully hard to do this after Crapanzano's work and indeed the whole newer ethnographic writing that explicitly or implicitly critiques the method of methodological objectivism. Thus in *Medusa's Hair*, as Crapanzano with *Tuhami*, I bring the voices of informants and frame that discourse and interpret it in terms of psychoanalytic theory. Unlike *The Words to Say It*, it remains an ethnographic narrative and not that of the informant; nevertheless, it brings the informant's own story within the interpretative discourse of the ethnographer.

AM: In the course of my research, one of the gaps I've found in the work of anthropologists engaged by psychoanalysis is the near-total lack of familiarity with developments of the last 20–30 years, and particularly with the output of the British Independent tradition. Both you and Kathy Ewing at Duke, for instance, make the point that the primacy of *logos*, or the privilege the West accords to language, is not a sufficient tool through which to understand, or even mediate, *experience*. Ewing, for instance, takes issue with Lacan on this score, arguing that the symbolic register cannot be presumed to provide any kind of privileged access into inordinately diverse and rich realms of experience. It seems to me that both of you are hinting at the possibility that other visions or versions of psychoanalysis might be able to provide a way for talking about the immediacy of experience without reducing it to the primacy of language. You both seem to hint, for instance, that Winnicott . . .

GO: Winnicott is the obvious person there . . .

AM: . . . and Christopher Bollas is another, among the contemporary theorists . . . but neither you nor Ewing, for example, spell out Winnicott's name or look to develop or apply his insights . . .

GO: Well, I think that if there is any lack in current anthropological research of this kind, this is where it is. Bollas, you see, I'm not familiar with. And personally, I'm still trying to sort out whether I can articulate Winnicott in terms of my interests. It's something I'm still playing around with. Several people have pointed this out to me, by the way, including an English psychoanalyst of note. But I do want to say that with Winnicott I have many of the problems I have with the notion of Ego or Self, both of which are central to his work. Many of Winnicott's ideas make sense in a Euroamerican cultural context but not in relation, say, to Sri Lanka. For example, on the one hand, the word for 'self' is *atman*, but that has all sorts of other reverberations in Buddhism and Vedanta. On the other hand, take an obvious notion such as the development of self-awareness in childhood. I would as a Buddhist make the claim that if one takes out the word *self* and simply uses 'awareness', then one has made a very interesting move. Thus the issue would be a development of *awareness*, which means awareness of many things, including the self, the body, and the world that emerges within the field of consciousness. One is removed from the narcissistic preoccupation with self as all those hyphenated words indicate. I'd like to think I can take statements from Winnicott and others and, without using the restrictive term 'self', simply retranslate them into English, to make even greater sense.

AM: In trying to make these connections, it also seems that you are using Buddhism as a way of both engaging psychoanalysis and, at the same time, to find a vehicle other than language to get to something like the primacy of experience . . .

GO: Yes, that's correct, as I'm also looking to uphold a sense of the intrinsic primacy and integrity of Buddhist thought itself. Of course, the other point where Buddhism and psychoanalysis intersect is in the theory of desire, and while Buddhist desire is epistemologically broader than the psychoanalytic one, there are some Buddhist thinkers who did formulate sexual desire as primary or as ideal, typically representing the wider notion of desire.

AM: I wonder if I'm now beginning to understand more about what you call your 'disengaged identity' . . .

GO: Well, part of my disengaged identity again comes from the Buddhist sense that you should be able to stand outside of yourself in some way. The term itself is Charles Taylor's, which I borrow. His is a reaction to the postmodern and the occasional hermeneutical dilemma which states there in no such thing as objectivism in the human sciences. While sympathetic to this position, Taylor makes the case that one cannot write without something like a 'disengaged identity'. At the risk of repeating myself, I would retranslate this in Buddhist terms; for meditative experience is *par excellence* both the engaged and disengaged identity at work.

AM: One final question. You've mentioned to me in private that you have, over the years, pointed several students of yours in the direction of the New York Institute for psychoanalytic training, to complement their anthropological pursuits. Did you have any such psychoanalytic training yourself? There was no such mention in revisiting your biography earlier . . .

GO: No, I did not. You see, to some degree I resisted this, because one of the criticisms of psychoanalysis when I was in graduate school was simply that you got brainwashed in the process. I mean, psychoanalytic training invariably involves an implantation of sorts, in the consciousness of the trainee, of the models and theories and doctrines of psychoanalysis.

I always felt that if psychoanalysis has validity it must stand on its own, outside of its particular learning situation, in the same way that any other conceptual system, or any other metatheory, must. This is not to suggest that we are at all immune to our conceptual systems: we all learn from our teachers and we all identify with them. We are all victims, to some extent, of certain kinds of dogmas that fall our way. But at the same time, much as I don't have to become a shaman to want to study shamanism, you see, neither do I want to have to be a psychoanalyst to appreciate and apply psychoanalysis.

I should say, in any case, that I do not object in principle for an anthropologist to undergo training analysis. I have known several who have done so, and while some made very little headway with that experience as far as their creative work went, others benefited quite clearly. But I do think it is a mistake to insist on one; that is a kind of authoritarianism that I resist . . .

### Note

1. Alan Roland has pointed out that Obeyesekere's equating of self psychology (Kohut) and object relations theory (Winnicott) reads as a 'highly inaccurate view of psychoanalysis'. My own sense is that Obeyesekere, while failing to distinguish between the two theoretically, combines them on the basis of a shared understanding of a Western-centric 'ego' for the purposes of his critique.

# References

Cardinal M (1994) The Words to Say It. Cambridge, MA: Van Vactor & Goodheart.
Crapanzano V (1980) Tuhami: Portrait of a Moroccan. Chicago: University of Chicago Press.

Durkheim E (1970) Suicide: A Study in Sociology. London: Taylor & Francis.
Erikson EH (1993) Childhood and Society. New York: W.W. Norton.
Freud S (1921) Group Psychology and the Analysis of the Ego. In: J. Strachey (ed.), The Standard Edition of the Complete Psychological Works of Sigmund Freud, vol. XVIII. London: Hogarth.
Jones E (1924) Psychoanalysis and anthropology. Journal of The Royal Anthropological Institute, 54.
Kaplan B (ed.) (1961) Studying Personality Cross-Culturally. Evanston, IL: Row & Peterson.
Leach E (1961) Pul Eliya: A Village in Ceylon. Cambridge: Cambridge University Press.
Parsons T (1964) Social Structure and the Person. New York: Free Press.
Reynolds F, Capps D (eds) (1976) The Biographical Process. Berlin and New York: Walter de Gruyter.
Ricoeur P (1986) Freud and Philosophy. New Haven, CT: Yale University Press.
Rivers WHR (1999) Psychology and Ethnology. London: Routledge.
Weber M (1993) The Sociology of Religion. Boston, MA: Beacon Press.
Whiting JWM (1966) The Field Guide to Socialization. New York: John Wiley.
Whiting JWM, Whiting B (1975) Children of Six Cultures: A Psycho-Cultural Analysis. Cambridge, MA: Harvard University Press.

CHAPTER 2
# Vincent Crapanzano

Vincent Crapanzano is Distinguished Professor of Comparative Literature and Anthropology at the Graduate Center of the City University of New York. His extensive field research, often and profoundly informed by a far-reaching critical appreciation of psychoanalysis, includes work with the Navajo in Arizona, with the spirit-possessed in Morocco, with whites in South Africa, and most recently with Fundamentalist Christians and legal conservatives in the United States. This research has been documented in a number of acclaimed books, many translated (into French, German, Italian, Portuguese, Spanish, Polish, Japanese, and Hebrew), including: *The Fifth World of Forster Bennett: A Portrait of a Navaho* (Viking, 1972, 2002); *The Hamadsha: An Essay in Moroccan Ethnopsychiatry* (California, 1973); *Tuhami: A Portrait of a Moroccan* (Chicago, 1980); *Waiting: The Whites of South Africa* (Random House, 1986); *Hermes' Dilemma and Hamlet's Desire: On the Epistemology of Interpretation* (Harvard, 1992); and *Serving the Word: From the Pulpit to the Bench* (New Press, 2000).

In addition to his present academic post, Professor Crapanzano has also taught at Princeton, Harvard, the University of Chicago, the University of Paris, the Ecole des Hautes Etudes, the University of Cape Town, the University of Brasilia and the Federal University in Rio de Janeiro. He has been a recipient of a Sherman Fairchild Fellowship at the California Institute of Technology, a Poynter Fellowship at Yale, as well as grants and fellowships from the American Academy in Berlin, the Rockefeller Foundation, the Fulbright Commission, the National Science Foundation, the National Institute for Mental Health, the Wenner-Gren Foundation, the CNRS in France, and the Commission Nationale de Cinéma, also in France. In 1998, Crapanzano delivered the Jansen Lectures in Frankfurt am Main, on the theme of the anthropology and poetics of the imagination. His most recent book, *Imaginative Horizons: An Essay in Literary-Philosophical Anthropology* (Chicago, 2003), is loosely based on those lectures. He is presently completing a study on the articulation of life histories/experiences after dramatic changes, such as religious conversion, a bout of insanity, or an alteration in sexual identity.

The following interview with Vincent Crapanzano took place in his New York City apartment on 8 December 1995.

Anthony Molino: Can you talk about your fascination with psychoanalysis? When did it originate, and where does it stand chronologically in relation to your pursuit of anthropological interests?

Vincent Crapanzano: My interest in psychoanalysis grew as I began reading Freud after college, where I didn't study anthropology but philosophy, and was mainly interested in literature. When I graduated, I spent close to a year in Vienna, and it was there that I began to read Freud seriously . . . Later, at Columbia, where I went to graduate school, I didn't find much interest in psychoanalysis. Margaret Mead was sympathetic, but most of the other faculty members and the students were hostile to any kind of psychological anthropology. They had a very simplistic understanding of psychoanalysis. Yet, ironically, despite their limited theoretical interest in the field, they – many of them – had had psychoanalytic therapy at one time or another. Somehow they split off this dimension of their experience from their professional life. In any case, it was at Columbia that I began to develop a more systematic interest in psychoanalysis and its relationship to anthropology.

My Moroccan fieldwork was concerned with curing systems as a whole. My aim was to find a place, a kind of institutional setting, where I could work, over a long period of time, with people who were suffering from any malaise *we* might call 'mental illness'. At the time I was more interested in psychoanalysis as methodology than as theory; that is to say, I wanted to use free-association as a way of learning how people related to various curing practices. It wasn't that psychoanalytic theory didn't interest me; it was just that I found it reductive and simplistic. I was unimpressed by the kind of culture-and-personality use of psychoanalysis the Whitings put forth. But I was interested in psychoanalysis as a kind of interpretive schema against which to reflect. That's what psychoanalysis gave me: a mode of and for reflection. It helped me meet the ethnographic challenge the Moroccans I worked with posed. It was only later, when I was writing *The Hamadsha*, that I began to struggle with exactly how 'psychoanalytic' I wanted to be. I felt uncomfortable with certain of its assumptions, and yet, in a way, much of the work I was doing was premised on these same assumptions.

Before starting to teach at Princeton, I spent a summer in France preparing a graduate course on structuralism. I read Lacan for the first time – in a completely untutored way. Confronted with his *Ecrits*, I was overwhelmed, excited, in agreement, in disagreement, mainly impressed by how strikingly different a picture of psychoanalysis he had from my own and that of the American and English analysts I had read. Lacan's extravagant re-reading of Freud opened up for me the possibility of different readings. What struck me then was the importance he placed on language, and the idea, indeed the fact, that a recounted dream is after all not a dream but a dream text, and that it's this text that is analysed. Now this all seems naive, but at the time it got me thinking about how language as the medium of both psychological expression and analysis could serve as the basis for developing an epistemologically sophisticated, psychoanalytically inspired anthropology. It struck me that through Lacan one could rethink the whole anthropological project.

AM: In an early article of his, entitled 'Psychoanalysis and the movement of contemporary culture', Paul Ricoeur makes the point that the human sciences remain far from achieving an integrated hermeneutical model that can account for the discoveries and insights of Freud, Marx and Nietzsche. You yourself, however, in the essay entitled 'Talking (about) psychoanalysis', in *Hermes' Dilemma and Hamlet's Desire*, cite and take issue with what you call the 'romantic hope' of Abram Kardiner, who similarly aspired to a unified social science. In this context, how do you see the *agonistic* element of dialogue that you call for invigorating the crosscurrents between psychoanalysis and anthropology?

VC: The idea of unification I was disputing was that of a totalizing social science. I don't see why science should be 'unified' in the first place. Why shouldn't 'science' be pluralized? Why shouldn't these sciences be at one another's throats – asserting, debating, challenging? A unified science would be the death of science. I prefer a baroque vision of science. It's the debate, the dialogue, the challenges, the multiple angles of vision, the divergent viewpoints, their refractions and mirrorings that make for good science.

As for the relationship between anthropology and psychoanalysis – I think both disciplines should be pluralized: the relationship between anthropologies and psychoanalyses. It's the tension within and between them that is creative. The power of their 'relationship' lies not in unity, as people like Mel Spiro would want, but in disjunction. It's their disjunction, their divergent perspectives, that calls attention to their respective limitations. I prefer a more agonistic view of their relationship to one of complementarity, which can only breed complacency.

AM: In an article written several years ago, 'The self in a world of urgency', Unni Wikan contends that anthropology's fascination with the problem of multiplicity is itself a product of the Western academy's own experience of fragmentation and discontinuity. In questioning the operative postmodern paradigms of much contemporary ethnography – in which she says the problem of representation vs experience 'has simply ceased to exist' – Wikan contends that the problem of wholeness disappears by a sleight of hand or, as she goes on to say (as you yourself have):

'Personally, I cannot see how if a person is unaware of such discontinuity there is at all a problem of experience.' How do you respond to this kind of critique, and is this fascination simply the latest expression of our own ethnocentrism?

VC: We must not forget that a statement like Wikan's, where she says that the discipline's fascination with the problem of multiplicity is a product of the academy's own experience of fragmentation and discontinuity, is itself a product of that very experience. Of course, what Wikan says has always been true. What we see seems always to be governed, to a certain extent, by our own situation. I've often said, somewhat ironically, that if one wants to study territoriality, or notions of taboo and pollution, we might consider *starting* with the academy. Just imagine a study that concerned itself with the phenomenon of intellectual pollution! But I wouldn't want to push this too far, because it's only part of the fascination. Ultimately, we are not simply projecting our own situation. We are also responding to our experiences of what's out there. Call it difference or otherness or the other.

When Wikan says that 'the problem of representation vs experience has simply ceased to exist', I want to know what her evidence for this is. I don't know that it's true. I think it's precisely one of the major questions anthropologists are asking today. Of course, there are some of them who are trying to deny — or ignore — the conjunction or disjunction of representation and experience by focusing on, indeed asserting only, surface representation, in Baudrillard's fashion. That's 'with-it' anthropology. Wikan's critique, impassioned as it is, strikes me as simplistic if only because she does not read — that is discuss carefully — the work of the people she criticizes. (She's not alone in this. Most anthropological critics of postmodernism do the same thing. You seldom know whom they're attacking.) A good ethnographer has to ask the questions Wikan does, but as a good ethnographer, he or she has to look at the evidence — and read deeply. It's embarrassing to have to say this. By looking only at the surface, in a funny way, Wikan ends up being more postmodernist than many of those she critiques.

To do justice to Wikan, however, I do think she is right to point out that if someone is unaware of the discontinuities in his or her life, we cannot declare them to be a problem of experience for that person. If the decentred self is not a problem, then it's not a problem. From the psychoanalytic angle, however, this 'problem', is more interesting if only because psychoanalysis aims at uncovering that which is hidden, masked, out of awareness, unconscious. Someone may not be aware of the fact that he is really troubled by experiences of discontinuity. He may suffer from other symptoms that lead him to a psychoanalyst and may discover during their analysis the role of discontinuity in his life. Of course, this raises the specter of construction. To what extent is the new awareness – experience – of discontinuity a product of analysis? To what extent has the patient been seduced by this construction?

Anthropologists have paid less attention, at least traditionally, to this problem. Notwithstanding the enormous difference between what psychoanalysts are 'supposed to do' and what they do in their offices during sessions, they have thought through their practice in a much more sophisticated way than anthropologists, who have succumbed to a series of banalities about what they do. They talk a lot, for example, about participant observation, which is obviously a catch-all phrase for a whole lot of attitudes and field practices that are contradictory, discrepant, disjunctive, and in a process of continual change. So what you have, then, is a label for a supposedly common practice that doesn't really have a sound basis in fact.

What's needed is a much more careful reflection on the process of fieldwork. Unlike psychoanalysis, where, because of the simplicity of the setting, it's easier to describe and legislate what goes on, in the field – which is much more complicated – it is harder to describe what goes on. What is needed is a continual reflection on what's going on in the field, and on how this notion called 'the field' can itself determine events and perceptions, as well as their understanding. We can no longer afford to be naive fieldworkers, if only because the people we work with will not let us. I think, however, there are still anthropologists who believe, in a Geertzian fashion, it's possible to be 'invisible' in the field; indeed, that it's possible not to ask 'leading' questions. But no one, including Geertz, has ever been invisible in the field. The delusion is extraordinary. Everyone 'in the field' is certainly aware of the anthropologist. Similarly, the idea of a 'non-leading' question is absurd because every question – even silence – frames what is being questioned. Minimally it frames whatever it questions as being questionable. Rather than try, then, to use pseudo-scientific methods for avoiding influence, you have to plunge right in and look at what in fact is happening as honestly as possible, reflecting critically on how what is happening is determined, among other things, by the extent and intensity of your presence and your interventions. You have to admit from the outset that you will never know fully what your influence is, if only because you are *engaged*, if only because no interpretation is ever final or fully justifiable.

To return then to your question – I would say that when you are confronted with a situation in which a person doesn't experience himself as being disjoined (and has a corresponding self-representation), your questions, as an anthropologist, might well produce a sense of being disjoined and – who knows? – a questioning of self-articulation. The anthropologist may play the role of dreams and nightmares – as pointing out, indeed creating, at some level, another, or a new, awareness: new anxieties. I think we have to be much more careful in theorizing about the field to take into consideration the effect of our own presence. This is a serious problem, with which we have not successfully grappled. And it is not only an epistemological problem; it's also ethical.

But before you ask me another question, let me add that we mustn't give ourselves too much credit either. We are, for the most part, working with people who are living successfully, who are quite autonomous, well-defended, capable of reflecting, of evaluating us in their own terms – terms which might well be more stabilizing than our own.

AM: Psychoanalysis explores dimensions of experience, like the unconscious, not readily subsumed by anthropological models. In this context, I wonder if you could discuss your understanding of *shadow dialogues* and their relevance to fieldwork. More specifically, can ethnographic theory and practice integrate into their respective domains the distinctly psychoanalytic, yet arguably ubiquitous, shadow dialogues of the transference and countertransference?

VC: The first thing that has to be acknowledged is that these dialogues do in fact exist, rather than attempt to deny them through all kinds of pseudo-scientific methods, or dismiss them as depth metaphors, or through emphasis on surface phenomena. We have to ask a series of questions: How do we articulate such phenomena? Where do we locate them? In the psyches of individuals who are listening with a 'third ear', so to speak? Are there varying degrees of awareness of such phenomena? I may have it wrong, but I think there are two ways of conceptualizing transference and counter-transference. One, the orthodox Freudian position, attributes the transference to the patient and the countertransference to the analyst. This formulation, of course, reaffirms the co-presence of two different selves engaged in a process known as a psychoanalysis, which both asserts individual autonomy as it acknowledges the effectiveness of dialogue (however truncated by psychoanalytic practice). There is a contradiction here. At one level, you have these two autonomous beings who enter a dialogue that is somehow independent of them, or contained by them, or determined by them; and at another level, you have transference and countertransference phenomena, the dynamics of which suggest that something else is going on – which puts into question autonomy and control of the dialogue.

Lacan, if I understand him correctly, offers a second way of understanding transference. Transference is containing. It is within the transference that the dialogue occurs and the participants manifest their autonomy or lack of it. Lacan doesn't talk about counter-transference, because he sees it – or interpretation in terms of it – already as part of the transference. From an anthropological point of view, this makes for a more interesting conceptualization, because it doesn't insist upon the centrality, or existential priority, of the individual participants as individuals, in the engagement. One understands, then, why many contemporary studies of the decentred or multiple self are more sensitive to a Lacanian understanding of the transference.

And, if I were to fault my own theorizing, I would have to admit that my dialectical approach probably has over-emphasized the individual self and not been as sensitive to the effect of dialogical containment. It seems clear that my theorizing reflects my individualism.

As in some of the essays in *Hermes' Dilemma*, I'm reluctant to use 'transference' and 'countertransference' – and their metaphors – to describe non-psychoanalytic or psychotherapeutic encounters like the ethnographic, because they reflect a particular practice which may well be different from, say, the anthropological, from what happens in the field; and because they are derived from and relate to psychoanalytic theory or metapsychology, and are thereby, in a certain sense, self-referential if not self-validating. I prefer not to have to rely on that element of self-validation. I don't think we should describe what normally happens in the field as transference and countertransference, at least in the traditional psychoanalytic sense. No doubt, similar dynamics occur. But the 'metapragmatic talk' that references the pragmatic processes defined as transference and countertransference may be better metaphorized in different ways which integrate with other kinds of understanding. This approach is open and allows us to acknowledge ethnographically the function, if you will, of the particular metaphors for understanding pragmatic relations like 'transference' in different encounters. We can better appreciate the integrative, indeed the theory-confirming, role of calling certain of these relations – of 'father' transferences, for example. It conforms to psychoanalytic theory and practice – and to the cultural and historical conditions of the genesis and continuance of that practice and theory. I think if we start applying these conceptualizations and metaphors to other practices, we risk distorting them – rendering them psychoanalytic-like. We might miss countless other ways in which the pragmatic processes are referenced and metaphorized – and the implications of these references.

We also have to recognize that the awareness and articulation of pragmatic practices, that is context-constituting practices, like transference, vary from society to society. The fact that Freud began to concern himself with transference and countertransference only after investigating the symbolic meaning of dreams, jokes, and other events, cannot be explained simply in terms of his own intellectual trajectory but as a symptom of the language community in which he lived – which has always privileged symbolic over pragmatic and rhetorical uses.

AM: Concerning dreams, you develop in your work what you call a 'Moroccan dream theory', which presents us with the disjunctive idea that the soul leaves the body at night. According to the maxim you cite: 'When a man sleeps, his soul leaves his body and walks around. No one sleeps with his soul . . .'

VC: I am not at all sure that the Moroccan theory of dreams, of the soul's wandering, is in fact disjunctive. It's a theory. I'm not sure how reflective of experience, except perhaps of dreaming, it is. We have to be careful not to view a people's theorizing about what we would call psychology – their ethnopsychology – as an expression of their experience. It may be. But we have to establish the linkage.

'Ethnopsychology' is already a misnomer, acting as it does as a framing device. We're really caught in a situation where almost all of ethnography should be written – in Derridean terms – under erasure. All our terms impose a philosophical understanding that may well be alien to the culture being described. Of course, we'd get nowhere if we did that, so we selectively pick certain terms, according to our interests and orientation, and we question them. It's the framing that's important here. The very idea of a 'psychology' presupposes an economy of knowledge, a classificatory system whose presuppositions are probably quite different from those of the Moroccans I worked with. It isn't that they don't have 'inner' experiences. It isn't that they don't have a 'reality' that we would describe as psychological. But it's the framing – and the staging – of such realities that's different. What's understood in terms of demonic intrusions, being struck by a demon, possessed by one, married to one, is experienced differently from what would be understood were it described in some other idiom, say, a psychoanalytic one. (I don't want to enter into the problem of a psychological idiom's self-realization.)

Would such a difference affect the nature of reflection, of self-reflection? Would expressive or dramatic reflection be more likely in a world articulated in terms of demons? I doubt it. But we should pose the question. The problem of self-consciousness has always been a big one, especially in interpretative anthropology. It was for Victor Turner. *Has* a person to be conscious of reflecting for there to be reflection? Or is it possible to enact 'reflection' without being fully conscious of what one is doing? I'm not saying this well. I'm referring to something like 'acting out' in psychoanalysis.

From a political standpoint, I feel there has to be a kind of self-consciousness for something to be reflected upon – at least critically. There's a lot of talk today in anthropology about *resistance*, in a political sense.

Anthropologists are declaring all sorts of things 'resistance'. It seems a bit promiscuous. To me at least, for an act to be one of resistance, political resistance, it has to be recognized as such by those who perform it. To say that a people making a pilgrimage to some shrine is a form of resistance is so only if they see it that way. It may well be understood as such by a dictator or an anthropologist. But the pilgrims may just be seeking escape from tyranny, or doing what they have always done or been obliged to do by some supernatural entity. If they are not consciously resisting, then there is no sense of the autonomy, which I take to be what resistance is all about.

Of course consciousness of what one is doing is always problematic. We may be acting in bad faith, denying what we know, wishing not to know what we know we know, etc. I'm talking about all those quasi-conscious knowledges, those semi-awarenesses, which you psychoanalysts are concerned with. Think, again, about acting out. Does or doesn't the adolescent boy who breaks the windows in the row houses his father is building know he is acting out his anger at his father? Do I ever understand why I do something? I may say why I've done it, and then years later, after having been in analysis – or having been questioned by an anthropologist – I discover what I said was my reason, was not my 'real' reason! I discover it was motivated by my desire not to admit my 'real' motivation. And perhaps, after my analysis is completed, after the anthropologist has finished his interview, I discover that my motive was not after all what we came to believe it was. Self-understanding – and interpretation – occurs over time and changes with context. Our understanding of any of our acts, of our motivation, has, I believe, to be seen in terms of an imaginative horizon that gives us an inkling of other possible understandings and motivations. Through some intervention, some contingent experience, we may come to understand what we did and why in terms of what we had only had an inkling of. In terms of what we dimly imagined. This is perhaps why we can say, 'Yes, I always knew that but never thought of it before' when we come to understand something in a new way or acknowledge motivations we hadn't acknowledged before. Such understanding has to be seen in terms of power – the power of our interlocutor, of the circumstances which determined our 'new' understanding. It has also to be seen in terms of the power that controls our imaginative horizons. They're not entirely free. Suppose I asked one of the pilgrims if his pilgrimages were a form of resistance. He might laugh at me, at the absurdity of my question. He might agree with me. 'Yes, you're right, but I never thought about it before.' Or he might just shrug his shoulders.

AM: This brings me to another question, concerning the issue of politics. Dorinne Kondo, in another conversation, questioned 'the historically specific and unproblematized categories of psychoanalytic foundationalism'. You yourself, in discussing psychoanalysis, have guarded against the use of what you call 'extra-systemic metalanguages' to describe the intrasystemic (or *indexical*) process of the informant/informer's own experience of the encounter. In your words: 'This indexical process is granted a kind of existential priority legitimated by the "scientific" or other privileged status of the interpreter's hermeneutic.' As an anthropologist whose work is informed by psychoanalysis, how do you grapple with such a tension? And does this cautionary note of yours validate Kondo's suspicions regarding a master discourse such as psychoanalysis?

VC: No doubt it does. I should add that I don't 'guard against' 'extra-systemic metalanguages'. I don't believe they are possible. We can only approximate them but have to resist being conned by them.

But remember my own perspective on psychoanalysis has changed. I was first interested in using its methods and then in its hermeneutics. I look at it ethnographically, the way I would look at any system of interpretation. Yes, I believe psychoanalysis, like Marxism and many other systems of interpretation, is 'closed' – totalizing, all-comprehending. It is foundational insofar as it postulates certain basic dynamics, like the Oedipus complex, certain basic drives, like the sexual. Of course, Lacan recognizes up to a point, but only up to a point, the metaphorical status of these postulated dynamics, these basic drives. I'm not sure Kondo's criticism would be as applicable to Lacan as to Freud. In any case, I don't think she herself is as ironic as Lacan is, at least some of the time. Irony is perhaps the only escape from foundationalism because it recognizes the artifice of its own foundations – or the denial of those foundations – and the artifice of its own stance. Kondo's critique rests on assumptions, which can no doubt be understood in terms of foundationalism. We mustn't accept what one says one is doing as what one is in fact doing. Her criticism, like that of many postmodernist theorists (and I am not saying she is one of them) rests on a narrative too. It's just a different sort of narrative. Don't the Spanish refer to postmodernism as neo-baroque?

In a more positive, more down-to-earth vein, anthropologists can use – and have used – psychoanalysis in several different ways. It can be used as a methodology, as I tried to do in Morocco. It can be used as a hermeneutics and risks being reductive in its universalist pretension. Or it can provide a sort of allegory – a counter-story against which other explanatory stories are 'measured'. In this respect, it functions as an 'illuminatory hermeneutic'. As such it aims not to reduce one narrative, one sequence of events, to another – the psychoanalytic – but rather to illuminate these narratives, these events, their interpretation, by contrasting them with another narrative, series of events, or interpretation, those of psychoanalysis. It gives us, we say, insight. This illuminatory hermeneutic relies on montage, on metonymy. It is undervalued in our culture – our academic, scientific culture. But it is not in fact absent in even our most causal-reductive hermeneutics. It is most developed in gnosticism and those literary-critical approaches that rely on some sort of epiphanous experience. We see it in divinatory practices like the I Ching. The I Ching provides a contrasting story to the story one habitually tells, in however an inchoate fashion. It crystallizes that story – puts it in perspective, gives it meaning, modifies it.

Ethnography can also play this role. We assume, for example, that we have one soul. Then suddenly an anthropologist tells us there are people who believe in multiple souls. How do we respond? We may dismiss these people as 'primitive'. Or we may try to find ways of explaining why we believe in one soul and they in several souls. We may correlate our belief with individualism, with a particular family structure. We may correlate this individualism, the nuclear family, with a particular economic formation. Capitalism, for example. And we may correlate their belief with – for lack of a better word – communalism, with lineages and relate this communalism, the lineage organization, to another economic formation. In doing this – and here I am only playing with explanations – we are making a lot of assumptions about causal priority, about the relationship between economic formations and social and familial organization, about the relations between social and familial organization and the articulation of the person, the self, and about the relationship between person or self and souls. Such explanations are of course familiar. They translate the unfamiliar into the familiar. They domesticate it. But can we have any confidence in them?

I'm suspicious of such explanations. However seductive they may be, I want to know why I find them seductive (if I do). Of course, ultimately I can't find out why, simply because I'd be advancing similar – unsupportable – arguments. I prefer not to speculate – or to recognize my speculations as speculations. That's my discipline. I prefer the illumination that reveals new possibilities, other worlds, and is perhaps creative. It's a bit scary, if taken seriously. But is it really so scary? I am never so disengaged from my own world as to float in a world of pure, unjustifiable possibility. But, enough of my own philosophy of life.

AM: You've written quite a bit about dialogue, and actually review in an essay the etymology of the word, relating it to the agonistic potential that you invite. One gathers from reading *Tuhami* that you and your Moroccan friend somehow managed to dialogue in just that ideal way. Can you discuss the evolution of that special relationship from which the book evolved, in both its transformational as well as its oppositional elements?

VC: I can try. You know, it's been a long time since I wrote that book. As with all books, so much went unsaid. I think everyone has had the experience of meeting a person with whom, for some reason, something simply 'clicks'. The chemistry is just right. Encounters like these present an intrigue, an interest. I had this experience with Tuhami. There were many other Moroccans whom I befriended, but with Tuhami there was a sense of depth, of closeness, I'm sure we both felt and never doubted. I don't know how else to put it. Oh sure, we were annoyed with each other at times, but this sense of closeness persisted. You know, I never even bothered to understand this friendship, how it came about. Tuhami may have understood it as something fated. But this may be my fantasy. If our encounter was 'fated' for him, it was fated the way the she-demon A'isha's coming to him was fated. But I wouldn't want to push this line of speculation too far.

AM: In thinking about *Tuhami*, what struck me most was your apparent 'decision' at one point, as you and your wife prepared to leave Morocco, to intervene directly in the life of your friend, and to function, as you put it, as a 'curer'. The psychoanalytically inspired position you assumed was certainly an unorthodox one – at least with regards to more traditional understandings of the ethnographer's role. Along these lines, I have several questions, in rapid fire. How did you come to the decision? Was it Tuhami's facility with the dreams that seduced you? What was it like to subvert your initial position as ethnographer and to recreate yourself, not only professionally, but existentially as well? And lastly, what was the response of the anthropological community upon reading of this dialogical move of yours?

VC: Well, let me begin with the idea of change. I think it goes back to what I was saying about the special relationship Tuhami and I had. I think it's within that context – which I don't want to romanticize – that my 'decision', as you put it, has to be seen. I think that human relations are both too complicated and too simplified in most sociological understandings. I don't think one can generalize very easily about how one engages with other people. And I also think that the kinds of interventions anthropologists make in the field are, to a very large extent, determined by the nature of their relationship with the people they meet. I would not advocate the kind of intervention I made in Tuhami's life. I would probably not try it again with someone in even greater need than Tuhami. Again, what I did, what we did, grew out of our special relationship. I simply felt it was right.

I used the word *curer* because it comes as close as any to how I imagine Tuhami understood my role when I decided to intervene. It should be remembered that despite my psychoanalytic orientation, I was not the immediate instigator of all the talk about illness. When I met him, Tuhami was already seeking something, he was already going to sacred sites where people *were* being cured. He talked a lot, and quite spontaneously, about his illness. He was obviously troubled. I am certain that the pressure of my then-imminent departure compelled me, at least in part, to act as I did on his behalf. But had I stayed, I'm sure, I would have had to intervene. My attempt to 'cure' Tuhami was a response to both a demand from him and from within myself. I knew that if we were to remain friends, I had to change the terms of my/our engagement.

I'd like to make another, more general observation. When Americans describe their personal experiences, they tend to assume a confessional voice. I think this is an indulgence. There are times to confess, but there are always ways in which one can use one's own experience in a non-confessional way – to reveal the intricacies, the dynamics, of personal relations, of a change in perspective, or to critic a given practice. My experiences with Tuhami made me question all I had been taught about fieldwork and anthropological methods. In those days, at Columbia particularly, there were a lot of 'do's and dont's' that even in my first fieldwork with the Navajo made me uncomfortable. I was sure there was a lot more intervention going on than anybody was willing to admit. How couldn't there be? If you didn't intervene, you'd be a creep and taken for one, or its equivalent, by the people you were studying. I found myself caught, as I am sure all sensitive anthropologists do, between trying as objectively as possible to make sense of the people I was studying and their world and being human, being attentive, being caring (in Heidegger's sense of *Sorge, sorgen*). I guess I came to realize that you couldn't really do the former without the latter – without concern. I wanted to illustrate this, and I used my experiences with Tuhami (here I can say 'my') to do so. I wanted also to show – ultimately an impossible task – how that conflict affected how we interpret and how we write.

In a field methods course with Margaret Mead, we talked a lot about medical intervention. That always seemed to be a crucial topic in those days. What did an anthropologist do when confronted with somebody sick? Did you give him penicillin if you had any? There were anthropologists, certainly students in that class, who argued no. Most argued yes. Medicine was the privileged domain for discussing the ethical dimension of fieldwork. No one talked about mental illness or suffering. The body was clearly privileged. War was another topic of discussion in those days. Not in Mead's class, but in other classes I took. People debated questions like: 'Ought an anthropologist try to prevent a war?' 'Or ought he to observe it?' (They were talking about tribal wars, mainly in New Guinea.) Some anthropologists argued that it was more important to observe it because we would then understand war better! Here again the focus was on the body – on bodily harm. What this says about American society I don't even want to contemplate.

With Tuhami it was different. In writing *Tuhami* I wanted to call attention to the fact that a lot of anthropology was constituted on either the denial or the dismissal of realities like Tuhami's, whose suffering would not have been deemed worthy of intervention. I think anthropology has come a long way since then. We are more realistic about fieldwork, more open to 'looser' research methods, and can recognize the absurdity of some of the conventions of fieldwork that were promulgated at the time. Of course, questions about objectivity rightly persist. I think feminism, perhaps more than any other factor, along with the war in Vietnam, radically changed the way anthropologists thought about what they do. They both helped raise questions of engagement and commitment. But there was another part to your question, about Tuhami's dreams . . .

AM: Yes. I was wondering if Tuhami's own facility with dreams, as an expression of what we might call his 'inner life', may have facilitated the kind of intervention you chose and perhaps even 'seduced' you, in a way . . .

VC: Oh, I think the dreams definitely played a role, though I was generally more fascinated by Tuhami's overall articulateness.

AM: What was it like for you to subvert and redefine your role in this field dialogue, moving from the professional ethnographer to 'curer'?

VC: I didn't find that a problem. I was so convinced of the importance of what I'd decided to do that I wasn't at all troubled from either a personal or a professional standpoint. What did worry me was failing.

As for *Tuhami*'s reception. Does an author ever really know? At first, I think readers were upset by it, less because of my intervention, than – and this is a sad symptom of academic anthropology – because I questioned the discipline itself, its claims to objectivity, the genres through which it conveyed its findings. They were jolted by my deconstructing the anthropological experience. Other issues, concerning ethics, for example, seeped in over time. Many people seemed finally to be moved by the book, by Tuhami himself.

AM: How did the book write itself, so to speak, as both an anthropological document as well as personal testimony and homage? What was the evolution of the project, from its original conception to the kind of psychoanalytically mediated testament that it is?

VC: You're on to something here, because there is no term, or genre, in which to classify the book. I tried to resist genre-containment. I'd already confronted the problem in a paper entitled 'Mohammed and Dawia' that I'd written before *Tuhami* and which I included in *Hermes' Dilemma and Hamlet's Desire*. In writing that paper I was bothered by the way in which the genre I was writing in – a case history – seemed to predetermine my understanding of the couple I was writing about. As I began to write about Mohammed's sexual life – his fear of fellatio, his experiences of circumcision, homosexuality, bestiality, defloration – I realized that my conventional organization of these themes was setting up the interpretations I would make. This disturbed me, but it was only in writing *Tuhami* that I came to grips with the fact that what really obliterates cultural differences is the way we frame the differences we write about.

In this sense, in revisiting the book over the years, I kept finding new dimensions of the 'original' experience. How can I now separate the experience from the text? All I can say is that in some perverse way that text, its rigidity, has precipitated Tuhami and insofar as 'he' has resisted that textualization, he has remained alive for me. There is nothing mystical in what I am saying. Such is the capriciousness of memory and its expression.

AM: A closing question, as a way of both summing things up from a theoretical and philosophical standpoint, as well as addressing the issue of the genre within anthropology. Can we as ethnographers envision a model, perhaps at the frontier of psychoanalysis and anthropology, which can attempt to re-present or enact the psychic landscapes of the Other, to render him, as you put it, 'less bloodless'?

VC: The big problem is institutionalization or routinization of genre. We tend to routinize what happens in an agonistic arena – which is where our expressions as well as our illusions of creativity take shape – and to integrate what we have 'routinized' into our received wisdom. We have to resist, as best we can, this routinization and integration. One of the paradoxes of experimental ethnography is that it can only occur once. Afterwards it's a repetition. That's the danger. I should add, however, that I don't see anything necessarily wonderful about innovation for innovation's sake. Like everyone else these days, anthropologists are constantly looking for something new. But when I use the word *innovation*, I mean it to refer to a practice – a gesture – that resists routinization. That, I think, is our primary task: we have to avoid routinization, for routinization destroys creativity. (And we must not conflate creativity and innovation. They're not the same.) It's a task – this struggle against routinization – that is inherently dialectical. It is always doomed to fail. The innovation either falls by the wayside or is integrated at some level into the prevailing culture. Rarely if ever do we have revolution, though we can theorize about revolution.

We ethnographers have, at any rate, to balance the actual human experience at the core of our work with the kind of theorizing that same work demands. Theorizing should never replace or substitute for the experience itself. Ideally, theory ought to illuminate the experience as it derives, paradoxically perhaps, from the experience. Admittedly, there's a kind of circularity here, which I think important to recognize. We seem to be going through a period in which theory is so privileged as to deny the illuminatory experiences from which it originates. Experience is denied, crushed, eliminated. What becomes important, then, is to structure what we communicate, whether through text, film, or any other medium, in such a way as to preserve the tension between theory and experience – without surrendering to the one or the other. I'm as appalled by the idea of surrendering to experience for experience's sake as to theory for theory's sake. I think a 'touchy-feely' kind of approach to anthropology, or to experience more generally, is suspect. It avoids the theoretical – and what the theoretical can evoke: a transcending dimension to the particular experience.

We have to cultivate our ability to empathize with requisite courage, to acknowledge our fear of empathy, of what we experience and discover. (I think we need to use old-fashioned words like *courage* and *fear* in our evaluation of what we do.) I imagine it takes a certain courage every time you intervene in psychoanalytic treatment, if only because you have an inkling of failure. This is also true for anthropologists, but they are less often in a position to make such interventions. They do require courage for empathy. Unlike the psychoanalyst who usually works in his own culture, accepts more or less its diagnostic categories and evaluations, and is supported – protected – by institutional structures and a relatively systemic theoretical bulwark from the temptations of the patient's world, the anthropologist, working away from home, in an alien culture, forced (professionally) to question diagnostic categories and evaluations as well as his own theoretical edifices, has no such protection. He requires a confidence – what Keats called 'negative capability' – to be able to enter another's world without losing his own bearings. If he were to lose them, he would be able neither to enter that world, empathetically, as a native even, nor to depart from it. He would just hover in a sort of no place – a *Zwischenwelt* – edging, always edging, on the psychotic. I don't want to romanticize the anthropologist. There is in fact nothing particularly romantic about empathetic understanding or the risk of failure. We have simply to recognize the anthropologist's position.

How do we convey all this? I don't know. I do know, however, that some anthropologists have succeeded in doing so. Psychoanalysts have been, I believe, less successful in conveying their encounters, the risks inherent in them, the danger. Perhaps they have been hampered by the 'case' and the 'case study'. It is an imprisoning genre.

I've asked many analysts, over the years, whether or not their transference relations with one patient are carried over to other patients they see during the day. All of the analysts I've spoken to, more than two dozen over the years, are startled by the question! Every one of them has denied any kind of interference, any kind of contagion. It seems incredible.

Which reminds me, before we finish up, there is one thing I'd like to add concerning the matter of 'the third'. By the third I don't mean a particular person in a triad. I mean a function. I remember a Lacanian once criticizing me on the grounds that I reduced what he saw as a four-part dynamic to a single function, and I think he misunderstood what I meant: because by the third I don't mean a function that is the same for each of the participants in a given context or situation. The third, as I see it, is that towards which two people are aiming to construct and control: usually, as an element of stability. But they see this element in different ways, inevitably. There can never be a merging of horizons.

# References

Lacan J (1977) Ecrits: A Selection. New York: Norton.
Ricoeur P (1974) Psychoanalysis and the movement of contemporary culture. In: The Conflict of Interpretations. Evanston: Northwestern University Press.
Wikan U (1995) The self in a world of urgency and necessity. Ethos 23(3): 259–85.
Wilhelm R (transl.) (1967) The I Ching (or Book of Changes). Princeton: Princeton University Press, 3rd edn.

# Chapter 3
# Katherine Ewing

Katherine Pratt Ewing received her PhD in Anthropology from the University of Chicago in 1980. Her training also included four years as a research candidate at the Institute for Psychoanalysis in Chicago, as well as three years of training in psychotherapy at the University of Chicago Hospital. Presently, she is Associate Professor of Cultural Anthropology and Religion at Duke University, where she has been on the faculty since 1991.

Much of Professor Ewing's work has focused on the cultural shaping of authority relationships, cultural inconsistency, and linkages between concepts of self and the politics of identity formation. In *Arguing Sainthood: Modernity, Psychoanalysis and Islam* (Duke, 1997), which served as the basis for much of our discussion, she examines how the Sufi mystical tradition has been a focus of religious and political controversy in Pakistan and how this controversy plays out in the lives of individuals. In point of fact, the book is an offshoot of her ongoing efforts to create a new synthesis of the perspectives of anthropology and psychoanalytic psychology by joining a dynamic model of cultural processes with her own model of multiple, culturally shaped, contextual 'selves' (developed in the 1990 prizewinning paper 'The illusion of wholeness: "culture", "self", and the experience of inconsistency'). From this theoretical stance, Ewing has studied Islam as a changing tradition in the modern world, looking to explore how its actors experience it, how they draw on it in the process of shaping personal identity, and how individual actions and creativity play a major and ongoing role in shaping Islam as an ever-changing religious tradition. Against this backdrop, she has also investigated the relationship among the 'selves' which informants present to others in specific interactions and how these concepts and manifestations of self draw on culturally specific premises and symbols and are shaped by Pakistani family dynamics.

Professor Ewing's other areas of specialization include South Asia and the Middle East, with field research in Pakistan, Turkey and among Muslims across Europe. Presently, in collaboration with anthropologists Rick Shweder (University of Chicago), Unni Wikan (Norway) and Garbi Schmidt (Denmark), Ewing is also developing a new project comparing the orientations of second generation Muslim youth in four countries (the US, Germany, Norway, and Denmark), focusing particularly on how families negotiate the pressures for assimilation, the differences in cultural orientation and social position between the first and second generations, and the place of Islam in this process of adaptation.

The following interview with Katherine Ewing took place on the campus of Duke University on 15 May 2000.

Anthony Molino: I'd like to start by looking at a statement you make in the preface of your book *Arguing Sainthood*, where you talk about having undergone psychoanalytic training, in part, because of wanting to complement your anthropological training . . .

Katherine Ewing: Actually my interest first developed in my undergraduate years. I was a philosophy major at Tufts University and got interested in phenomenology and the philosophy of mind. I went into anthropology because I sensed that there was a Western bias in philosophy, which often seems to be an effort to find universal truths based on Western cultural ideas. But then I found that my interest in the self and concepts of person, developed in my study of philosophy, really weren't being addressed in the cultural anthropology that I learned at the University of Chicago. At that time, the quest was to understand systems of meaning that were abstracted not only from any individual's experience but also from the sites and histories of their use. But when I was in the field, I found (like other anthropologists of my generation), that people were negotiating very complex situations, that they didn't have single sets of cultural symbols they were trying to operate with. Looking at how people were negotiating complex situations and how they were engaged in conflict led me to want to understand how people organized these complex issues in terms of their self experience. That's when I decided to look into psychoanalytic training.

Another factor was my personal experience of fieldwork, which I found to be extremely intense. When I left Chicago for fieldwork, I had the feeling that I was jumping off a cliff, leaving my own social world behind. Then I was in Pakistan for two years, looking at Pakistani concepts and experiences of self and how people negotiate complex situations. This led me to wonder what was going on with my own psychological processes. So, I was interested in having my own psychoanalysis as well . . .

AM: Can you be a bit more specific about what it was in your early fieldwork that may have played into the decision?

KE: Well, people used cultural ideas, like the image of the Sufi saint, in negotiating psychological conflicts. In one Pakistani family that I knew quite well, for example, it was clear that there were a lot of difficult issues. The mother had gone through a crisis in her late twenties . . . she'd had three girls, you know, and the family was hoping for a son, and she was getting a lot of pressure from her in-laws and such. Her reaction had been to withdraw into silence for an extended period of time. Various Sufi saints were brought into the family's healing efforts, though conflicts developed around decisions to visit various specific saints. Because of the saint's role as healer, I often met people with one kind of disturbance or other. In another situation I found myself interviewing a woman whose mother had committed suicide – I've written about both these cases in various papers. So there were a lot of issues that one could attach diagnostic labels to, though I was not particularly interested in doing that. Nevertheless, it seemed that without any tools from psychoanalysis, what I would do with these cases in terms of a cultural analysis was entirely inadequate. Furthermore, the way people were actually using cultural symbols for their own purposes seemed to be the most interesting thing about the interactions I was having with them. The woman whose mother had committed suicide when she was a child had all sorts of imagery around fire – her mother had poured oil on and immolated herself – that had cultural dimensions but clearly had a very strong affective charge and idiosyncratic significance at the same time. And it just seemed to me at that point that the interesting thing was how she personally used these symbols, and I thought, well, that's the kind of thing psychoanalysts look at.

AM: Can you say more about your psychoanalytic training?

KE: I was at the Institute for Psychoanalysis in Chicago, which at the time was very heavily influenced by Heinz Kohut, who was still alive then. I never actually had a full course with him, but he came in and did some guest appearances in some of my courses. So there was a strong emphasis on Kohut's self-psychology. I was still writing my dissertation when I was admitted as a research candidate. At that time it was very difficult for non-physicians to actually go through clinical training. So, I basically was doing the research training, with the idea that the Institute would use my case as one to put forward to the American Psychoanalytic Association for an exemption of the MD requirement for clinical training. Nevertheless, I did have a couple of long-term analytic therapy cases. I also did some work on an inpatient unit at the University of Chicago Hospital and went through a range of other experiences the Institute had set up for me. Along the way, I also did a psychological testing externship at Michael Reese Hospital, as part of a psychology programme I'd enrolled in at Northwestern, when I wasn't quite sure whether I was going to go into anthropology or pursue a clinical career.

In terms of analytic training itself, my most memorable experience of it was the overlap of the people – their multiple roles. The analysts who were teaching our classes also had the students in analysis. So there was quite a preoccupation about who says what about whom, a constant possibility that the boundaries between the 'private' analytic relationship and the 'public' teaching relationship would be transgressed, which felt very incestuous. But the part I found most valuable were the courses in technique . . . the how-to-do-it . . . how to listen, how to observe my own reactions, and the diagnostic seminars. They were more interesting to me than the theory because there seemed to be a better point of intersection between the technical methods and anthropological fieldwork, while I found that the metapsychologies presented in theory classes were several steps removed from the kind of data you get in a clinical situation. It's not that the models of the mind – metapsychological explanations of why somebody acts the way they do – are irrelevant, but they are answers to a different kind of question than I think most anthropologists are asking . . . For example, explaining behaviour in terms of the Oedipus complex or narcissistic deficits will make many anthropologists see red. There is quite an anti-psychological bias in anthropology. I wanted to find a point of intersection between research on social-cultural processes and the kinds of experiential observations that I was making in my interviews of people and in my participant-observation. I felt I could use this kind of clinical technique as an observational device without having to trace the psychodynamic history of why somebody is articulating this particular topic in a particular way. Focusing on observational techniques allowed me to look at the multiple things a person might be doing or accomplishing socially in a specific interaction with me.

AM: In your early essays there seems to be a predominant use of this how-to element to which you refer, albeit in the context of ego psychology. (You quote Hartmann quite often. I guess I'm struck now by the fact that the Institute was oriented towards self-psychology . . .) But by the time you get to *Arguing Sainthood*, your primary tools are offered by Lacan . . .

KE: Certainly the self-psychology training drew fairly heavily on ego psychology . . . it emerged out of that school and then took things in a new direction. The self-psychologists set aside some of the quagmires that ego-psychology had gotten caught in, like the increasing complexity of its models, and said 'okay, let's look at self'. But in fact, in the theory courses we read a lot of ego psychology. As I recall, we traced the works of psychologists whom Kohut had identified as the roots of his model. As far as my later attention to Lacan goes, I wouldn't say that in *Arguing Sainthood* I totally buy into a Lacanian perspective – but rather, I found that because Lacan incorporates Levi-Straussian structuralism in his articulation of language-based 'symbolic order', his work intersects with the sort of things that anthropologists have thought about. His idea of the symbolic order is one way of talking about the cultural in his model. But in many respects, that book is a critique of Lacan. My concern with the observational and the how-to stems from my concern for the experiential, how people actually experience their world. I look not only at how they use symbols, signs, but also at how they are doing multiple things whenever they speak. I have now shifted my focus since writing several of those technique articles. I am still less concerned with how to conceptualize the psyche, *per se*. Rather, I investigate how people project self-representations and identities, and how they negotiate these identities in politically charged interactions.

AM: Would you agree that most of the time, when psychoanalysis is brought to bear on anthropology, it is technique that is privileged? I'm thinking, for instance, of Herdt and Stoller's *Intimate Communications*, which I've read as something of a manifesto for what they call a 'clinical ethnography' . . .

KE: I certainly think that attention to the nuances of interviewing is important. But even psychoanalysts can miss the obvious. I did a review of that book at one point, and what I remember most was a woman they were interviewing who commented on the pleasures of nursing. These male interviewers seemed to have no clue that this was a very ordinary experience for a mother, that there is some sort of sexual pleasure associated with nursing. But I do agree with Herdt and Stoller that technique is important in anthropological interviewing. One of the things I teach is an interviewing course, for both graduates and undergraduates, and I encourage students to be very aware of controlling or power dimensions in their interaction. We devote much of our attention to strategies for getting the person being interviewed to talk about subjective experiences that are relevant to the topic the researcher is interested in, without shaping it by asking direct or leading questions. So we experimented with the open-ended question. We also tried, when setting up the interview, to tell the interviewee in advance about our general interest, so that the person might have an idea of what to expect. We'd then start the actual interview with something totally open-ended, like, 'tell me about yourself'. Sometimes it worked; sometimes it didn't. But it turned out that when the students were more directive, and especially when they asked questions because they were nervous or didn't want there to be silence, they got much less satisfactory answers. People were fishing for what the interviewer wanted much more than when the interviewer allowed silences or made it clear that whatever the person said was the right thing to say, or of some interest. Students would also do a series of interviews over time, something like four to six interviews, to see if there was any progression in the kind of interactions they'd been having. My own interviewing strategies, of this sort, were pretty much vindicated by their experience. The students who didn't quite dare do it the way I had suggested the first time would often try their hand at it later, finding that it worked much better, and that they actually got more interesting material on their research topic.

AM: I was wondering if you could talk a bit about what I see as the founding point of your enquiry . . . what I have come to call 'the Geertzian divide' and the split Geertz's work marks in the history of psychoanalysis and anthropology . . .

KE: Yes. Clearly there were people interested in psychoanalysis and in psychological anthropology more generally, as a major aspect of the discipline, through the 1950s, I suppose, and longer. I think what you get with Geertz is a turning back to an interest in issues like concepts of person and the significance of religion that had been set aside for a while, during the pre-eminence of structural functionalism and cultural materialism. There were several approaches that had moved away from enquiry about meaning . . . and Geertz returned to it, but he definitely wrote off the psychological as something that wasn't of interest to anthropologists. I wouldn't put it all on Geertz. I think structuralism played a role, too, with its focus on decontextualized systems of meaning. Researchers used individuals as vehicles for learning about the systems of meaning. So I remember that David Schneider, in teaching American Kinship, basically said that you can use anybody, say, in an interview situation or participant- observation, to find out about the whole cultural system . . . as long as they're a competent, functioning member of the community. He drew an analogy with doing a linguistic study: i.e. just make sure you don't find somebody who lisps when you try to decipher the phonemic system. So things were very decontextualized; probably most of my training involved approaches of this kind. The individual disappeared as a nexus of meaning and became simply a representative of a broader cultural meaning. You could talk to individuals; you could even study things like concepts of person; but you did not look at it from the perspective of the individual as a nexus, but rather you abstracted concepts of person from – with Geertz – a calendrical system . . . naming systems and the like . . . bringing together disparate aspects of cultural meaning and saying, 'this tells us something interesting about how this culture shapes personhoods'. The stress was on shared, public meanings rather than on conflict and disparate personal interests and perspectives. But now that anthropologists have moved toward a focus on practice, attention to the psychological has become even more important than ever.

AM: With regards to the word *culture*, you define it in *Arguing Sainthood* as 'a process by which individuals negotiate ambiguity and inconsistency'. How radically different a definition than the one employed just a generation earlier by Geertz, or even his students!

KE: Yes, but of course it's not just me. Renato Rosaldo in his book *Culture and Truth* had already defined culture as a process. I think what happened was that people were no longer trying to screen out outside influences to find a core 'culture'. In the previous generation you went to a village where it was possible to demarcate boundaries and you found and identified the shared culture as a 'system'. But a number of people in my generation did fieldwork in complex places – in big cities, for example. I think urban anthropology was something of a new thing then . . .

I myself was in a city where there were diverse people, the city of Lahore, Pakistan. There were people from lots of different parts of Pakistan coming in from villages, other cities, different social backgrounds, different ideological and political orientations. And so it was impossible to abstract a single system of meaning; not only was it impossible to abstract such a thing, but even to assume that somewhere underneath all of this complexity was a common set of assumptions – something that McKim Marriott, who had been my dissertation advisor, had really pushed for understanding in South Asia . . . that there were common, underlying assumptions about what a person is. So he was interested in a cultural conception of the person. He looked at a lot of different practices – such as astrology and caste rules – drawing on the research of a lot of his students who were looking at these different domains and activities, and said basically: 'from this array we can isolate certain conceptual devices by which people, probably all South Asians, organize experience – and they are fundamentally different from western conceptions.' What happened, I think, was that those of us who were confronted with trying to construct an ethnography out of all of these divergent opinions said 'this just can't be done'. So, I ended up in my dissertation laying out some competing systems of meaning and contrasting the perspectives of differently positioned people – men vs women, Christians vs Muslims, conformists vs traditionalists. I just kind of laid out the different systems. By the time I wrote *Arguing Sainthood*, my approach had changed dramatically – towards a more practice-oriented approach made possible by my psychoanalytic training. The book is based on additional research and is quite a distinct work. I think there are only maybe ten pages of overlap between the book and the dissertation. And the book took a fundamentally different strategy: instead of trying to find commonalities – such as the various subcultural systems that I identified in my dissertation – I focused on processes of negotiation . . . on arguments. And so I began to see 'culture' as a style of argument, a process of negotiating position . . . you could almost call it a toolbox for people's negotiations.

Now where I would differ from many anthropologists today – largely because of my psychological training and the roots of my training in psychoanalysis – is in positing motives behind people's negotiations. I think there's a tendency amongst anthropologists who are looking at culture as process, looking at conflict and negotiation and permeable borders and global processes and all, to simply assume an over-simplified motivational structure. There's an interest in power, for example, and there's a presumption that people's motives can be reduced to negotiations of advantage or power. While I think those are important, I also think that the psychoanalytic lens provides a sensitivity to the possibility that people's motives are not reducible to those dimensions. And motives actually are relevant to understanding how these social processes work. Take a question like, 'why is a political leader effective?' Well, you can't just explain it in terms of people's rational choice or strategic maneuvers. It's obvious that there are many other desires that are in play. And I think that's true of most negotiations. People are negotiating for status, as theorists such as Bourdieu have argued, but they're often negotiating other things as well.

AM: I was struck by the fact that even as you use Lacan's model to discuss what those negotiations might be, you also criticize that aspect of Lacan that insists on the element of recognition. In fact, you argue that it's not language exclusively that mediates the subject's relationship with the world, and refer in this context – albeit fleetingly – to Winnicott and the kind of direct experience with the world he advocates. And yet in the Preface you cite the shortcomings of Winnicott's theory *vis-à-vis* Lacan's . . .

KE: My criticism of Winnicott, and Kohut for that matter, was that there's too much reliance on the idea of a cohesive ego. I stress in my work the fact that people are extremely variable and not as cohesive as that model asserts. I feel that even more strongly as I work among immigrants and watch when people successfully negotiate all kinds of different positionings . . . different kinds of self-representation. And so to say there's something cohesive there is not something I find very useful. But what I think is useful in Winnicott is the emphasis on a kind of a presence that he stresses . . . on the relational tie that comes not out of trying to get something from the other person, or from trying to establish a position of status *vis-à-vis* the other person, but rather a simple kind of . . . of being there.

AM: Being with . . .

KE: A 'being with', exactly. And it's that dimension that I try to bring up in the book. The difficulty is that articulating anything like 'being there' moves things into another domain. Nevertheless, I think that there's a pure sociality that gets lost in an over-emphasis on the verbal, or in negotiating power and status. I mean, I think that there's a kind of pleasure being in the presence of somebody else that doesn't depend on strategizing for advantage . . . it's not always a power game. There are lots of ways that people interact.

AM: One of my aims is to explore the conspicuous absence of object relations theory in ethnographic applications of psychoanalysis. Your book stood out in this sense, partly because of the cited but limited references to Winnicott, and partly because – where you talk about play, for instance – you use Kristeva extensively and again ignore Winnicott altogether! . . .

KE: I did not deliberately say 'Oh I'm not going to work with Winnicott's use of play.' I was thinking about Kristeva in relationship to the work of other theorists that I was developing in that book; so yes, in that context, I was not really pursuing that line of object relations too directly. But it wasn't a conscious effort to go in one direction rather than the other. There are always choices and limitations to what one develops in an argument.

AM: Would you agree that French thinkers enjoy a certain status in anthropology circles? Even in your book, where psychoanalysis is concerned, it's the French model that seems to prevail.

KE: I think that's a very important issue, and I think it does play a role in the way that I use these people in the book . . . because there definitely is a politics of representation, and there are already two strikes against the psychological and the psychoanalytic, certainly. I experience it very directly in my interactions with other anthropologists. I've come to believe, I guess, that if anthropologists are going to listen to a theory that's coming from France and if it doesn't do violence to one's material, there is the possibility of being listened to. I found, of course, that I could work with these theories, and they did help me think. But, more fundamentally, because I was concerned with the issue of the decentred subject, I found that turning to Lacan and Deleuze allowed me a stance that was not compatible with theorists such as Winnicott – so there was a very good theoretical reason for it.

AM: Can you say more about those 'two strikes'? . . .

KE: Well, I remember being at a meeting of the Society for Cultural Anthropology . . . and it was a year when Robert Paul had organized the conference, so there were a number of psychological anthropologists present, but there were also a lot of non-psychological anthropologists, of course. At this meeting . . . somebody . . . and I have to admit I don't remember what the topic was, or who was presenting, but it was something about museums, and there was a kind of a psychological explanation embedded in the paper that had just been presented. And a prominent Chicago anthropologist got up after the paper and said, 'Well, I just don't find this kind of enquiry interesting'. There was no specific critique of our colleague's analysis or method, but just a dismissal . . . a wholesale dismissal of an entire line of enquiry. And I was so furious that this whole area I was studying had been dismissed that I got up and argued with her. We had a couple of volleys of argument and, in fact, she ended up coming around to my position without ever admitting it. To me, it was a watershed moment, telling me how much of an uphill battle it would be to do anything in anthropology involving the psychological. So I've always tried to bridge the two approaches and hope that I could disrupt a kind of narrowness where a line of enquiry . . . such as the Geertzian . . . will appropriate everything that the psychological anthropologist does but will call it something else and rule out the whole intellectual genealogy that is associated with psychological anthropology.

AM: Along these lines, I think I could count on one hand the times the word *unconscious* was used in your book . . . Were you sufficiently concerned about the resistances you might encounter in the anthropological community, to want to shy away from any explicit attempt to explore an idea of the unconscious?

KE: No, I would say that there's a deeper reason than that. The problem with the notion of 'the unconscious' is that it tends to get reified, just like 'the ego' or 'the self' gets reified. And it implies that there are things that are not accessible, they're not visible – they are in some deep place that is far away . . . I mean, far inside, or whatever. And I myself have tried, instead, to conceptualize things as all being right out there. They may not be explicit, but they're present. So I would rather use the word 'the implicit' rather than 'the unconscious', or 'something that's not articulated verbally'. Or, as I often stress, even something that's forgotten in two seconds but is present when it's present, rather than creating this reified thing or place . . .

Another way to think about it is that some phenomena can be perceived and experienced but not named. There's lots of stuff that we can't name, but which can be seen. And the reason I think that's important is that there is a tendency, if the unconscious is thought of as something hidden, as something that's not immediately visible, to feel that it's just not relevant . . . you know, 'we're not looking for that, we don't want to go further than that which is on the surface'. But I'm saying it *is* on the surface, it is *here*. An outside observer who's sensitive to the implicit can see things in the interaction which the person they're observing wouldn't be able to tell them about explicitly. So it's pretty analogous to thinking of culture as processes rather than culture as a thing that has to somehow be identified and reified. I think there is an analogy with Marriott's or

Geertz's way of looking for underlying cultural principles. They are public – 'out there' – but you have to be clever to find or notice them.

The model that I'm talking about now involves the idea that actions and meanings are highly contextualized, that the decentred subject is operating in terms of multiple cues in the environment. I think you will find that recent studies of brain functioning and the mind – and I really don't claim to be an expert on the recent research, since the material I studied dates back a few years – are really more consistent with a notion of contextualized and decentred processes, and that we're not going to find 'the unconscious', at some later time. Studies of memory, for example, are quite consistent with the idea of things being highly contextualized. Responses to specific situations and habitual responses are, again, not necessarily something you can put into a single idea of a 'self' or some single 'unconscious' that's giving rise to different clinical phenomena. My experience of psychoanalytic training was that efforts to find a particular complex, such as the Oedipus complex, in a specific psychoanalytic case, or to confirm a particular diagnosis, were really imposing a kind of theoretical order on the therapeutic or clinical process. The instructor at a case conference would say, 'follow the red thread'. Well, what that means is to impose a certain interpretive framework on data that's coming out of this interaction – emphasizing certain things and overlooking others.

AM: In this context, a strong aspect of your argument is your critique of the pervasiveness of so-called hegemonic discourses and how they might shape ordinary persons' experience. You counter with an argument that goes like this: if something is not experienced as hegemonic, we have to wonder if indeed it is . . .

KE: Okay. Well, my focus has been on the vicissitudes of everyday experience. I see constant shifts, not just in an individual's positioning, but in the premises or terms out of which people operate. I experienced inhabited – and contested – multiple discourses, even when the people I was interacting with did not directly acknowledge them. And as an observer I do take a certain privilege. For instance, why must I believe someone when they say that they don't experience multiplicity? If I see this person claiming a certain identity in one situation, or hear them saying that they're having a certain experience, and then I observe them in another situation when they're saying something completely different and describing a different set of memories associated with a given self-representation, there's plenty of reason to doubt such a claim . . .

If their experience is highly contextualized then, yes, they may not experience the shift because each self-representation feels natural in its own place. One of the points I make, in an article entitled 'The illusion of wholeness', is that it is when somebody is concerned about consistency and resists making that kind of contextually appropriate shift in self experience that you're going to have somebody who's maybe not managing life comfortably. When they're conscious of inconsistencies and try to prevent them . . . then somebody like that may have more difficulty than somebody who simply 'goes with the flow', so to speak, no matter what the situation. To argue that it is presumptuous, if somebody doesn't articulate an experience of multiplicity, to claim that the person does indeed make such shifts, is to remove any ethnographic authority . . . I think that we should have and do have such authority: by trying to observe a whole situation and not just the overt content of people's utterances. I don't think it's presumptuous to claim such authority, and I think it's inauthentic to deny the legitimacy of such a claim.

AM: You also make the case against a facile dichotomy between modernity and tradition, and say at one point: 'My goal is to deconstruct the premises that lead to the conclusion that modernity gives rise to a distinctively new form of consciousness.'

KE: A prevailing idea is that, if you have a historically new form of consciousness, presumably it has been constituted by the condition of modernity. But I think that the presumption of the distinctiveness of modernity ignores the kinds of situations that people have found themselves in throughout human history . . . The idea of 'the native' who is shaped or determined by the hegemonic discourse of his or her culture comes out of anthropology, but does not reflect experience, anybody's experience. I mean, everybody has constantly experienced different orders of reality, even before today's 'globalization'. There have always been contacts; people have always moved around, there have always been traders. And so there have always been moments when discourses confront one another, when cultural habits are denaturalized. Reflexive consciousness is not a new thing.

AM: In a similar context, you also talk about the pragmatics of the transference/countertransference matrix. And when I read the word pragmatics, I couldn't help but think of Crapanzano's work and wonder what, if any, influence his thinking has had on yours; and what about Obeyesekere who, from a very different angle, was one of the first to explore psychoanalytically the nexus between the private and the public spheres?

KE: Well, actually Vincent Crapanzano was probably my first mentor. He happened to be a visiting professor at the University of Chicago right after I came back from fieldwork, and he taught a course which I audited that became the book *Tuhami* – in which he stressed a kind of fluidity of interaction. Indeed, his emphasis on disrupting the idea of fixed subjects, or of fixed culture, by looking at the space between the person and the interlocutor, was really very influential for my work . . . that aspect in particular . . . And he also helped me make contacts with the psychoanalytic community along the way.

I've also followed Obeyesekere's work very closely. Initially, I took more Crapanzano's direction than Obeyesekere's, in the sense that in Obeyesekere's psychoanalysis there was a very strong emphasis on frustrated sexuality, and a tendency towards explanation of cultural phenomena in terms of psychological phenomena in a way that I'm not quite comfortable with. He wouldn't just reduce one to the other, but in doing both culture analyses and psychological analyses he has some trouble, I think, in getting them to really come together. It's that intersection that we have all struggled with, though he has come up with some interesting solutions. Still, I'm left with a sense that the broader social and political scene somehow was not sufficiently emphasized in the more explicitly psychological work such as *Medusa's Hair*. Also, I think that the kinds of explanations that he gives, in terms of the meanings of symbols, are more orthodox than those espoused even by certain schools of psychoanalysis. But he's a great thinker and a major figure in anthropology. He's also been very helpful for me in my career.

AM: You made a reference earlier to the power relations between ethnographer and informant in sensitizing your students to the intricacies of that relationship. It's a point you also explore in *Arguing Sainthood*, where you discuss how that 'othering' gaze of the Westerner cannot help but influence what happens in the field . . . What about those delicate aspects of fieldwork, and how did psychoanalysis help you mediate or negotiate them?

KE: I actually talk about the power dimension quite explicitly in the book, and contrast what I was trying to do with Geertz's statement of claiming a kind of objectivity, of being neither the village atheist nor the village priest. There was another scholar who came along later and said, 'Well that really was not an accurate reflection of Geertz's actual positioning.' This person visited with people Geertz had worked with and asked them how they saw Geertz's attitude toward religion. He was told, 'Oh, he was the scientific atheist'. So, I really played with . . . not played . . . but seriously entertained the truth of people's experience of their own religious beliefs and practices . . .

Psychoanalysis of course helped . . . but it didn't really help in the first fieldwork because I hadn't been through it at that point . . . it helped later, during the next fieldwork I did for the book, when the psychoanalytic training I'd had gave me the tools for noticing my reactions, so that if I were uncomfortable or feeling anxious in a situation, instead of responding automatically to evade that anxiety, I would try to note it and figure out what was creating that kind of response. In that sense, I think psychoanalysis has a lot to offer for anthropologists learning to be self-reflexive. Much of reflexive anthropology, I think, has been a dismal failure because people really didn't know how to be self-observant.

In fact, in some of the early reflexive ethnographies, there's an effort to be self-confessional and present that does not enhance the reader's understanding of the people being studied. The way I see reflexivity as being useful is when you are able to use your own reactions to tell you something about the people with whom you're interacting.

AM: You've probably heard a joke that I first learned from Elmer Miller, my dissertation advisor. 'What did the postmodern ethnographer say to the informant? "Enough about you, let's talk about me!"'. . .

KE: Right. Exactly. I've really felt that some ethnographies are like that. As an example of how a reflexive text can miss something in the interaction that really could be revealing of the person, there's a section in Dorinne Kondo's book *Crafting Selves* that I've written about . . . There's a passage where Kondo describes a student, a young male high school student that she was tutoring in English. In this episode, to the author's surprise, the young man asks her advice about what career choice he should make. And Kondo goes on to make observations and comments about the interaction.

She uses it as evidence of the kind of crisis young people go through in Japan, of the power of parents to try to impose their intentions on the child. She took the fact that he raises the issue in the conversation with her as proof that the making of a career choice was a life crisis in a way that it wouldn't be for an American child. But what Kondo misses is the specific significance of their relationship that may have encouraged his openness. In fact, the young man at one point overtly mentions a role model from TV, a teacher, whom he says doesn't really exist in Japan. Given that Kondo was acting as a kind of teacher to whom he *did* open up, it is not a great leap to surmise that his comment on the TV character was an expression of his fantasies about Kondo and America. What she doesn't notice is the function that she's playing in their interaction. Anyway, this is all written up in a new paper, 'Revealing and concealing: interpersonal dynamics and the cultural production of identity'. It's an example of how a real reflexivity that's informed by psychoanalytic issues of transference and countertransference would have opened up the interaction and revealed something about who the boy was, the kinds of decisions he was making, and the kinds of role models he was using. In so doing, this is a kind of reflexivity that goes potentially far beyond Kondo's decontextualized analysis of the interaction.

AM: I'm thinking of an interview of mine with Michael Rustin in London, who makes the argument that psychoanalysis is a very specific practice whose terms, techniques, and vocabulary are best located within the clinical setting. Do you believe we can usefully speak of transferences and countertransferences, say, in terms of actual fieldwork?

KE: I do, and I would say that, first of all in traditional psychoanalysis, the idea of the full-blown transference is considered to be something that only emerges after months of psychoanalysis, and that's really not what I'm talking about. I'm talking about the kind of perceptions and feelings that get transferred onto the observer or the interviewer . . . It's pretty obvious that there are certain patterns of interacting that repeat aspects of a person's earlier relationships . . . and that I as interviewer would have countertransference reactions to some of these . . . You don't even have to use the word 'transference' – I mean . . . a structure of feelings and assumptions about who I am that are not based on direct observation. For example, if somebody talks to you as though they've got a chip on their shoulder from the first moment of the interaction, you can figure there's something going on. Now, the anthropologist is usually not concerned with tracing the history of that particular structure of feeling, and so in that sense, I'm not going to say, 'Well this person was transferring their feelings towards their father onto me in this interaction', unless there's some specific evidence within the interaction, some hints that there may be some specific issue that I can identify. But, otherwise, I just say, well, clearly there's a transference/countertransference element in any interaction. You can identify the parts that affect the interaction and shape its meaning without necessarily having to trace the history of the transference.

AM: Along these lines, I also liked your emphasis on narrative and the argument that identity gets negotiated, renegotiated, slips . . . Indeed, you cite at one point Freud's *Interpretation of Dreams*, and while you shy away from actually saying that it provides a model for fieldwork, there are one or two paragraphs where you almost seem to suggest as much . . .

KE: I think that stories are one of the main ways that people communicate, and telling a story is pretty analogous to telling a dream, and I imagine a lot of the same things are going on in the telling of a story. Furthermore, stories are a place where I think identity is negotiated and presented. And in a story, identity is not necessarily a fixed thing . . . It's a process, and in the telling there can be shifting positionings. So it is a vehicle . . . Actually one of the theorists that I find useful in thinking these ideas through is Benveniste, in the way he analyses the word 'I' . . . the way the meaning of 'I' shifts, even within a single sentence. Freud does a similar thing in analysing the dream . . . He says that the self or the dreamer is located in many different places in the dream. I think that this is true of narrative as well.

AM: You make a nice point of establishing a relation between what you call identity and ideology, on the one hand, and between subject and narrative on the other. I found that juxtaposition to be a really compelling device for exploring these tensions.

KE: Yes, in a story you have a subject who wanders through it and takes different identity positions. In ideology, the identity of the subject is more clearly articulated, and is more fixed. If I were to really analyse particular ideologies closely I might not say that ideology is as fixed as I tend to picture it in my mind, but I think that there is a tendency to try to fix positioning. But, the reality is that ideologies are also adjusted to specific situations.

AM: It seems to me, nowadays, that while everybody talks about the subject, there's a real tendency to reify that concept too and give it an immediacy of meaning which I always don't see. Why talk about the subject, for example, and not the unconscious? Why privilege this otherwise unlocatable entity?

KE: Well, I think agency is an element of the concept . . . but I too think it's dangerous to simply equate the subject with agency because there is the Foucaultian position that the subject is discursively constituted. I wouldn't go that far, in that I do see a certain fluidity in the idea of the subject, as that which is never fully captured by a positioned identity. The subject is always escaping, moving on, leaving collapsing structures in its wake. That's how I would picture it. The word 'subject' is a kind of a marker for that which evades articulation. So my notion of the subject is coming out of Deleuze, as well as my early training in existentialism and phenomenology . . . and it's also coming out of Sartre . . . Sartre's notion of the self, though there is a lot of Sartre I would not go along with because I think he also has a unidimensional understanding of motivation and an insufficient consideration of the constraints on the subject in his emphasis on freedom.

AM: Back to the Freudian model of the *Interpretation of Dreams* . . . though you may shy away in your writing from a term like the unconscious so as not to reify it, when you're doing fieldwork are you, Kathy Ewing, working with a sense of the unconscious?

KE: I guess that in the sense that there are things that people truthfully say about why they think they are doing something, but that do not correspond with what I observe, I could say that the motivations are unconscious. Still, I'd be more comfortable saying that I think defences are operating. I can see people evading things, for example, or defending themselves against some kind of slight. But if I were to ask them, they would not be able to represent that defence system in words. To think of 'the unconscious' as an explanation would be to assume something with a causative force such as a certain structure of sexuality. I mean, I find this, perhaps, paradoxical in Freud's theory itself: the unconscious is both structured and unstructured in his various models. Clearly, I imagine that there are desires, that there are different sorts of impulses that people have that they cannot recognize or acknowledge . . . so in that sense they are unconscious or implicit . . . but I don't see what you gain by locating the unconscious as a thing or a place. It's not that I'm rejecting psychoanalysis, which does make sense to me. . . but in the specifics of people's particular interactions, I can't think of when I would impute something to somebody as being unconscious, that I couldn't just as easily characterize in some other way.

AM: At one point in your book, you criticize Fanon's notion of the dichotomy between the public and private . . . a split that he argues is induced in the subject by colonialism. You counter with the notion that these different discursive spaces are not so clearly demarcated . . .

KE: That's right, but my main concern was not making this division between public and private, because that's chopping things up in a preconceived way, rather than finding the implicit being present in both. The implicit permeates both sides, the public and the private.

AM: I guess what I did was to place your work in a continuum of sorts . . . Obeyesekere was not addressing anyone like Fanon explicitly, let alone any colonialist influences . . . And yet he seems in a way to establish the groundwork for your enquiry . . .

KE: That's a good point. It would have been a good sequence to trace out, I think.

AM: In the final chapter of *Arguing Sainthood*, you again cite Kristeva and talk about how she argues for domesticating the logic of the discourse of the other without dominating it . . . which I thought was quite lovely . . . Could you say more, as this seems to be an apropos definition for the contemporary anthropological project?

KE: I think that much anthropology doesn't succeed in doing that, and that many anthropological encounters do involve a kind of domination of the other. The whole idea of leaving the other as something uncontained by words is the theme that underlies my whole project in the book. I'm not sure if I cite Levinas directly in the book, but he was another inspiring influence in terms of choosing a stance from which to proceed in my enquiry . . . of somehow trying to depict the other, or open a window onto the people I'm talking about without presuming to explain or diagnose them. I think there is something irritating about case histories in psychoanalysis, and in other disciplines, in that they do try to turn the person into a diagnostic object – it's like capturing a butterfly with a pin. In the introduction to *Arguing Sainthood* I hint about the uneasiness I experienced even in my own analysis . . . Basically, I remember having the sense that any of the profound experiences I'd had in trying to study Sufism, when brought into the setting of a psychoanalysis, are explained in terms of – reduced to – one's past history and unconscious complexes rather than being an opening out into the future. And I think my basic aim is to represent these people as having something wise and insightful to say: to me and my audience. They are not just trapped in modernity. They are people who bring the richness of their experience to today's world, who have just as much to say as the rest of us.

# References

Crapanzano V (1980) Tuhami: Portrait of a Moroccan. Chicago: University of Chicago Press.

Ewing K (In review) Revealing and concealing: interpersonal dynamics and the cultural production of identity.

Ewing K (1990) The illusion of wholeness: 'culture', 'self', and the experience of inconsistency. Ethos 18(3): 251–278.

Freud S (1900) The Interpretation of Dreams. J. Strachey (ed.), The Standard Edition of the Complete Psychological Works of Sigmund Freud, vol. IV. London: Hogarth.

Herdt G, Stoller RJ (1990) Intimate Communications: Erotics and the Study of Culture. New York: Columbia University Press.

Obeyesekere G (1981) Medusa's Hair: An Essay on Personal Symbols and Religious Experience. Chicago: University of Chicago Press.

Rosaldo R (1989) Culture and Truth: The Remaking of Social Analysis. Boston MA: Beacon Press.

CHAPTER 4
# Paul Williams

Paul Williams is a Member of the British Psychoanalytical Society, Visiting Professor of Psychoanalysis at Anglia Polytechnic University (UK) and Joint Editor-in-Chief of the *International Journal of Psychoanalysis*.

Prior to becoming a psychoanalyst, he trained in social anthropology at London's University College where he was a distinguished scholar. His anthropological fieldwork for his doctoral thesis was undertaken at London's famed Maudsley Hospital, where he was a participant-observer on 'Ward Six': an in-patient psychiatric 'therapeutic milieu' for 'last resort patients', all suffering from psychosis, where treatment was along psychoanalytic lines. In his thesis, Williams attempted to elucidate the role of psychoanalytic thinking in the understanding and treatment of psychosis within the context of a psychiatric institution influenced primarily by a biological model of the mind. An offshoot of his doctoral research became the book *Unimaginable Storms: A Search for Meaning in Psychosis* (Karnac, 1994), co-authored with Murray Jackson, a fellow psychoanalyst and psychiatric consultant on Ward Six. This book, which is used widely in the teaching of psychiatrists and psychotherapists, is a graphic clinical exposition, using actual clinical case examples, of how psychoanalytic thinking can be applied to psychiatric practice.

Paul Williams has written and edited numerous papers and books, primarily on the psychoanalytic treatment of serious disturbance. These include *Psychosis (Madness)* (Institute of Psychoanalysis: London, 2000); *Key Papers on Borderline States* (Karnac, 2002); and *A Language for Psychosis* (Whurr, 2002). He is one of the editors of the volume *War and Terrorism: Unconscious Dynamics of Mass Destruction* (Karnac, 2002) and, more recently, of *The Generosity of Acceptance: Eating Disorders in Children and Adolescents* (Karnac, 2004). Awarded the Rosenfeld Clinical Essay Prize by the British Psychoanalytic Society in 1995, Williams will be Visiting Professor to the San Francisco Psychoanalytic Institute for the year 2005. As readers will gather from our conversation, his principal interest is in the internal object relations crises of severely disturbed individuals and the internal and external influences that give rise to these, distorting the sense of personal identity.

The following interview with Paul Williams took place in the suburban London village of Northchurch on 8 December 1996.

Anthony Molino: I was wondering if you could talk about your background and training in anthropology, and about how anthropology and psychoanalysis are connected in your life and work.

Paul Williams: My interests in psychoanalysis and anthropology combined in the course of my postgraduate training in the Anthropology Department at University College, London. I'd decided at the time not to go halfway across the world to study a small-scale society, as did many of my colleagues. Instead, I found one inside a mental hospital in the heart of London. I went to the Maudsley Hospital, Britain's main psychiatric teaching hospital, where there was a psychoanalytically oriented ward which took in serious, often tertiary referrals who were chronically ill, mainly psychotic. The ward used psychoanalytic and psycho-social methods to treat them, in addition to basic general psychiatry. I did my anthropology PhD study on this ward, where I tried to find out what the psychoanalysts were doing, using talking treatment, to treat these very ill people in what was the most biologically oriented of institutions.

AM: What defined the focus, the parameters of your research? What did you seek to study?

PW: I did two and a half years' fieldwork as a participant-observer, living more or less as a member of this residential ward. I made fieldwork notes and interviewed patients and staff, participated in the therapeutic groups, and so on. The objective was to try to find out what these staff and patients were doing in this multi-disciplinary setting, *vis-à-vis* orthodox psychiatry. Here were a group of talented people trying to treat some of the most ill psychiatric patients using analytic methods – a rare undertaking. They held very different views from the conventional psychiatrists and had different values: they were challenging psychiatry in a variety of ways, particularly through the use of nursing. The nurses did most of the treating of patients. The nurses were 'nurse-therapists' and wielded far more clinical authority on a daily basis than did doctors. I documented the staff's stated attitudes to their work while studying their and patients' behaviour and the problems associated with the work: particularly in the areas of relations of authority and in processing the powerful emotional consequences of dealing with psychosis. I tried to see phenomenologically, as it were, what they were doing and how far this matched up to what they said they were doing.

I discovered that the staff were trying to produce a durable, lasting improvement to psychosis through a restructuring of psychotic patients' internal worlds, using talk and relationships. This is simplifying things terribly, but the ward had recognized that psychotic patients only improve significantly if they are involved in ongoing relationships with key others.

They were employing the social ideas that are inherent in psychoanalytic theorizing about the unconscious and object relations formation, and using them in the transference and in a social setting to reconstitute an object-relating capacity in these patients. This is a tremendously ambitious undertaking when you think about it, especially for a standard acute ward in a public hospital. The ward experienced deeply the impact of psychosis on the staff – close contact with psychosis can make people quite ill, and how you deal with exposure to psychotic communications is crucially important in any treatment milieu. Generally, psychoanalytic units or wards do this by having supervision and staff groups where a process of detoxification, if you like, or metabolization of the impact, can take place. And so did this ward. But they did fail to take seriously enough the impact of psychosis on staff, and this generated conflicts in individuals and in the ward community. These kinds of things are very important because they are relevant to all the mental health professions and their relationship to psychosis. There's something about psychosis that is so threatening, that the majority of mental health workers deal with it by avoidance. If people do try to face it like this ward did, you come up against unpleasant, disorienting experiences, internally and collectively. People's internal worlds become disturbed, staff fall ill, the community can be disrupted, all that kind of thing, and you have to have ways of managing these problems if you are to avoid conflict and, in extreme cases, chaos.

AM: How many years removed are you now from the experience?

PW: It was 1985 when I joined the ward.

AM: How might Paul Williams the ethnographer – who participated in and documented the experiment – reflect on the ward's story, as opposed to the psychoanalyst looking back on it more than ten years later?

PW: I found myself in the kind of position that the staff found themselves in, to an extent. I experienced the ward as shocking, difficult to understand and enormously demanding, emotionally and intellectually. When you live with patients who are disinhibited, perhaps pissing all over the place, masturbating in public, fighting, becoming terribly distressed or violent, it's difficult to cope with, emotionally and intellectually. If anything I was probably at something of a greater disadvantage than the staff because I hadn't had their experience or training. The impact of the ward affected me greatly. I was confused for a long time, frightened, and I often felt threatened. This was partly due to the fact that my role was controversial. I was alternately seen by the ward staff and patients as a kind of saviour or rescuer or else as a useless interloper. The staff regularly tried to get me to join up with their views and practices, and could be very disappointed when I had to maintain my role as a participant-observer.

I also became someone who was vilified at times of social crisis, which I think was also linked to my indeterminate status. I realized that there was nothing personal in this at all. As the least important person on the ward, I was a useful target for the release of tensions and conflicts. As an ethnographer, I felt that the ward could be such a mad and stressful place that all I could do for a long time was to witness the experience and record whatever I saw. I decided to wait and see what emerged from these experiences, as I was incapable of making informed or clear inferences from my work as I went along. By the end of the two years of fieldwork, the main thing I had discovered was that there was something in the air, permanently on the ward, that could not be talked about but which the ward made strenuous efforts to talk about. This entity was moved around and located in different places, usually in patients but sometimes in doctors, managers and others. I later realized that this entity was madness, and that everyone – staff and patients – were engaged in the personal and collective management of madness. Gradually, I came to understand something about the ubiquity of madness and how we are all struggling with it in one form or another. On this ward they shared the endeavour, with interesting results which influenced much psychiatric practice in Britain and elsewhere.

AM: You've mentioned to me that you knew you always wanted to be a psychoanalyst. What was the path, what were the motivations, that led you from anthropology to psychoanalysis?

PW: The two were initially distinct for me, but they joined up later. As a teenager, like many people, I read whatever I could get my hands on, and Freud was the most coherent account of human motivation I'd come across. Freud's ideas are the most precise and elevated analysis of common-sense psychology one can imagine. They are a wonderfully detailed understanding of the human condition, expressed in ultimately ordinary ways. I think Freud took what people knew intuitively and formulated it in an inspired fashion which was accessible to many people. There and then I knew I wanted to be an analyst! I was obviously far too young to train to be one, so I just keep reading, including everything I could on psychotherapy and psychoanalysis . . .

I think, on reflection, I was also taken by Freud's interest in anthropology and archaeology. I eventually got the opportunity to study anthropology, which I felt would be a complementary discipline to psychoanalysis. During the analytic training, I discovered the social dimension to psychoanalysis – beginning with the formation of unconscious identifications – and I became increasingly interested in the ways in which group relations – you might even say culture – become represented internally in the psyche. Eventually the two disciplines came together in a practical way in my postgraduate work. I had to drop quite a lot of anthropology during my training to be an analyst, but it remained with me as a counterpoint to psychoanalysis, and I've now gone back to it, in that I teach a university course on anthropology as it relates to psychoanalysis. I am also researching into what one might term the phylogenetic evolution of object relations – when and how hominids acquired an enduring mental representation of the other, and how this related to our behaviour and our capacity for symbol formation.

AM: Can you say more about your teaching and research interests?

PW: The Institute of Psychoanalysis in London and the Department of Psychology at University College London have instituted a Master of Science course in the theoretical study of psychoanalysis, and it's taught by British Society analysts. I teach psychoanalytic technique and psychoanalysis and culture, as well as seminars on psychoanalysis and anthropology. In psychoanalysis and anthropology, I try to understand some of the differences in the theoretical perspectives of the two disciplines which create links but which also make them uneasy bedfellows. They don't fit in any obvious sense because of the different subject matter and historically distinct methodologies. The history of both disciplines has many features in common linked, as we know, to the rationality debate. Nevertheless, people do seem to have managed to link the disciplines productively, particularly in areas of symbol formation and the relationship between internal and external objects. The social theory of psychoanalysis is something the social sciences have not pursued to any extent. In psychoanalysis and culture, I think more about the place of psychoanalysis in contemporary culture, for example the way in which the notion of an individual self, of unitary subject with one body and one mind, has really evolved into an axiomatic datum in our culture, and how this has underpinned orthodox psychoanalytic theory, giving rise to whole and part-object theory, object relations, subjectivism and the current debate on constructivist relativism. The trauma-affect model and developmental experience are often closely linked to these phenomena. Trauma produces affects which disturb the psychological equilibrium which then produces symptoms which have to be addressed. This highly specific model of the human mind is readily understandable when you look at the history of psychoanalysis, but it is a model which is increasingly challenged and on which anthropology can throw some light.

AM: How so?

PW: Different meanings of terms like 'the self' are extremely important to consider, in my view. We analysts may have something to learn from ethnographers' accounts of different methods of construction of the person or self, if only to caution us against the automaticity with which we employ politically, morally and culturally laden notions to depict the contemporary self of psychoanalysis. One way of thinking about the emergence of Multiple Personality Disorder in the US is as a faultline in our definitions of the self, a concept which now carries far too much for the term to bear. Anthropology can help analysts situate their models in ways which I think can be helpful therapeutically and which can widen our horizons.

This is difficult, of course, as one must return to the question: what does any information mean psychoanalytically? But this does not imply that the task is therefore invalid. Alternatively, psychoanalysis may be able to help anthropology take more seriously the tremendous structuring influence of the internal world and its relations to social action, which most anthropologists have trouble thinking about. Why is the struggle in the late twentieth century in psychoanalysis with borderline patients and narcissism – conditions and themes which are reflected in different forms of cultural discourse? How do we account for the power of pathological narcissistic organizations, which are uncannily similar to fascistic groups? With what model can you explain them, let alone treat them? Why do patients and illnesses change over the years and take different forms? What is the relationship between the evolution of illnesses, of the unconscious and of the external world? These are questions that interest me and which bring analysis and anthropology closer together.

AM: Joel Kovel, in a 1995 paper titled 'On racism and psychoanalysis', makes the case that the unitary model of self is a distinct historical product, maintaining that – for all of Freud's colonizing ventures, first and foremost into the female 'psyche' of his time – his models ultimately reflect what Kovel posits as an originary, universal, polycentric self. Kovel goes on to suggest that Freud's tripartite model somehow points to a deeper understanding of what may have been an originary, shared sense of self than psychoanalysis can even hope to approximate today.

PW: I think so. If you look at *The Three Essays on Sexuality*, Freud's understanding of the development of human sexuality is, I think, quite revolutionary. The polymorphously perverse self, the process of acquisition of sexual identity, the indeterminacy of it all and the interplay of constitution and environment, these were all very original ideas. I would certainly agree with Kovel in that, if I understand him, he would see the notion of a modern self as an attribute of a post-enlightenment product of scientific knowledge, industrialization and concomitant individualization.

AM: Yes. He traces the notion back to the trickster archetype, which in the course of Greek history splits and yields the dualism of Hermes and Dionysus, thus splitting off and compartmentalizing for the first time the sexual dimension of being human. The body, then, is ripe for castigation, the mind is exalted, and sexuality repressed in a line that runs from the Greeks through the early influences of Christianity and up to Descartes, before finally being consolidated in the wedding of Protestantism and capitalism.

PW: One of the big questions in psychoanalysis today is: what's happened to sexuality? People don't interpret sexuality anymore. Why not? Something has happened to cause us to leave out . . . increasingly leave out the sexual self from our lives. Perhaps it's part of that process Kovel talks about. But what you remind me of, in terms of my own work, is how the primary instincts – sexuality and aggression – perhaps even the rudimentary compulsion towards predation and reproduction, are alive and visible within the contemporary human psyche.

AM: Why is it, in your opinion, that psychoanalysis has been – at least in recent decades – banished to a great extent from anthropological discourse? Is this true of contemporary British anthropology as well?

PW: The same holds true here. The unconscious continues to be, if not dismissed, then largely ignored by academic anthropologists, with a few exceptions. I think it's the inherent problem of the unconscious ultimately . . . it's not psychoanalytic theory that anthropologists attack, it's the notion of the existence of an unconscious that they find so uncomfortable. They would argue, I would imagine, that we have sufficient difficulty depicting and researching consciousness and conscious behaviour to need the idea of an unconscious. So it's not included. You know Gellner's work: he is a classic exponent of the British view. This is why psychoanalysis doesn't get studied in university anthropology courses any more. 'Freud will be dead and gone in ten years' is something I remember several anthropologists telling me once during the 1980s, rather like a war chant.

AM: Are you suggesting that the question, ultimately, is one of representation? That is to say: 'How am I ever going to write anthropology if I have to factor in the unconscious as well?'

PW: I think representation is crucially important. Psychoanalysis deals with emotion and fantasy. I suppose the British empirical tradition of research, which prides itself on its rigour and objectivity, cannot deal with the use of emotion as a measurable entity, as an observable reality, because it's such a fluid idea. British anthropology is wedded, in my opinion, to a fairly orthodox scientific model. Even in the most liberal of anthropology courses there is always a kind of conventional lip service paid to observing the conventional scientific method, to achieve a purported objectivity in the work. The use of the subject and the subject's world in the work – however it is you employ the term 'subject' – is not one that is addressed by anthropology except in higher order terms. The reflexive nature of the work is acknowledged, but is not properly investigated, in that it is not an explicit part of the work itself. It is not considered a problem within the work worthy of exposition. And yet the representational significance of the unconscious, of dreams, of fantasy, is tremendously important. I admire Obeyesekere's work, in that it addresses these problems of representation in a way which links social and psychological forms.

AM: Would you say then that, as a group, anthropologists remain somehow threatened by psychoanalysis?

PW: I would guess so. As I said a moment ago, I remember when I was an undergraduate that many of the anthropologists in the department I was in were preoccupied with predicting the end of Freud . . . 'in ten years' time Freud won't exist . . . in fifteen years psychoanalysis will be dead'. This was a typical attitude, and I wondered why people got so worked up about Freud . . . he must be important to incite such behaviour. I concluded that anthropology had not yet addressed the internal worlds of subjects. In fact, I think it has a horror of the internal world because, in my view, the content of the unconscious is, in a research sense, so startling and challenging. Anthropology has not yet got the methodological means to deal with this and therefore it simply doesn't. Whereas this is the heart of psychoanalytic study.

AM: How would you respond to an anthropologist colleague who, in a prior interview with me, whenever I tried to raise issues concerning the unconscious, mind, internal worlds, etc., repeatedly responded that these were foundational categories that somehow needed to be exploded, in a Foucauldian manner of sorts? Her critique challenged such elementary, ready-made binary oppositions as inner/outer, maintaining that such categories could not be attributed and projected onto the people and worlds anthropologists study.

PW: I could go along with that view, if one is speaking meta-theoretically or meta-philosophically about, say, the definition of the subject or methods of categorizing human thought. Everything needs historicizing and situating, obviously, but this must not be used to explain away bodies of knowledge or different perspectives. Otherwise you soon find yourself on the well-worn treadmill of 'scientism', which I find lifeless – simply politics. Whether we like it or not, we dream, we dream of murdering babies, sleeping with our mothers, implicating ourselves in the most impossible of situations, and so on. Serial killers display predictable fantasy systems. Women have different psychic dispositions than men, etc. These things exist, and are not rendered much more intelligible by describing them as mere foundational categories, which they may well be. Explanation and meaning of clinical evidence and the behaviour of subjects is of the utmost importance to try to understand. If an anthropologist were to sit with a psychotic patient and try to make sense of that person's internal world, s/he would need a paradigm, a way of thinking, concepts with which to consider the internal experiences of the patient. Psychoanalysis does have a coherent basis for addressing the internal worlds of subjects and no other discipline, as far as I know, takes the representational significance of the internal world seriously.

AM: I'm sure, however, that our colleague would question the 'exportability' of such a paradigm. There are always concerns about the universalizing claims of psychoanalysis. To the extent, then, that it is a distinctly Western paradigm, can we assume it to operate in or be applicable to the field?

PW: I sympathize with that view because I think some psychoanalysts have tried to universalize the Oedipus complex or certain 'core' developmental states. I don't know whether they are universal, but I would guess not – although I think that polymorphously perverse sexuality does seem to feature in just about any ethnography you read. Also, I think that sexuality and aggression may be universal traits, but how they are constructed and utilized by the subject and by a social group in different societies, I imagine would be very different. Thus the application of a psychoanalytic model would not be automatically helpful. I wouldn't want to impose a Western model in this way. At the same time, I would want to promote the study of what Matte-Blanco called 'the infinite sets of the unconscious', whereby he suggests that there is a primordial level of mentation which exists in and is expressed by individuals and groups in different personal and collective ways. Finding ways of understanding these non-conscious states interests me.

AM: But would you assume that what we'd call an 'unconscious mind' does indeed operate everywhere, however it is articulated?

PW: Not necessarily an 'unconscious', as we analysts define it, but perhaps a version of it. There are forms of mentation beyond consciousness or immediate awareness, and these have profound implications for motivation and agency. We need ways of addressing these not only from the point of view of overt behaviour, their expressive significance or role in social action. We have relatively little knowledge about what all these states mean from the subject's point of view: psychoanalysis helps with this problem, I believe.

AM: Can anthropology make room for psychoanalysis? and if so, how?

PW: I hope so. How do you ride two bicycles at the same time, and stay upright? We need to talk more between us about the rationality debate, subjectivity, the role of agency, the organization of the internal world. Much research is being done on the structuring processes of infantile development, including the psyche – work which locates these issues within social action and an environmental context. I'm thinking, for instance, of Mary Main's work on child development, and of Daniel Stern's *The Interpersonal World of the Infant*. This research is extremely exciting and offers an opportunity for bridging the disciplines. There is also the central psychoanalytic tenet of transference, which has caught the imagination of some anthropologists, as it is so vivid and discernible in a fieldwork context. Transference is a living component of the internal world, dependent for its effects on a social context. This has profound significance for psycho-social theorizing, I think.

AM: During your own fieldwork, was an awareness of such applications integrated into your research plan?

PW: I wouldn't say integrated – I think I was incapable of integrating anything at the time! But I think you've touched on a central issue for anthropology. If we can learn to address the phenomenon of transference, which occurs everywhere ... in social settings, in personal relationships, intra-psychically, I think we can begin to formulate a more comprehensive theory of personal action. Transference cannot be explained simply by descriptions of social behaviour or theorizing about social action. These are necessary, but we need to consider: what is the origin of transference? How is it represented, psychologically as well as socially? Why do people make these compelling relationships with each other that can lead to social conflict (or other forms of unintended action)? If there were a way of introducing anthropology to the power of transference and the unconscious origins of transference, I think it would be helpful. Anthropologists might begin to do fieldwork on the internal object relations world of their subjects *vis-à-vis* the external world, for example. I don't mean that you can examine the internal world of one or two individuals, no matter how thoroughly, and extrapolate the findings into a social context. But to do an extended mapping of the internal worlds of a group of people, observing over a period of time how these worlds are constituted and how they evolve . . . I think that this would make for a psychoanalytic anthropology of an original kind . . .

The question of counter-transference has increasingly been taken up by anthropologists, often implicitly, in the realization of the reflexive nature of participant-observation. The impact of the experience on the fieldworker's internal world is an inherent component of fieldwork knowledge. In the past, the main use to which anthropologists have put their counter-transference seems to have been in writing novels as an expurgation of the fieldwork experience!

AM: I realize that we're talking at the level of conjecture and imagination, but how might such a mapping be represented?

PW: The internal world of human beings goes on existing in terms of internal populations of individuals, in each individual, in social relations, in attitudes and in personal and collective behaviour. These are amenable to being recorded. We know that when these have been recorded in detail, psychoanalysis has produced explanations, similar to what James Hopkins calls commonly understood semantic agreements about meaning. Psychoanalysis specifies areas of meaning, subjective or internal meaning, forms or categories of meaning for groups, according to what Hopkins and his colleague Sebastian Gardner called 'conceptual strings', which can be seen to reflect repeated themes. Anthropology produces categories of meaning for social action and external behaviour. I wouldn't think it was beyond the wit of man to construct a system of a set of criteria for specifying shared or agreed meanings of internal states amongst subjects, which could be studied alongside expressive forms of social behaviour.

AM: Did anything of this sensibility inform your work at Maudsley over ten years ago?

PW: My specific interest on the ward came through the way in which the internal psychotic states of the patients, which I took to be the core of the ward's activity, interacted with the internal and external worlds of the staff, with the staff as a group, and the consequence of this for collective behaviour on the ward and within the institution. The Tavistock Psycho-Social studies by Trist and Murray were predicated on similar lines. I was studying ward life from an anthropological point of view, that is to say its social action, and in the process I was trying to understand what the differences were between the ward's overt claims and its actual behaviour. But at the same time, I was trying to keep an eye on what was happening to staff working in these unusually stressful circumstances. Staff were often ill, they sometimes fought with each other, they acted out in covert ways with each other, there were splits, factions, alliances and problems with the institution, internal crises which could only be partially addressed and accounted for by explanations of social action. In other words, there was the added problem of madness and its location. How do you account for, measure, understand the impact and role of psychotic anxieties on human action? It's an important subject as it is manifested in everyday life in many ways. It is not enough to categorize the behaviour as deviant or in relation to prevailing social rules. There is an embodiment of an unmanageable state, located within an individual (for good or ill) which then becomes a major issue for everyone else. What do they do with it? Where do you put it? Historically, medicine and society have colluded in agreeing that it is the patient who is mad and that it's a medical responsibility. By implication the hospital will cure it. There is no cure for madness. The whole process is about negotiating something quite unmanageable, which also has a live, even vital existence within the patient. Psychoanalysis knows about the disturbances in object relations that occur in psychosis. Neurobiology knows about levels of pathology. Anthropology witnesses the system within which these phenomena occur. Conceptual bridges are needed between these disciplines if we are to arrive at a comprehensive understanding of psychosis. I tried to look at it a little in a hothouse environment, a ward in which the internal and external manifestations of psychosis were placed at the centre of the stage.

AM: I don't mean to read into your words, but you seemed to be hinting before that the psychotic self, if you will, is sort of a testament to the insufficiency of our unitary understanding of self. I was wondering if you could comment on this idea, both theoretically as well as from the perspective of your experiences at Maudsley.

PW: You can look at it from a number of points of view, but historically, psychiatry and psychoanalysis have not been conspicuously successful in coming to terms with psychosis. I don't think anyone else has, for that matter. There is no comprehensively agreed cure of psychosis, and there remains controversy over definitions. Great advances have been made in our understanding of possible genetic constitutional contributions. But I think it was Bob Lewontin or Tienari who said that genes are tendencies . . . they are not in themselves determinative. The environment can modify genetic constitution. Tienari has done good work on this to reveal the interplay between constitution and environment in the area of psychosis. Psychoanalysts and psychotherapists have made advances in understanding psychosis, but because of our unitary model of mind we've had difficulty in knowing how to think about and address clinically the divisions that exist within the psychotic mind. Where we have addressed them, we have tended to try to shoehorn these experiences into our prevailing model of neurotic functioning. The psychotic's experience is not unitary. In a sense, why should it be? The evolution of mind is not a unitary phenomenon. The unconscious is characterized by representational pluralism of its instinctual structure, which has led to such difficulty in discussing it in an interdisciplinary way. Yet psychiatry and psychoanalysis proceed according to the premise that the body of the patient contains something called a self and a mind which can be discerned. I know these problems are not new and are continually debated; my interest lies in ways in which psychotic patients demonstrate for us in graphic form the non-unitary substrate of human experience. Maxwell Jones's work with the therapeutic community at Belmont in the 1950s, and Robert Rapoport's book *Community as Doctor*, both reveal something of the problem and how it might be addressed through a combination of fieldwork and psychoanalytic knowledge. There are other writers too, who have tried – Wilfred Bion first and foremost, of course, then Menzies-Lyth, Spillius, Clark, and so on.

AM: Perhaps you're suggesting, as American psychoanalyst Michael Eigen does, that there is a psychotic core organization that is common to us all. And yet somehow the people you worked and lived with incarnate alternate visions or versions of self which aren't simply and tragically alternative to the dominant one . . . It's as if there's something in those versions of self that remind us of our own . . .

PW: I think it's an extension of Freud's view of the universality of psychotic anxiety. We all carry around some sense of underlying madness. We might be walking along only to sense that there is a storm brewing inside us, but out to sea, as it were, and we are like a cork bobbing along the surface, taken along and relatively powerless against this, only able to experience some intimation of what might be happening or going to happen. We may find ourselves behaving strangely, or driven to think in ways we cannot understand. These phenomena are unconsciously derived, and I think point to an alternate domain which has links with but is not co-terminous with consciousness or the relatively advanced capacity to symbolize.

I think 'self' has become one of these terms that may have lost its significance because it can mean so many things, including the encompassing of all domains of internal experience. But is this really the case? Isn't there something called 'primary process' – a beautiful concept from Freud – which acts as a backcloth to our lived experience, creating opportunities, connections, disjunctions and a host of turbulences about which we still know comparatively little? I find it useful in my work to follow Bion's notion of a psychotic or primary process personality and a non-psychotic personality. These ideas are derived from Freud's

'Formulations on the two principles of mental functioning'. Bion's theory of thinking and his differentiation of psychotic and non-psychotic personalities makes it more or less clear that he feels that there are two personalities in the individual psychotic, one non-psychotic and the other psychotic, and both have to be addressed. Traditionally, we've addressed the non-psychotic personality as though it is capable of appreciating 'its' capacity to be psychotic, and I don't think you can do this in practice. The two states are fundamentally different. This can create problems for patients in therapy, if the therapist hasn't understood this.

For example, quite often psychotic patients, when they're being psychotic, or rather when their psychotic personality is in the ascendant, are taken by the therapist to *be* that personality. You perhaps know the kind of thing: 'I think you are doing this or being like this (whatever it is) because you can't bear facing your feelings of needing me' – that kind of interpretation. Whilst this may be correct as far as the non-psychotic personality is concerned, it can actually make the patient feel despair, and as though the therapist is in need of therapeutic help from the patient. The reality of the non-psychotic personality of the patient is not doing anything of the kind. I would see the non-psychotic personality as being engulfed at that moment by the psychotic personality, and unable to convey a non-psychotic communication. It's the job of the analyst to try to help extricate the non-psychotic personality from the psychotic, so that communication can take place about the patient's feelings and motives. So I'm not at all sure about simple notions of a unitary self. I'm more concerned with types of personality, and my interest is in how you help the non-psychotic personality in relation to psychosis, and what techniques can do that.

AM: On the matter of what we might call the psychotic and the non-psychotic aspects of the personality, what can psychoanalysis learn from the ethnographic record and the healing rituals of other societies?

PW: I don't feel personally qualified to comment on that because my time has been spent with Western patients, although I'm sure what you imply is relevant. An area where I think psychoanalysis can learn from anthropology is in the way in which anthropology has the capacity to identify and specify transformational states through analysis of ritual, myth, collective behaviour, rites of passage, healing ceremonies, and so on. Anthropology demonstrates how, despite the group's conscious motives or actions, there is a structure which generates momentum and determines action, the expressive forms of which may be handed down. If psychoanalysts can bring themselves to think of the unconscious as not just a personal endowment, but as having structural forms which act and react in the world in the sense that myths impact on social behaviour, and analysts can document ways in which the unconscious responds to certain social situations, then the question of psychosis may become more understandable. It is as though there is a dimension of thinking, a domain of registration of the world which may be called primary process, unconscious, or psychotic, which needs to be understood as a legitimate but opaque reaction to events.

AM: This may be a flight of fancy of mine, but you seem to be bringing Lévi-Strauss and Jung together!

PW: I wouldn't want to go quite as far as that, but I am interested in what is the adaptive significance of paranoia, for example. Every therapist deals every day with paranoia. It is a ubiquitous experience in the consulting room. It seems to pervade human experience too, and takes compelling social forms, whichever way one approaches the phenomenon. Institutions contain it, social action expresses it, so where does it come from and what function does it perform? How appropriate is the term, or is it multi-dimensional? What does it mean phylogenetically to be endowed with such a component to the personality? – because we now know there are genetic markers for certain aspects of disposition. It seems to me to have meaning. I don't only mean meaning psychodynamically, but meaning culturally, biologically, historically, anthropologically. Perhaps this is all too ambitious, but Lévi-Strauss made strenuous efforts to transcribe these internal forces and their social place, as did Jung in his own way, and I think the endeavour is worthwhile even though destined to be an impossible task.

AM: You were talking to me recently about a theory you were developing, concerning psychosis as a phylogenetic residue. . .

PW: Yes. It derives from my interest in symbolization. It's not quite that I see psychosis as a phylogenetic residue. Psychosis is a term denoting pathology. I see the problem more in terms of there existing constitutionally a form of pre-symbolic mentation which acts with our more evolved capacities for symbolization and cognizing of the world. Consider that aspect of our work as therapists where we are concerned with the facilitation of processes of symbolization in our patients. When we see a capacity for symbolization growing and developing, we feel satisfied in our work, and rightly so because we're helping to produce more complex representational systems which reflect the potential of the patient, and which can be used to advantage in complex social relations. That's why they evolved within the genome. Yet, concrete thinking, symbolic equations, psychotic thoughts are also very common in more disturbed patients – what Melanie Klein called paranoid-schizoid responses to being alive. Environment, learning and development are necessary for these childhood states to be transcended sufficiently to enable an individual to function adequately, yet in many adults they persist. It's possible that the psychotic anxieties these people display are not only products of infantile crises but also represent the breakthrough of poorly bound instinctual charges which attach themselves to the patient's insufficiently developed symbolizing capacities. The more raw and undifferentiated these instinctual representations are, the more I think they reflect precursors of symbolization, or primary process phenomena. I don't think that's a revolutionary or original thought. Hanna Segal talks about psychosis as being a very early attempt at symbolization. I wonder whether these phenomena are not only the products of crises in object relations in childhood, as we analysts think they are, but that they also may be the mental representations of a kind of pre-object relations substrate which characterized the hominid species for a long time as processes of symbolization evolved. The capacity for symbolic representation, archetypally expressed through language, is comparatively speaking a recent phenomenon. If there is anything in that idea, it would be fascinating to research, from an anthropological point of view as well as from a psychoanalytical one.

AM: We know that any number of societies make room for what we call psychosis without it having anything of the pejorative or pathological label that we attribute to the term and the 'reality' it denotes. As Foucault has evidenced, our social space can't seem to make room for psychosis . . .

PW: In Western society, to study what happens to psychotic anxiety is important, including how it gets sequestered and allocated, often to the most vulnerable groups. There are societies where access to psychotic states is included and is even felt to be indicative of productive social meaning, when linked to dreams, rituals or visions. Presumably it has an adaptive, explanatory significance socially, along the lines Hopkins describes. We seem to have lost that in the West. Although psychotic anxiety seems to infuse the way we interact socially, and is prevalent in our social system, the allocation of psychosis to so-called patients has become an industry!

AM: I'm wondering what the implications are of such a predicament. Can a society as complex and articulate and repressive as ours, at one and the same time, make room for psychosis even as we're so invested in 'curing' it?

PW: Big question. One way for me to think about it might be to transpose that very dilemma to the consulting room. Isn't that what every psychotic patient is required to face up to if they go into treatment? They have no intention, it would appear from their behaviour and history, of addressing their psychotic illness, and yet they want treatment. They sincerely need help, often to the point of demanding it through action. They get to see someone, and in addition to medications there are but words available to deal with the dilemma. How does each side react? Can the psychotic person be open to benefiting from his analyst's failures? Can the analyst open himself to the illumination and insight that comes from tolerating his patient's and his own psychotic anxieties, without trying to 'cure' them? How can we construct ways of approaching psychotic states, in individuals and in groups? I'm not sure you can address the problem of psychosis directly. It seems unamenable to view, as it registers to a greater extent as an experience which requires mediation. It's a necessary task, because psychotic people receive a very raw deal. They are neglected, misunderstood and very little serious health expenditure goes to them. They are a non-technological problem with no solution – the least appealing of categories.

AM: Nancy Chodorow argues that if a 'person-centred ethnography' is going to make any sense and be taken at all seriously, it has to make room for, if not psychoanalysis, psychoanalytic understandings of the person. She and others – Herdt and Stoller primarily – talk about a clinical ethnography, emphasizing the dynamics of projection and introjection as well as other identificatory processes. What are your views on the matter of a clinical ethnography?

PW: I find the idea stimulating. I think psychoanalysis and intra-psychic processes would have to be central to such an ethnography. First, a person-centred ethnography has to define what a person is, and a person is a complex phenomenon. . . it's not self-evident. This goes back to the problem of psychoanalysis' role in understanding social formation . . . this can take me into another area, but projective identification, the formation of identification, the world of internal objects and their use in social relationships . . . these are valuable fieldwork tools, if only anthropologists use them. Psychoanalysis has a social theory built into its very foundations through these concepts. We exist on the basis of our identifications with an other, so a person-centred ethnography would be at once a social and biographical interplay between fieldworker and the object of study, through which both would be altered, and a third creation, the ethnography, would emerge.

AM: While reading your book *Unimaginable Storms: A Search for Meaning in Psychosis*, I realized that it is an offshoot of your doctoral research. Would you consider the book an ethnography? I realize the problem of genre is a difficult one . . .

PW: It would be a generous description to call the book an ethnography, but maybe there are some ethnographic elements in it. It's more a reportage of clinical material, which is interpreted and discussed. It's a transcript of an absorbing experience on a ward, written to give, I suppose, clinicians mainly the rare experience of 'seeing' verbatim interviews with psychotic patients by a psychoanalyst with experience in this field. This is exciting and illuminating for clinicians. It does give a flavour of the ward and the degree of tolerance and concern employed by the staff. So, in that sense, it's ethnographically interesting.

The thesis from which I derived the book tried to delineate a remarkable attempt by a group of people to use psychoanalytic concepts to create change in a very serious mental illness within a general psychiatric frame; in other words, to effect greater and more durable improvements in psychotic patients than had hitherto been managed by orthodox psychiatry. To a great extent, this ward was successful. An innovatory model for the psychiatric treatment of psychosis evolved which has since been taken up by a number of units around the world. I wanted to know about the paradigms and values being employed, the departure from conventional psychiatry, what kind of social formation permitted this to happen and what were its failures and inadequacies. Out of the thesis came a kind of proposal, as I saw it, or a more refined model for the treatment of psychosis in the community. That was a by-product: anthropologically, the objective was to show this small-scale, complex society as fully as I could and compare it with its peers and competitors. I am glad I did it, as it disappeared in 1987 and nothing like it has been created since, so it is also an ethnographic record of a vanished social formation.

# References

Eigen M (1986) The Psychotic Core. Northvale, NJ: Jason Aronson.
Freud S (1905) The Three Essays on Sexuality. In: J. Strachey (ed.), The Standard Edition of the Complete Psychological Works of Sigmund Freud, vol. VII. London: Hogarth.
Freud S (1911) Formulations on the two principles of mental functioning. S.E. Vol. XII.
Hopkins J, Savile A (1992) Psychoanalysis, Mind and Art: A Prospective on Richard Wollheim. Oxford: Blackwell.
Kovel J (1995) On racism and psychoanalysis. In: A Elliott, S Frosh (eds), Psychoanalysis in Contexts: Paths between Theory and Modern Culture. London & New York: Routledge, pp. 205–22.
Matte-Blanco I (1998) The Unconscious as Infinite Sets. London: Karnac.
Rapoport RN, Rapoport R (1960) Community as Doctor. London: Tavistock.
Stern DN (1998) The Interpersonal World of the Infant. London: Karnac.
Trist E, Murray H (1990) The Social Engagement of Social Science (2 vols). London: Free Association Books.

CHAPTER 5
# Michael Rustin

Michael Rustin is Professor of Sociology in the School of Social Sciences at the University of East London, where he was Dean of Social Sciences from 1991 to 2001. A Visiting Professor at London's Tavistock Clinic, his work has contributed considerably to the integration of psychoanalytic and broader social scientific thinking in the United Kingdom. He was co-director of a European Union-funded research project on Social Strategies in Risk Societies from 1996 to 1999, and of an Economic and Social Research Council project on Childhood, Urban Space and Citizenship from 1999 to 2000, both projects involving biographical and case-based research methods. His many books, widely translated, include *For a Pluralist Socialism: Essays on British Politics* (Verso, 1985); *The Good Society and the Inner World: Psychoanalysis, Culture, Politics* (Verso, 1991); *Psychoanalytic Sociology*, Vols 1 and 2 (edited with J. Prager: Edward Elgar, 1993); *Reason and Unreason: Psychoanalysis, Science and Politics* (Continuum/Wesleyan University Press, 2001); *Mirror to Nature: Drama, Psychoanalysis and Society* (with Margaret Rustin: Karnac, 2002); *Biography and Social Exclusion in Europe: Experiences and Life Journeys* (edited with P. Chamberlayne and T. Wengraf: Polity Press, 2002).

Professor Rustin has been a Visiting Fellow at Princeton University's Institute for Advanced Study, and has lectured in many countries. A contributor to many psychoanalytic and social science journals, he is also co-editor of *Soundings* magazine. The following conversation with him took place in his London home in November 1999.

Anthony Molino: In your book *The Good Society and the Inner World*, you talk about the 'neighboring human sciences' of psychoanalysis – implying, clearly, that psychoanalysis qualifies as one. Can you talk about that classification?

Michael Rustin: I take the view that the development of sociology and anthropology of science from the 1960s has produced a more multivalent idea of what sciences are than was previously held. The established model was, I think, extremely prescriptive – it was philosophically driven and controlled. It had a set of rules which said that these people were scientists and everybody else wasn't, especially those people who were trespassing into being scientists, and trying falsely to claim the scientific legitimation. Of course, Marx and psychoanalysis were held to be the chief offenders against all of this. Karl Popper was the most important of these philosophical legislators.

Then in Thomas Kuhn's *The Structure of Scientific Revolutions* in 1962, we had a description of what scientists actually do and how scientific paradigms have evolved through procedures which are much more consensual, socially regulated, and socially determined than had previously been imagined, and in ways which paid little regard to the orthodox prescriptions and anathemas that philosophers had put forward. Following this, it became possible to think about psychoanalysis in a different way – as perhaps not as unlike other sciences as people had imagined it to be. The more complex the idea of science, and the more different kinds of science there are recognized to be, then the less abnormal and peculiar psychoanalysis has come to seem. The work of writers like Ian Hacking and Karen Knorr-Cetina on the diversity of scientific practices has been important to this understanding. This work in the sociology of science made me feel that there was much less reason to be defensive, and that rather than trying to decide whether psychoanalysis passed the test of scientificity, why not instead, try to find some description of what psychoanalysts actually do? Then see whether it conforms to the idea of an orderly and rational process of knowledge generation, which I think it does.

What is science? It's a process which consists of the orderly generation of verifiable knowledge, empirically testable knowledge. I think psychoanalysis is an activity of that kind. It investigates deep structures of mind which determine various kinds of surface effects. Freud's topographical models of the mind set out a map of these spaces, and his theories of such configurations as the Oedipus complex show how these structures give rise to various effects, which include pathological states, symptoms and dreams. Psychoanalytic explanation depends on the positing of such deep structures. The philosophical realism of Roy Bhaskar has made it possible to see psychoanalysis as based on procedures of inference from deep theoretical structures to surface effects. I wrote about this in a chapter in *The Good Society and the Inner World*, and David Will has done so at greater length in a couple of important articles.

What has also influenced me in thinking about psychoanalysis as a science has been Bruno Latour's work on Pasteur and the process of knowledge generation. Latour is a remarkable French anthropologist of science. There is a wonderful paper of his called 'Give me a laboratory and I will raise the world', in which he describes the way that Pasteur, in order to do what he did, had both to cultivate his bacillus in the laboratory – it was the anthrax bacillus – and also impose a set of routines and procedures on the farms, such that the properties which the bacillus were shown to have displayed 'indoors' in the laboratory could also be made evident and measured 'outdoors' on the farms. What he argues in the paper is that the discovery of the bacillus enabled Pasteur and his fellow scientists to, in effect, completely remake the world. Remake the world in what sense? Well, we purify our water-supply, we organize our hospitals like large-scale laboratories in which we carry out experiments and clinical trials, we immunize our children, we follow rules of hygiene, we keep records so that we can trace the incidence of infection among people and animals. Latour has shown how the discovery of the bacillus has led to the reorganization of the world. One says the discovery, rather than the invention of the bacillus, because the bacillus plainly existed before Pasteur observed it growing in cultures in his laboratory. But for all intents and purposes, it might as well not have existed until its properties had been recognized by scientists. Once recognized, it becomes an active agent of transformation, in a different way from when it was merely causing diseases!

And so what, you might say, what has this to do with psychoanalysis? Well, I argue that the unconscious is from this point of view rather like the bacillus. It existed prior to its discovery by psychoanalysis, having the effects that it did on human beings around the world. But it only became usable as something to think about, and act upon, when analysts became able to investigate it in 'laboratory conditions'. This is when the unconscious became an agent of change, which was how Latour described the role of Pasteur's bacillus. Freud always said that the consulting room was a laboratory. Well, it is, in a fairly precise and specifiable sense. In this 'laboratory', one can observe the unconscious as one has no chance of observing it outside, because in the consulting room one can distinguish between phenomena which can be attributed to the unconscious, and phenomena which can be sufficiently explained by reference to the surface world and do not need explanation by reference to unconscious processes such as repression, projective identification and other mechanisms of defence. The analyst can see, in the controlled conditions of the laboratory where 'external' stimulus is kept to the minimum, which states of mind in patients are observable or inferrable aspects of their inner world, and what are not. It is the gap between inner and external reality, as this can be made manifest to analytic patients, which makes it possible for them to recognize the reality and effects of their own unconscious states of mind, and thus become able to modify these to some degree.

There is an additional argument I make about these issues, in my book *Reason and Unreason: Psychoanalysis, Science and Politics*, concerning how psychoanalysis has spread. The paradox developed there is that psychoanalysis, with hardly a decent statistic to its name in 100 years of existence, has nevertheless spread over the world, and become part of the common sense of our culture.

AM: Like a germ . . .

MR: A widely recognized germ . . . exactly. How can this have come about? I think what explains the mode of diffusion is that people were continually given the opportunity of coming into this laboratory and discovering for themselves, as patients or therapists, that the unconscious indeed existed. Some defenders of psychoanalysis used to say of their critics – well what do they know about it? It always seemed a cheap kind of response to say that people had no right to criticize psychoanalysis unless they had been psychoanalysed, it seemed too similar to a dogmatic defence of a revealed religion. But there was also a way in which that response had a justification. If the context in which one best observes the effects of the unconscious is the consulting room conditions in which they are visible in their 'purest' form, then if one doesn't expose oneself to these conditions, one isn't going to know very much about it. We don't after all think it unreasonable to expect critics of laboratory science to have some experience of what happens in laboratories, and some capacity to understand what goes on in them.

There are surrogates for the clinical consulting room for the observation of unconscious processes. The development of infant observation is interesting from this point of view. Baby observation has been introduced in England, more or less universally, as a prerequisite, precursor or component of psychoanalytic training. What happens in baby observation? Trainees visit a family once a week for one hour. They're told to keep their thoughts to themselves, to be ordinarily friendly, and on no account to interpret or become actively involved as clinicians. They are there just to watch and learn. What usually happens? They become aware that the feelings present in the family – of mother for baby, of baby for mother, of themselves for mother and baby, for example – are more intense than they had expected or anticipated them to be. They may find themselves becoming unexpectedly anxious, or jealous. They make reports of what they see, hear, and feel, to a seminar, where other students (who are also observing in families) and a supervisor discuss what is happening, and seek to interpret it. Let's say that Mother is told the observer is going on holiday for a fortnight, and will be missing two visits. Lo and behold, the observer turns up for the session after the break, and Mother isn't there, everyone seems to be out. What has happened? The observer feels concerned and disconcerted that her appointment seems to have been forgotten. The seminar explores what this might be about, later taking in what the observer reports of the next visit that she does make, once the misunderstandings have been cleared up. One possibility is that Mother is pushing on to the observer her unconscious feelings of being rejected, when she misses her visits. The observer has encountered the strength of Mother's unexpected transference feelings towards her, and her own countertransference experience of Mother's feelings of abandonment. So the baby observation setting becomes another laboratory in which the existence of unconscious emotion becomes visible, available for reflection. Group relations events have similarly been constructed as settings for the investigation of unconscious states of mind.

Thus as people continually revisit these quasi-laboratories where the unconscious can be seen, so the unconscious remains alive and generative as a concept. Those specialists who work in these laboratories – psychoanalysts and psychotherapists – are able to use their experience to elaborate, refine and develop the theory of unconscious or inner world processes, in relation to this or that category of patient or state of mind. And, of course, from there, these ideas have spread outwards, to 'outdoor' settings. Although one can't regulate the whole world in the way that a hospital is regulated, the unconscious can be managed outdoors to a degree, one can pay some regard to its implications for human relations. Uses have been found for psychoanalytic ideas by those who work in personnel, in social work, counselling, teaching or nursing. People who have learned to recognize unconscious phenomena in its 'pure' form in the consulting room laboratory gain an enhanced capacity to recognize and notice its existence outdoors – in themselves and in others. My view is that the clinical consulting room, and the possibility of learning from experience within it, is the principal setting in which psychoanalytic ideas have been able to develop in a systematic, structured, and cumulative way. That is, as a human science.

AM: Among the neighboring human sciences of psychoanalysis is anthropology. Is there a way in which you see it being enriched, particularly where fieldwork is concerned, by the distinctive tools of psychoanalysis?

MR: Well, I'd better say something about my most recent encounters with fieldwork. For three years, I was involved in a project on the sociobiographical analysis of the socially excluded. I didn't myself do any of the interviews – it would have been better if I had – but I was involved quite a lot in the analysis of the narrative interview data. At the University of East London we had six other European partners and we conducted about forty interviews in each of seven countries. We had chosen six categories of socially excluded people – early retired manual workers, unemployed graduates, unemployed unqualified young people, single parents, migrants and members of ethnic minorities. Our approach to our interview subjects was to ask them to tell us their life story. We gave them a prompt – for example, 'we are doing research on social exclusion and we're interested in single parents'. We now think it may have been a mistake to offer so definite a prompt. The problem with such prompts is that they encourage subjects to structure their life stories in relation to what they think interviewers want to know about them. But what we actually wanted from our methodology was for them to tell us their life story as they constructed it, not as a response to our presumed interests. For us, the way that subjects construct their life narratives becomes an important aspect of their identities, of how they see their 'life journeys'. This method deliberately looks at the relation between the chronological facts of a life, as reported to us, and its thematic structure, and reflects on apparent discrepancies between them. The emphasis given to a life-episode, or an unexpected silence about it, can each be evidence of its significance.

There is a third dimension of analysis too, namely the different rhetorical forms which subjects give to different parts of their narratives – their different 'speech acts'. We distinguish for example between description, and argumentation and self-justification, in the narrative. Which aspects of a life-history seem not able to be reported descriptively, but instead evoke anxiety or passion in the subject, and what might this signify? This multi-dimensional approach to narratives has links with, and indeed its origins in, psychoanalytic ways of thinking. What the socio-biographical method does is to 'triangulate' (the term, now standard in qualitative research, is Norman Denzin's) these three dimensions of the narrative texts, to put hypotheses about their meanings on solid ground.

Now, adopting a receptive or containing mode – a 'feminine' mode, if you will – has been important in learning how to do these interviews properly. The difficulty is for interviewers to remain relatively silent, whilst continuing to give interview subjects the sense that they are being properly listened to. Interviewers had to learn to contain their questions – just encourage their subjects to talk – and only to come in to explore apparently unclear or missing episodes at the end of the interview, once the subject's own narrative had been concluded. One similarity between this method and the psychoanalytic is its commitment to an approach which is receptive to subjects' own states of mind and feeling. It needs to be non-judgemental, capable of absorbing tensions and anxieties which people feel when they start to talk and think about themselves. Our methodology was developed in postwar Germany, principally for the study of subjects whose experience had been formed by life under the Nazi regime. Part of the reason for the 'indirection' of this method – whose initial approach was 'please tell us your life story' – and not, for example, 'were you ever a member of the National Socialist Party?' – was to make it possible for subjects to explore and tell their story, whether they had been victims, perpetrators, or neither. This method, like psychoanalytic free association, though with a more sociological than psychoanalytic frame of conceptual reference, gave subjects space to explore their experiences without imposing fear of external judgement upon them.

Now, in our social exclusion project, we were not interested specifically in traumas, but in more ordinary experiences, less drastic experiences of social exclusion. But we thought that this method would nevertheless enable us to explore moments and episodes of stress. Quite subtle distinctions could be made, in analysing these narratives. For example, one of our subjects was a London Transport worker who had been 'early retired' after many years in the same job. He described how London Transport imposed a kind of 'speed up' on its maintenance workers and their routines, and how he had found himself unable to cope with the increased stresses of the job. He became ill through working night-shifts, so they moved him to another department and a lighter job, and so forth. They treated him in quite a considerate way, but finally the demands of the work meant that he had to go, so he was offered early retirement. He was forced out through the implementation of a carefully administered policy of 'downsizing', achieved through negotiation with the trade unions, and with some regard for established custom and practice. The way it was done was such that, by the time his early retirement was decided, both he and his fellow-workers had come to think it was inevitable, there was even a sense that it was his own choice. One interesting aspect of this was observing him, through his narrative, trying to decide who was to blame for what had happened to him, for this premature end to his chosen lifetime's work. Although he felt some bitterness, he tried hard to avoid giving way to this. He seemed to want to protect in his narrative both himself as someone who had been a good worker, and also to a degree his employers to whom he had given twenty-five years of his working life. He had started his interview by saying that his father and brother also worked for London Transport. It was difficult for him to protect in his narrative of his life both his own self-respect, and his wish to feel that he had not been totally betrayed and let down by his employers, which would have undermined his sense of a working life well spent. In fact, he became most angry after his early retirement, with the Employment Office, which he felt had treated him abusively and had infringed his rights. He had told the Employment Office that he wanted day work, and they sanctioned him for refusing to accept a job which required night shifts. He became angry, and also ill again from the stress, but he sought redress via the Citizens' Advice Bureau, feeling that he had been treated with a degree of indignity that he had not experienced previously. We saw evidence here that his years in public sector employment had left him with a sense of legal entitlement. Our narrative method enabled us to look at the complexities of self-definition and self-esteem in this changing social context.

But although we were interested in these multiple levels of meaning, and in our subject's ways of protecting his self-esteem from psychic injury, I was at the time reluctant to use an interpretative frame that one could think of as directly psychoanalytical. There were arguments in our group, between some who were more inclined to seek explanations in patterns of family influence which drew on psychoanalytic ideas, and others (like me) who preferred to seek explanations in the social and cultural context. I felt that our transcripts did not provide good enough evidence to support psychoanalytic explanations. However, having since taken part in analysis of these narratives with psychoanalytic clinicians, who are especially sensitive to the emotional and relational implications of personal narratives, I am no longer so sure. It certainly seems clear that where narratives are primarily generated and structured by their narrators, they can lend themselves to different kinds of valid interpretation. I now think it would be interesting to re-analyse these narratives making use of the interpretative skills of clinically expert researchers.

All this is to say that psychoanalysis as a methodology depends on its context of observation. The consulting room is a context of observation. The organizational study in which one observes people and practices in an institution is another context in which one can make use of evidence of unconscious states of mind. But the existence of unconscious states of mind must be supported by evidence. The question is, where is this evidence to be found? Throughout our socio-biographical project on social exclusion I was sceptical about whether even unstructured biographical narratives provided such evidence, but now, after its completion, I am no longer so sure about this. I may have been right to resist the temptations of 'wild interpretation', to which our clinically untrained research group might have fallen prey. But I may also have underestimated how far interpretation depends on the methodological resources and sensitivities of the researchers, and how far our data would lend itself to analysis from perspectives other than our sociological points of view.

The answer to your question about how far anthropological and sociological fieldwork might be enhanced by a psychoanalytic approach has thus now become less clinically 'purist' for me than it might once have been. Although the main location of psychoanalytic discovery has undoubtedly been the clinical consulting room, there are sufficient parallels between the socio-biographical method and psychoanalytic approaches to suggest that these might be productively brought together. This might also be true of other anthropological approaches as long as there is data which provides good enough evidence of subjects' states of mind, and researchers well-enough trained to interpret it psychoanalytically.

Researchers who try to use psychoanalytic ideas extramurally, even if they try to maintain contact with the fount of these ideas in the clinical tradition, may nevertheless find themselves treated with some discouragement by psychoanalysts, because of the demands of those inside this tradition for a fine quality of empirical inference. The clinical tradition trains its practitioners in detailed reflection on spoken and observed detail. It requires this too of applications of psychoanalytic ideas to social or cultural materials. But this doesn't mean that such further applications should not be attempted. It is just that they require the same respect for detail, and the same precision of inference to and from theoretical concepts, as is necessary in good clinical work. The psychoanalytic paradigm is very powerful and fertile, and it can be extended in responsible and useful ways to non-clinical settings.

AM: Are you familiar with Paul Williams's work?

MR: Yes! I was his supervisor for the latter part of his PhD work.

AM: I'd like to quote him on one such possible application of psychoanalysis to anthropology, and see what you think. In an earlier interview with me he said:

> If there were a way of introducing anthropology to the power of transference and the unconscious origins of transference, I think it would be helpful. Anthropologists might begin to do fieldwork on the internal object relations world of their subjects, *vis-à-vis* the external world. For example, I don't mean that you can examine the internal world of one or two individuals, no matter how thoroughly you can extrapolate the findings into a social context. But to do an extended mapping of the internal worlds of a group of people, observing over a period of time how these worlds are constituted and how they evolve, I think that this would make for psychoanalytic anthropology of an original kind.

Is what Paul suggests workable, in your view?

MR: I suppose the first thing I would say is that Paul's own study, of a psychiatric ward for the acutely ill, does do this successfully. But it does so in a context which is, nevertheless, very close to the core concerns of psychoanalysis. What interested him was the extreme difficulty of social organizations in handling, tolerating and managing states of extreme psychotic distress. He did very good work on the difficulties of the hospital where he worked in coping with these extreme states of mind. His work in this respect continues earlier efforts by Goffman and Spillius on the disturbance and pain that is engendered by contact with insanity. In Paul's view, what happened by way of this therapeutic community approach to psychosis was that patients on the ward managed to achieve a substantial degree of improvement in functioning and well-being while they were actually still in the hospital. This was because of the quality of support and understanding that was available to them, and because of the sharing (we could say *containment*) of psychic distress among the community in the ward, among patients as well as staff. But when the patients left the hospital, things became very difficult for them, because the so-called 'community' to which they returned was rarely adjusted or adapted to providing the level and intensity of support that these individuals needed. (Going back to my earlier analogy with Pasteur's laboratory, one could say that while it proved possible to manage psychosis in the hospital setting, it was not possible in the 'outdoor' world, since virtually no part of it could be recreated in the image of the hospital.) Paul's view about these patients, as he states in his writing, is that psychosis is often an incurable condition, and that therefore the best that can be done is to enable it to be mitigated and rendered tolerable to its sufferers.

This is a brief description of Paul's own application of what he is proposing. That is, of his own application of anthropological methods which investigates and takes account of internal object relations of an extremely disturbed kind, but which also shares the clinical concerns of psychoanalysis with mental pain, anxiety, and psychotic disturbance. And of course, Paul Williams is a psychoanalyst, as well as an anthropologist. I don't know what other topics Paul would propose as analogous topics for anthropological investigation, further from the field of mental illness, but there must be many that are possible.

I think the crucial requirement of this work is to remain clear about the dimensions of experience one is investigating. There are, as we found in our social exclusion research, social and cultural dimensions to the formation of a life-experience. But to be sure there are also 'inner worldly' ones, if one has the capacity to study them. There are some risks in mixing these together – one could lose at the same time the rigorousness of both sociological and psychoanalytic kinds of inference and interpretation. For this reason I think methodological and theoretical pluralism may be a more attainable goal than theoretical integration. In the field of applied psychoanalysis, there is certainly a risk that poor work will be done, which will not help the development of the field very much. Do you see what I mean?

AM: I do, but I wonder if there might not be a germ of contradiction here. I was thinking about what you were saying earlier, as you cautioned against applying psychoanalysis outside of its traditional setting of the consulting room. In the context of baby observation, the intrusion, if you will, of an outside observer into something of a micro-culture (that between mother-and-baby) does not involve necessarily any investigation of a pathological expression – which is the *raison d'être* of the consulting room. At what point, then, ought psychoanalysis to limit its excursions into such micro-cultures? There are people as different as Gilbert Herdt and Nancy Chodorow who talk about a clinical ethnography, and extend to fieldwork a model very similar to that of baby observation. Their argument is that through proper training, through proper sensitization and through a psychoanalysis of one's own, ethnography can be enhanced by observation of the kind that takes place, say, in Tavistock trainings . . .

MR: Well, I agree with that. Why I think baby observation works is because it tries as far as possible to reproduce the conditions of the consulting room in regard, say, to neutrality and repetition; the possibility of holding conditions constant such that one can compare variants with one another. That's why it works. In other words, it's the fact that the observer goes on going, week after week, and has to think about the meaning of the differences between experience in week one and experience in week two, that enables it to lead to understanding. This gives some possibility, as it were, of isolating the germ – namely, the unconscious state – from the conscious state. Now, there's no reason why that couldn't be done in other settings, in classrooms, in narrative interviews, or wherever else. The precondition, however, is that observational conditions are created in which there is the possibility of comparing mental states perceptible in one setting with those in another. The difficulty, the delicacy of the task is to clearly identify the space between the manifest and the latent. That's what is essentially psychoanalytic. It is what is *not* obvious, and what is also defended against and disguised, which is the key topic of investigation. So you then need measures which enable you to repeatedly test – well, is that the correct explanation of why this is happening, or is there some better explanation? And going around, more or less guessing, about the unconscious meanings of events in the outside world is not going to be good enough, even if trained analysts are the ones trying to do it. Guessing never is good enough. So my problem isn't with the idea of extending psychoanalytic observation to other settings. It's with the need to establish protocols for conducting observations which are as neutral and careful as, I think, those of the clinical consulting room have become. That would be my qualification.

Now, I could just say one further thing about the method of infant observation. At the Tavistock Clinic we're much involved with how observation works as a way of sensitizing and training observers to use psychoanalytic language with perception and accuracy. It is a context in which trainees can see or experience a set of feelings and learn what names to give to those feelings. You learn what paranoid-schizoid or depressive feelings are, or catastrophic anxiety, or the infantile fear of falling-to-pieces, or whatever. The lexicon of psychological concepts can be learned, or some of it can be learned, through many sessions of baby observation. What goes on in baby observation can be described as a kind of 'naming of parts'. In the first place, discriminating one feeling from another, deciding to whom the feeling belongs. Is it my feeling? Is it Mother's? Is it Baby's? Is it shared by more than one of us? This learning, at quite a deep and internalized level, does I am sure take place for many students.

Much less established at this point is how far this context of infant observation is one which will make possible the development of psychoanalytic ideas, in new ways. It is one thing to create a setting in which the descriptive and explanatory power of these ideas can be reproduced for many people; it is another to see this setting as a laboratory in which ideas can themselves be developed in response to new evidence. You see, the normal context for elaborating psychoanalytical ideas is the clinical setting, in which interpretations are offered to patients, and their response, whatever it is, is taken as an indicator of their state of mind, and also as a measure of how well the analyst has understood it. Responses to interpretations do sometimes convince analysts that they have got their patients plain wrong, or that the ideas they are using to understand them are insufficient to what they are trying to understand.

Now if the cardinal rule of infant observation is that one doesn't interpret, then one is restricted to a passivity in trying to grasp and make sense of mental phenomena. This is quite unlike the more active stance of the analyst in the consulting room. That's the difficulty from a research point of view. In infant observation, the observer does not set out deliberately to encourage a flow of thoughts and feelings in the mothers and infants they observe, even though the attentive, sympathetic gaze of the observer may sometimes have this benign effect, and enable mothers to think aloud more than they otherwise would. The experience of observation can even help mothers and babies get together, and have a more active emotional contact with one another, than they otherwise might. At this time some work is being done at the Tavistock, and in Caen, in France, to develop 'therapeutic observations', mainly with seriously 'at risk' families, to see if these can help, with very limited intervention except the containment of a reliable listening presence, to put troubled relationships between mothers and babies on to a better footing.

But because the purpose of infant observation is not to set going a process of thinking about feelings in those observed, it may have its limitations as a setting for the generation of psychoanalytic knowledge. After all the object of psychoanalytic research is the active mental processes, conscious and unconscious, which are revealed primarily through the transference relationship! The transference relationship exists in infant observation, but it is incidental or auxiliary to it, and is not its principal resource. My view about how psychoanalytical ideas evolve – which is another way of describing the respect in which psychoanalysis is a science – is that a person working in the consulting room starts out with a received body of ideas, usually learned from analysis, clinical supervision, and reading and didactic teaching. Most of the time what they do is to make reference to these ideas to understand their patients as particular individuals. They bring different ideas together to make sense of their patients. This may be with a unified focus, if they are versed in a specific theoretical paradigm, or more often, perhaps further away from their trainings, in a kind of synthesis or mosaic of ideas, each therapist's choice no doubt reflecting what ideas they find they can best work with in practice. It seems to me that genuinely new and original ideas evolve when received theoretical templates, the resources that the analysts have, are found insufficient to serve a clinical purpose. Something is going on that an analyst finds they can't understand. Sometimes after prolonged struggles with this painful situation, involving reflections on the patient, on the clinical and theoretical literature, and on the analyst herself, a new idea may emerge. This new idea may even initiate a new departure and a period of theoretical development, as for example in the work of W.R. Bion. My view is that this usually happens at the interface between a body of ideas (all psychoanalytic perceptions are dependent on ideas) and a body of 'empirical' or clinical material which cannot be contained adequately by them. (This is a sense in which the container-contained idea of Bion's also refers reflexively and recursively to the development of psychoanalysis itself.) This is what has happened in the development of psychoanalytic ideas in England, in the Kleinian tradition, but also with the work of Winnicott and many other original psychoanalytic thinkers.

What one has, then, is a connected development of ideas where new 'evidence' puts pressure on established theoretical formulations. This is exactly what happens in other sciences, isn't it? People start out saying, as their evidence appears, oh yes, our theory works! Then they discover, oh no, we have a problem! When something doesn't quite work, the body of ideas has to evolve in response to the evidence of fact. So, while I think there are important specificities in the way psychoanalysis works as a science, I don't think its fundamental mode of development is unlike that of other sciences.

AM: I can appreciate your insistence on the dynamics that generate knowledge, especially since a clinical ethnography does look to verify and 'document', if you will, something like the workings of the unconscious within a 'field' whose reliability as a scientific setting you have reason to question. This reminds me of a literature professor who used to tell me that you have to read a work like *The Divine Comedy* on the basis of faith. You don't question whether heaven or hell exist, or if Dante made the afterlife journey or not. You take that fundamental premise, as it were, on faith. In a way, the same argument – an 'unscientific' one, surely – applies to the unconscious. For when we try to talk about it in anthropology, the objections raised are that it can't be observed, it can't be classified or quantified . . . *ergo*, why concern ourselves with its purported existence? As a result, it has rarely been part of our sphere of study. However, once subjectivity becomes a concern for anthropology – as it has in recent decades – then the case can be made that there is room for psychoanalysis to prove its viability as an ethnographic tool . . .

MR: Well, for a start, I don't think anthropology owes much to quantification. In this respect, in their shared preoccupation with what Clifford Geertz once described as 'local knowledge', anthropology and psychoanalysis are quite close relations.

My view about psychoanalysis as a body of ideas is that it's been incredibly fertile. The thing which is most depressing and irritating about much of the criticism of psychoanalysis today is that many of its critics seem to be not in the slightest bit interested in how it has developed, or in what it has achieved in its history. In the terms in which you have just put it, they read psychoanalysis as if they were reading Dante from the perspective of a dogmatic atheist. They tend to read Freud alone, and they go on about him in various ways, but it's not enough to do this. The main interest of psychoanalysis lies in the fact that over a hundred years its ideas have continued to evolve. That is why psychoanalysis is much more interesting, significant, and indeed influential, than hypnotism, for example. Now, of course, people can say, in respect of its development, that it is still more of an art, like literature or painting, than it is a science. Well, that's a different and worthwhile debate, to have – psychoanalysis does in truth exist somewhere on a borderline between the human sciences and the arts. But at least one has to acknowledge that one is not dealing with an unchanging, static orthodoxy, but with a continually evolving set of theories and techniques.

So far as parallels and links between contemporary psychoanalysis and anthropology are concerned, I must say I am not very well informed. I have already mentioned Geertz's *Local Knowledge* as a resource for understanding the particularity of psychoanalytic understanding, and its reliance on the case-study. Bion's work is likely to be the most fertile from the psychoanalytic side in developing other such parallels. One could think for example of his theory of 'catastrophic change' – by which he means a necessary exposure to uncertainty and the possibilities of new development, with its necessary risks – and one of the formative concepts of modern anthropology, Victor Turner's idea of 'liminality'. Turner describes the social and cultural framings of key transitions. There might be a useful way of bringing together these anthropological and psychoanalytic ways of looking at crucial life transitions, and transitions of other kinds.

AM: Speaking of Bion, I'd like to refer to an article of his, 'Reality sensuous and psychic'. I have tried thinking about the field as – and here I'm quoting Bion – 'an expression of O . . . incommunicable save through K activity'. Incommunicable, that is, save through the kind of knowledge activity brought to bear by the ethnographer. Bion, as we know, also emphasizes that what is required of the psychoanalyst is what he calls 'a positive act' of refraining from memory and desire, noting that 'insofar as the function of memory and desire is to prevent transformation of the K into O order, the above characteristics cannot be indulged by the psychoanalyst without impairment of analytic capacity'. In a way this calls back to a very early attitude in data collecting that Boas himself espoused for anthropologists, which makes me wonder about some possible parallels . . .

Bear with me as I think aloud and bounce these ideas off you. Again on the receptivity to O, Bion writes: 'If he, the analyst, is able to be receptive to O, then he may feel impelled to deal with the intersection of the evolution of O with the domain of objects of sense.' I'm reminded here of the anthropologist Michael Jackson, whose research aims to bring the objects and dimension of sensory experience into ethnographic focus. In short: might not someone like Bion, at a level of theory, or maybe even metatheory, have something to offer anthropology?

MR: Well, the trouble is, you see, that I think what you've been describing is more a principle of method than a principle of theory. I think what Bion is saying is that there are many temptations, in undertaking psychoanalytic work, to impose our own theoretical preconceptions on the material. That is, not to recognize the difference, the specificity of both the nature of the patient and the emotional experience with the patient. And what he provided was an insistence that authentic analysis requires a capacity to completely suspend judgement and open oneself to experience. This has been a very inspiring idea for analysts, and especially perhaps to young entrants to the field, representing the idea of a pure commitment to analysis.

As an aside, I am reminded here of the way Wittgenstein's writing inspired philosophers in the 1960s, by its repeated demonstrations, as in a conversation, of philosophy-in-practice. Of course many of Wittgenstein's books were in effect transcribed philosophical conversations. Psychoanalysis shares with some kinds of philosophy an attachment to the live master-class: F.R. Leavis's interrogative method of 'practical criticism' generated some of the same intensity of commitment in the English Literature departments of the 1950s. All three of these very 'English' approaches of this period can be described as shared empiricisms of language, in which ideas become useful only through their manifestation in the particular.

But back to Bion. His aphorism is a warning about the pitfalls of merely reproducing a set of ideas as opposed to exposing oneself to a deep analytic experience – which also has essentially to be an emotional experience. Bion pointed out that one of the equivalents of this idea was the poet Keats' idea of 'negative capability'. Meg Harris Williams and Margot Waddell have developed the parallels between Bion's theory of mind and the Romantic poetic tradition in their book *The Chamber of Maiden Thought*. The idea is that the great artist needs to have the capacity to respond to the other, to respond to experience, in ways that allow new thoughts to evolve. They cannot simply impose onto these experiences pre-existing ways of thinking. This becomes for Bion a methodological precept, about how to think, in psychoanalysis, and elsewhere. New thinking requires being able to tolerate the undermining of one's preconceptions, and the anxiety which goes with the emergence of new ones. Bion wrote about new thoughts needing a thinker to be thought, as if the individual subject has to make himself a passive receptacle for something which comes essentially from the outside, or we might say alternatively from deep inside oneself. Bion has this idea of thought processes which evolve – if they are allowed to – in response to new experiences, of which the most vital kinds are emotional experiences. As a methodological precept for creative work, I think this is wonderful.

You could then say, well what is the theoretical presupposition underlying this way of putting things? In fact, Bion seems to retain in his mind, even while he's saying that we should empty our minds of all ideas, a theoretical structure which is deeply rooted in a particular psychoanalytic tradition and lineage. Recognizing the deep theoretical continuities in Bion's work is somewhat like recognizing the innumerable reworkings of Old Testament prophecy in the narratives of the New Testament!

I don't think Bion is saying, if analysts merely suspend memory, desire and preconceptions in their consulting rooms, they will have new thoughts, though he perhaps does hold this disposition of mind to be a necessary if not a sufficient condition of psychoanalytic thinking. Bion's writings, often explicitly addressed to psychoanalysts, suggest that he thinks that those who are being enjoined to do this, have already been well trained and formed in a rich tradition of ideas and techniques. The implicit notion is that the ideas of psychoanalysis are fertile and capable of further development, if reflected on with imagination.

This idea of creativity could be compared with that which might be applicable to the work of a poet or dramatist. A poet or playwright may be the inheritor and bearer of a specific literary tradition, but in order to do original work, she has momentarily to eschew traditional forms, and respond to her experience as it is. Subsequently, what artists have achieved will be seen as having taken place in dialogue with their chosen predecessors. Even a break with the past is usually shaped by an active engagement with it, and bears many of its marks, even if as negatives. Harold Bloom, the literary critic, has described the relationship between writers and their predecessors in quasi-Oedipal terms, as a struggle with the 'anxiety of influence'. The point I am making is that new psychoanalytic work does not start from scratch.

AM: In a way you're supporting my own thoughts, even as they look for a thinker! Christopher Bollas talks about psychoanalysis as a micro-ethnography of sorts, as a way of entering a private culture of meanings, a cosmology of objects that we originally cannot presume to understand. This idea connects for me with a nice phrase of Bion's, who somewhere refers to psychoanalysis as 'the domain of hallucinosis' – not unlike fieldwork, whose strange and alien domains no ethnographer (also working within and against a tradition) would ever presume to understand upon entry. I guess what I'm trying to do is take from your work the inspiration to think along comparative lines and just see how far these lines can be extended. You yourself make the case, in fact, for parallel moments or developments in social theory and psychoanalysis . . .

MR: What I don't understand, or what I think needs to be elaborated in the position you're taking, is what would count as the theoretical framework or object of study which is involved in the idea of ethnography. You see, if you think of psychoanalysis as an ethnography of a particular situation, the argument I've been making is that it is an ethnography which already embodies a very particular theoretical structure, an elaborated notion of what kinds of things you're likely to be looking for and are likely to be puzzled by in this particular setting.

Now, for me, ethnography is too general a term. Ethnography describes a method, not a theory, and if you're going to do an ethnography, my question would be: an ethnography of what and with which problem in mind? You could say that Arthur Hyatt Williams, working in prisons in Britain with long-term offenders, was doing an ethnography of the world of the prison and, in particular, of the mental world of the long-term prisoner. In his book *Cruelty, Violence and Murder* he's interested in states of unresolved mourning, guilt, and a kind of destructiveness which cannot be mentally processed or digested by the offender. He has a whole repertoire of the kind of things he thinks are likely to be there. His work emerges from psychoanalytic theories of paranoid-schizoid and perverse states of mind, but also from a long practical and clinical experience of working with violent prisoners. So his ethnography starts out with a frame of reference. Now, in fact every ethnography starts out with a frame of reference, but you've been talking about an ethnography as if it's not necessary to specify the frame of reference in order to understand how psychoanalysis might be useful to it. Now, it seems to me that if you specify the frame of reference – which then will involve some kind of elaboration of whatever the concepts and categories might be – then borrowings or influences from psychoanalytic methodology become more possible.

This does not exclude the prescriptions we've been describing, such as the suspension of belief, the openness to countertransference experiences, and so on. These are precepts, to be added to other methodological resources which can be drawn from psychoanalysis – close observations compared with each other, maintaining some invariance in the setting in order to reveal invariances, etc., even the measured use of interpretation, and the transference and counter-transference. There are all kinds of things one could imagine taking, as an ethnographer, from the consulting room or infant observation setting, and making use of 'in the field'. Once you specify what the ethnography is of, or about, the question becomes what theoretical concepts might be transferable, and might be useful, in this ethnographic context.

AM: You've hit on what was my major concern in interviewing you: whereas with someone, say, like Vincent Crapanzano, I could reference his fieldwork in Morocco, I was worried that our conversation could only be a theoretical one, as there'd be no *field* to focus on . . .

MR: Yes, but that's not quite the case. There is a field, as you say. You see, my main reference is to psychoanalysis itself. In as much as I am an ethnographer of any description at all, my field has been the development of psychoanalysis in England. And what I've had to say, both in some of the papers in *The Good Society and the Inner World*, and in *Reason and Unreason*, is about what happens in baby observation, what happens in consulting rooms, what happens in applied psychoanalytic study, and what happens in psychoanalytic organizations. The question 'what happens to psychoanalysis outside of its laboratory?' can be put in terms of the sociology of psychoanalysis, hopefully itself informed by psychoanalytic thinking as you think anthropology should be. I've tried to think about such questions as, how did psychoanalysis evolve in this way in Britain? Why does it take this form rather than that? How is it learned, how is it organized, how is it institutionalized, how has it extended its methods into other settings, such as infant observation? This has some empirical basis – empirical in an ethnographic sense – in the sense that I've been around this world, I've seen a lot of these settings at close quarters and I've tried to think about them systematically. It's a pretty loose ethnography but I am a sort of semi-insider, and I've been able to have quite a good view of it. More than many 'outsiders', anyway. If one looks for a concrete referent to what I'm all about, it's about looking reflexively at the field of psychoanalysis itself, although of course I'm not a clinician and therefore can hardly be fully reflexive about it. I don't know if that helps . . . but I think it does.

AM: Ethnographic texts, especially in recent years, have come more and more to reflect the fieldworker's own subjectivity, which becomes increasingly crucial to the narrative process. Could we perhaps reflect together on the ethnographer's production of such a text, or more specifically on the arc and process that move from the departure from one's culture of origin to a return there through the production of the text?

MR: What occurs to me is the fact that you can think of the transaction between an anthropologist and his/her subject matter as always a search for relevant identities and differences from what he or she already knows. You might take a view of the subjectivity of the anthropologist not just in terms of an individual subject, but as a bearer of his/her own culture, and as someone who is unavoidably saying something about that culture in investigating another one. The point is to say something which relates back to his/her own culture, which is, as it were, an expression of him/herself. You then get around to the question of what kinds of projection and projective identification are going on – both between the individual anthropologist and where he or she is, and in relation to what he or she is carrying to their culture in doing that thing.

A crude example would be Margaret Mead, going off and discovering all these sexual goings-on, as she thought. The fact that she was wrong, people say, is in a way all the more graphic. Why was she wrong in the way that she was said to be wrong? Because she wanted to be wrong. Why did she want to be wrong? Because she was looking for something . . . the other, as it were, of her own society. And you could say the same of Malinowski, I should think. Armed with Freud and a theory of sexuality, he goes to the Trobriand Islands, and discovers, 'Hey look, these people are different, there is no repression'. Well, whether this is true or not, it's a narrative which plays an important role in replaying and reworking the missing bits, or the unacceptable bits, or the hated bits, or the longed-for bits, of his own culture. It's back to noble savages . . . So I think that those dimensions of the other always having to be understood, in terms of some kind of transaction with what is already there, forms part of the principle of selection. The principle of selection is going to be related to some of the fundamental values which the anthropologist is engaged with in relation to his/her own society, as bearer or as critic – and to some of the fundamental values of the anthropologist as a person, as a subject with his/her own preoccupations. So you could say, to that extent, there could be both a cultural biography and an individual biography of an anthropologist, which would explain why they are making the sense that they are making in what they're doing. I think some psychoanalytic concepts, in relation to how objects are distributed in the narrative account, could be quite useful and actually quite instructive.

AM: I'm glad we got to this because this is what I've been struggling to communicate, even through my reference to Bion. You've just made the point about the preconception of fundamental values that an anthropologist invariably, and perhaps unconsciously, brings to the field . . .

MR: What this makes me think is that anthropologists are likely to be deeply engaged in some task of remaking, criticizing, re-sorting, rejecting or renewing . . . they're likely to be deeply engaged in that process, even if they imagine they're not. This is so because the characteristic stance of postmodern anthropology is to be above this struggle; to enjoy the reflective process, as if the anthropologist were not deeply engaged. Indeed being deeply engaged is defined as part of the problem. But I suspect that even lack of engagement may represent a form of engagement, in the same way that the enjoyment of cerebral pyrotechnics by certain kinds of poststructuralist cultural theorists is also a powerful rejection of another pre-existing morality which they are trying to get away from, or destroy. So I think if one considers any discourse as always arising from a relationship with some anterior discourse or some anterior objects, it seems to me one would have a powerful instrument for trying to understand what people are actually doing. It's quite interesting: if you think about the presentation of ethnographies, psychoanalysis also involves a continuing presentation of ethnographies in the form of case reports. Somebody does a case and writes it up. They're presenting an ethnography of their own experiences of a bit of the field, namely, their patient. What characteristic forms does this ethnography take? What are the characteristic rules of presenting clinical cases, and how are they different for different clinicians? My point here is that you could think about the aesthetics of ethnography in relation to case reports, as well as in relation to anthropological fieldwork. Who knows, after our work together, I may well find I've changed my mind about ethnographic applications of psychoanalysis . . .

# References

Bion WR (1970) Reality sensuous and psychic. In: Attention and Interpretation. London: Karnac, pp. 26–40.

Bloom H (1997) The Anxiety of Influence. Oxford: Oxford University Press.

Geertz C (1983) Local Knowledge. New York: Basic Books.

Kuhn T (1996) The Structure of Scientific Revolutions. Chicago: University of Chicago Press.

Latour B (1986) Laboratory Life. Princeton, NJ: Princeton University Press.

Williams MH, Waddell M (1991) The Chamber of Maiden Thought: Literary Origins of the Psychoanalytic Model of the Mind. London: Routledge.

Williams AH (1998) Cruelty, Violence and Murder: Understanding the Criminal Mind. Northvale, NJ: Jason Aronson.

Chapter 6
# Kathleen Stewart

Kathleen Stewart grew up in New England in a large extended family, did her graduate work in anthropology at the University of Michigan and has been teaching at the University of Texas since 1988. She has done extensive fieldwork all over the United States, primarily in coal-mining West Virginia, Orange County, California, and in Las Vegas.

Her first book, *A Space on the Side of the Road: Cultural Poetics in an 'Other' America* was published by Princeton University Press in 1996 and won honorary mention in both the Victor Turner Prize for Best Ethnography and the Chicago Folklore Prize. In taking up the question of the cultural poesis, or generativity, of everyday narratives in a poor, politicized and so-called 'marginal' place, the book experiments with new modes of cultural critique through performative writing: a form that draws readers close to its presumed ethnographic objects and vividly attempts to recreate for them field-inspired impacts and flights of fancy. It was Stewart's very emphasis on narrativity, and the swirling effects on me of reading her book, that compelled me to interview her. Indeed, by calling on processes that suggested for me the presence of a psychoanalytic sensibility at once romantic and postmodern (suffice it here to mention key terms of hers like *contamination, nostalgia, desire* and *fantasy*), Stewart readily confirmed the validity of my intuition by generating, in turn, an interview rich with resonances and possibilities for cross-disciplinary research.

Some signposts may well be in order to orient readers through the interview and highlight these very possibilities. It's important to note, for example, that the specific West Virginia 'performativity' of which Stewart speaks is an oral form, a stylized narrative expression. Such expressions are, as it were, the guarantors of a shared sense of what constitutes a vital selfhood (i.e., a self that is not fixed or unitary, a main theme of our discussion). The point could be argued that in an increasingly homogenized global space, where subaltern cultural forms – like those in West Virginia – are being systematically eradicated or absorbed, the practice of psychoanalysis is, perhaps sadly, one of the lone remaining spaces for the reconfiguration of self-experience through talking – that is to say, through a systematic reclamation project that seeks, among other things, to privilege and preserve a narrative dimension of storytelling and its pleasures. As Julia Kristeva reminds us, in her book *New Maladies of the Soul*

(Columbia, 1995, p. 43): 'Psychoanalysis goes against the grain of the modern convenience that calls attention not to the end of the Story of Civilization, but to the end of the possibility of telling a story.' And while many psychoanalysts have written on the idea of a multiple self, Roy Schafer and his book *Retelling a Life* (Basic Books, 1992) also come to mind, for its emphasis on narration, dialogue and their implications for selfhood. As Schafer writes (p. 29): 'We should be careful not to lose sight of the proliferation of selves in each person's construction of experience lest we begin to mistake our superordinate categories (i.e., what Schafer calls the ideal self and actual self) for entities discovered in Nature and observable without narrative mediation. In principle, no limit can be set on the number of experiential self constructions that it may be profitable to discuss in one or another context of inquiry.' One reads Schafer, and one could just as easily be reading Stewart.

I also want to suggest what I see here as substantial, important overlaps between Stewart's sensibility and the writings of Christopher Bollas. Consider, when reading Stewart's comments, Bollas's ideas on the generative unconscious and free association (*vis-à-vis* the rambling quality of Appalachian talk that 'remembers' and 'dis-members' objects and experience); or on the vitality, intensity, and integrity of objects: how the latter 'contaminate', transform, and indeed *fashion* (a key verb for Stewart) experiences of self, body and world. Outside of Stewart's timely rescuing for anthropology, in these pages, of a discourse on desire (that readily evokes Lacan, and opens the fluid sites of fieldwork to the Real), this convergence with Bollas's thought probably makes for the most fertile area of confluence between her work – and perhaps that of any contemporary ethnographer – and today's object relationists.

Professor Stewart has also written about nostalgia, conspiracy theory, apocalyptic thinking, daydreams, country music, gender, aesthetics, trauma, photography, whistle-blowers, hockey dads, dogs, TV repairmen, and the pitfalls of the American Dream. Her work has been performed in plays and it has been supported by the Rockefeller Foundation, the National Endowment for the Humanities, the School of American Research, and the University of California-Irvine Institute for the Humanities, as well as by the University of Texas.

She is currently completing a second book, *Vital Impacts: The Private Life of Public Culture*. This book tracks the circulations and impacts of public culture in the contemporary United States through close ethnographic attention to the intensities and sensibilities now emergent along the charged border between things public and private. In this work, Stewart asks how the political and economic transformations of neo-liberalism, advanced consumer capitalism, and the proliferation of publics and counterpublics are lived as everyday life, excitable senses, and emergent structures of feeling. Written in the style of vignettes that experiment with various forms of voice and personal address, it tracks impacts into seemingly disparate arenas and treats them not as a fixed body of elements and representations, but as vital forces and events. Already in our interview, that took place in Austin, Texas, on 26–29 October 1995 (long predating this recent research), readers will find prefigurations of Stewart's new work and intimations of its intersections with psychoanalysis. (Note: Unless otherwise specified, all quotes are from Stewart's *A Space on the Side of the Road*.)

Anthony Molino: Your work calls increasingly for a form of deconstructionist critique you call *contaminated* as opposed to 'constructive social science theorizing' – which, you write, 'sees its objects from a decontaminated distance'. How does your critique address the problems of the social construction of the subject?

Kathleen Stewart: Good question. It's a more complicated question than it might seem when you use the phrase 'the social construction of the subject'. In the anthropological literature, arguments about the social construction of things often say little more than that culture exists (i.e. things are not just nature); but often there follows no curiosity to wonder more about how things are constructed, or what the effects of these constructions might be. In proposing a contaminated mode of cultural critique, I am opening questions that might enable that kind of curiosity or engagement. 'Contaminated' critique is of course a polemical term, aimed at the unspoken norms and practices of academic discourse to disengage from its 'objects'. I am proposing that before we ask the seemingly straightforward question of the social construction of the subject, we first have to ask about the cultural-political charge given to particular notions of the analyst as 'subject' embedded in conventions of academic discourse – such as the practice of taking distance from one's 'object' of analysis, practices of self-control and transcendence, and particular ways of making judgements and choices which have come to signify intelligence and a kind of intellectual victory over other possible interpretations or findings. The point of a contaminated critique is to put the analyst (as 'subject') on a par with her 'objects' of analysis, to make the analyst more vulnerable to something that Bakhtin, in *The Dialogic Imagination*, calls 'trans-subjective relations'.

AM: Similarly, implicit in your critique is a redefinition of culture – no longer 'given', pre-constituted or 'out there' to be localized and discovered. As an anthropologist, how do you conceptualize 'culture'? and as an ethnographer, how do you go about the task of re-presenting it?

KS: I'm simply trying to keep that question open – the question of 'what is it?'. What is culture? What is meaning, or desire, or determination, or structure, or feeling, or any number of other 'things' that come into view in a particular instance? It's an ethnographic and historical question and that means interrogating these 'things' – 'ethnography' and 'history' too. All three – ethnography, history, culture – should be understood as a mode of questioning. They are not finished, fully present things to be operationalized and objectively reproduced. Nor do I think questions of representation are enough in thinking about the nature of culture; lately the question of what culture is or how it works has been displaced by a routine, compulsive critique of representations which ends up reducing culture to ideas, ideology, images, even as it dreams up a false utopia of finally someday getting the representation 'right'. I'd say rather that culture is something that's hard to grasp, because it has a vitality and a creativity which means that its 'meanings' are always in excess of what we can 'know' once and for all. Like the concept of simple 'social construction' *per se*, the question of how things are represented in culture or of how we as analysts represent the other, is not a radical enough question. It doesn't keep asking 'what is it?'. The problem is that all questions are caught in a political-economic context (such as the politics of academia at a particular moment – what gets jobs, what moves or claims to 'solutions' promote career mobility, what kinds of research are funded and not funded, and so on). One way or another, basic questions are too easily and too quickly closed. For me, as an anthropologist, the question is how to constantly re-open these questions that are always getting slammed shut. The key is the subject–object relations of ethnography and that deep and detailed thought and struggle that comes of sustained engagement.

AM: In your own efforts to arrive at a working conceptualization of culture, you identify it in your writings as that which 'inhabits the slippage of a gap between sign and meaning', or as 'a space of excess and desire'. This kind of language certainly isn't characteristic of much anthropology. Could you address the peculiarities of your terminology?

KS: It comes from this need to keep opening the question of what culture is. So I define my own role, as ethnographer and writer, as one of trying to track densities, forces and desires in culture: all things that are hard to grasp and exist in states of negativity or absence rather than a state of full presence. To see, or imagine, these aspects of culture requires a continuous gap in the certainty of anthropological knowledge of its 'objects'. Theory needs the same gap that exists in culture and is its nature – it has to have the same ontological status of a thing that is a questioning, a desiring, an argument, a resistance, a latency, and so on. I see culture as a motion of force fields. The question is how does it operate in an everyday life, what does it do to people in different positions, what is the source of its creativity or generativity, how does it structure events, what are its effects?

AM: Your writings teem with the language of Lacan – words like the real, gaps, lack, desire 'in-fill', as it were, the landscape of your texts. What is your relationship to psychoanalysis?

KS: Maybe not a direct, or at least not a systematic, relationship. I read Lacan before I wrote my dissertation. I then read Kristeva, who has had an influence, and Ross Chambers, a literary critic influenced by Lacan who has done some work on desire in literature. I also read Žižek. I've read a lot of literary criticism, cultural studies, and just that diffuse influence that has come to be called 'theory'.

AM: There is one term central to psychoanalysis which is conspicuously absent from your work. Though you do make frequent use of a notion of a cultural unconscious, I'm wondering if you've concerned yourself at all with the idea of the individual unconscious?

KS: Well, its meaning has changed. Personally I shy away from the assumed depth model of the distinction between conscious and unconscious states. But I borrow from Jameson the concept of a political unconscious in narrative form. To me the general idea of an unconscious – whether in the individual or in a society – holds open the more general space of the uncanny and unknown, and that I find important. But I think there is something about doing fieldwork which, at least in my case, makes me avoid the concept of an individual unconscious. For instance, there are topics that I didn't push at all in fieldwork, where you can't ask people direct questions. They don't like it and they don't answer questions. There's a certain sense of boundaries, of culture as a public phenomenon, in my work, and I think that's partly from the ethnographic practice of hanging out and seeing what it is that people talk about. I didn't push into areas that they don't talk about. Although, of course, I analyse what they say; I don't take it at face value. And I analyse it in terms of structures which they're not conscious of.

AM: In a broader context, how do you see the contemporary crosscurrents between anthropology and psychoanalysis? And, in light of your preceding answers, can anthropology make room for a notion like the individual unconscious?

KS: Well I do share the poststructuralist hostility to depth models which would accuse the concept of the unconscious of being a modernist conceit. On the other hand, it's ridiculous to simply avoid the concept because it's somehow tainted. Given the more interesting and sophisticated questions now being raised about subjectivity and meaning, there is probably a need for questions concerning something like the unconscious – as I said, the uncanny and unknowable now seem to me to be salient issues. But for me, the questions would become interesting at the moment when they eschew the dichotomy between 'deep structure' and 'surface phenomenon', so that they could talk about the uncanny within the everyday or the inexplicable at the heart of a known norm, or the excess that is not captured in any particular symbol or meaning.

AM: Of central concern to your work is the explosion of the subject–object dualism that has informed age-old Western and anthropological constructions of the Other. 'What if', as you write, 'identity itself proliferated in the gaps between word and world?'

KS: I am interested in thinking about the subject as performative space. This is something that I learned from fieldwork in West Virginia where everyday speech and sociality and agency are all organized to keep people from falling into any kind of fixed identity, so that different identities get played out in known expressive forms. Subjectivity is deeply a performance and an aesthetic – it's a way of marking the world and letting yourself be marked by it; it's a way, as they say in the coal camps, 'of making something *of* things'. People refuse to allow themselves to be characterized in fixed ways; they grow eccentric as they perfect their own styles of life-making. People who don't actively stylize themselves in performance are called 'no-account' – they don't offer an account of themselves, they become weightless. People who don't speak for themselves, who don't get out and go and talk to people, are suspect and they bring everyone else down. The performed self surrounds any residue of a fixed self or habitus and it is the vitality of the self. In West Virginia it's this that people actually identify with. You find this kind of thing everywhere and anthropology has long recognized it without really dealing with its ramifications.

AM: You occasionally make reference to multiple identities for a singular subject . . .

KS: I suppose I think of the self as an experiencing centre of things. But it's not singular because it's not fixed. It's the effect of tensions, desires, dialogic conflicts or debates between voices. It's political too. The subject, especially the subaltern subject, is an effect of contingency. The middle-class American ideology of the self as something that has a clear trajectory and is a kind of sheer agency that moves through the trajectory of a life is just that – an ideology, and one that is based on an imaginary arising in particular life circumstances. In the working-class coal-mining camps in West Virginia the operative idiom is not trajectory, but the accidental – things that impact people. The subject, or the self, then, becomes an effect, or a series of effects, in ways that are deeply significant. There are multiple sources of impact – many things happen – and so there are multiple 'selves': where 'self' is no longer a fixed, organized category at all. So our options in thinking about the self are not limited to this tired, always already bitter polemic between postmodern models of multiplicity and fragmentation and older but revalorized models of pure agency. There is also the equally 'political' model of selves who are subject to contingent events, but *because* of that, find themselves multiple, dispersed, generative, performative. So, to talk about the subject as effects is not just to talk about endless variation, unconnected to structures of power.

AM: I recall you quoting Bakhtin: 'What if the genuine life of the personality takes place at the point of non-coincidence between a man and himself?' A remark like that one echoes for me a statement of Lacan's having to do with the dislocation of the subject, as it speaks from a place in which it is not . . . How does this line of enquiry of yours relate to contemporary understandings of the postmodern self, *vis-à-vis* the split or decentred subject?

KS: I think the quote of Bakhtin's, and maybe the concept of the split subject too, are more precise than the decentred and postmodern subject, as it's used in the literature. In the split as well as in the performed subject, there is more of a sense of a self that is an interiority . . . that is being played with and constructed and deconstructed in very particular ways . . . whether the split is between conscious and unconscious, or whether a distinction prevails – of the kind that I'm making – between performance and fixed identity. The concept of a decentred subject in postmodern theory is, I think, vaguer – it's an attempt to make a very vague analogy between what is seen as a kind of socioeconomic formation . . . late capitalism . . . and a self that's something unmoored, but does not necessarily have this kind of tension within itself . . . that is, a tension that moves it away from essentialism.

AM: In your book, *A Space on the Side of the Road*, you expound on the origins of an individualist ideology – from which, you argue, was derived a 'bourgeois ethics of universalized personhood'. Can you clarify what you call the threefold operation that gave rise to what you call the bourgeois imaginary? I'm particularly interested in what you see as the third phase, involving the creation of a universal and impersonal subject.

KS: De Certeau, Habermas and others have written about the construction of the modern city and public sphere through a process of decontamination – of emptying space of its live historical difference and conflict and resistance to development by virtue of the existence of other life worlds already entrenched in space, or occupying it. The city meant the construction of a unified space by a process of cleaning out the physical environment and doing away with cultural difference and chaos. It meant creating a universal, unmarked space – a blank slate – and with it a universal, unmarked subject that would become the citizen in a civil society. The universal subject develops with an internally disciplined self – a self that is private, bounded, inside a skin and talks to itself. It should control itself. It should have internalized tastes that are marked *as* 'good taste' and it should valorize self-control as a virtue and a mark of distinction. The bourgeois public sphere is an imagined community predicated on this phantasm of the subject as an internally modulated and moderated thing that poses as a subject 'free' to discuss ideas and politics openly, with reason and without culturally situated motives or 'distortions'. This is the hegemony of a specifically middle-class self – what Richard Brown calls the 'bureaucratic self' to distinguish it from a more working-class model of the heroic self which reacts to events, accidents, or pressing, performative circumstances. The middle-class, self-disciplined self presumes a centred self with the power, or the opportunity, to create a trajectory for itself and to think of itself as moving along some path into the future. There's an idiom at work of getting on track and excluding things that happen accidentally or that could derail a person. It's a matter of becoming relatively rigid and unified, in that sense. It becomes more precisely bourgeois, in the sense of a subculture, when the excluded others develop an elaborate model of their own, in contradistinction to the model of the planning, plodding, self-controlled self who chugs along the track of a career and the 'progress' of a life.

AM: Is it your contention that in this threefold operation are to be found the origins not only of a Western or dominant notion of selfhood, but also the origins of our understanding of psychic life?

KS: Yes, though I don't really think the detailed historical research has been done.

AM: Apropos of this historical operation, you write on page 117 of *A Space on the Side of the Road*: 'A cultural diacritics, rooted in difference and social conflict, was displaced by an internalized struggle . . .' – for, as you've mentioned, self discipline, discerning judgment, good taste, etc. You use the word 'internalized' here – in attributing this struggle to the bourgeois imaginary. What confuses me is your willingness, at times, to recognize the space and place of interiority in what seem to be essentialist terms, while at other times you more than imply that the notion of interiority is a historical product. What about this apparent contradiction?

KS: I mean to say that there's a particular ideological spin on interiority in this bourgeois model, whereby interiority gets written with a capital 'I' – because it takes social, public, cultural, political polemics and rigidly internalizes them into a kind of moral discourse, or at least into something that lends itself to (or, rather, is actually constructed by means of) an exegetical discourse. So there are kinds of interiority, different processes of interiorizing.

AM: Given the poetic elaboration of so much of your language – infused as it is with words like *desire, enchantment, nostalgia* – how can so much of your work rest on such terms, even as you critique the notion of interiority as an ideological production?

KS: I'm critiquing a specific interiority that valorizes interiority *per se* as something that separates you and makes you invulnerable. The nature of desire varies in its essence. It can be something that people allow to affect them, or actively seek (and this can be done in an abject or aggressive way). Or it can be contained as a trait, or content, of a fixed, unshakeable self. It can be a ruminative state that one inhabits for a time and recognizes oneself in or it can be a short-term goal drive – a thing the self comes up with and spits out. It can be a collection of discrete forces residing in the self (but with a life of their own) and in complex relations with each other; or it can be a collection of things subordinated to the overall plan or map of 'the self'. It can move you out of yourself. Or not. It can spin the self out of control or it can become the subject of controlling judgements.

AM: Along these lines, in a 'desiring space' in-filled with traces and gaps, is there a way to model self-experience: of the subject, of the contaminated subject–object, or even of the ethnographer? Or, to put the question differently: from the 'extopic' place that you privilege, is it possible for subject–object contamination to convey, genuinely, the Other's experience of self?

KS: You mean can we escape the hermeneutic loop?

AM: Exactly.

KS: I think we presume that we can. But I would have to say 'no' – even though it's an enormously complicated question. In interpreting what's going on in another culture/self, particular people have particular insights and they pick up on particular things that are real. I think culture is extopic in the sense that it's objectivated . . . there are forms that people use to express themselves and produce themselves and so an analyst can see those things. What I do is to mimic them and then try to imagine their possible effects on people using them. Good ethnography depends on a very close attention to what people are saying and doing. For me, trying to write from within that close attention produces a double consciousness of who I am, as an analyst, and the kind of road-blocks that come up with being able to imagine what they're doing. But, I use the term 'imagine' because I think that it's a writing exercise or an analytic exercise and it's very much affected by enormous numbers of particular experiences that make up what I am and what it is that I see. But I do think that I see something. I think somebody else would see something different, and that that would be something too.

AM: Your own work clearly challenges those boundaries that you would have anthropologists transgress more readily and often. Specifically, I'm thinking of how you suggest that people in the mining camps and hollers of West Virginia fashion the self as a drama of encounter and desire. I find the idea of 'fashioning' appealing . . .

KS: Fashioning implies a kind of active and political, rhetorical, performative dimension to what it is people are doing. I think that they are aware of the many categories they have of ways of talking in particular situations and particular performative or political or rhetorical styles. It's actively fashioning something but out of given materials – the categories, the aesthetics and poetics of how things go together and form temporary unities. It reminds me of the ways in which the preachers can shift back and forth between supposedly relatively 'conscious' and 'unconscious' states. This is a rhetoric with a structure. The preacher talks in an ordinary neighborly tone and content for two or three minutes and then suddenly his eyes roll up in his head and he's in trance and jumping around the stage yelling for a couple of minutes and then just as suddenly he's back talking in this calm, ordinary tone. He's fashioning himself as preacher and medium – both calling on existing resources to produce an intended effect and carried away in the movement. The whole thing takes place in a heightened, performative state which is itself an expected cultural genre.

AM: Do you see a parallel between what you call 'the (historical) suppression of voices at the margin of "Otherness"' and Freud's quasi-concurrent discovery of the unconscious – with its own prominent mechanisms of repression? I also ask this because, in addressing this phenomenon of social suppression, you use a Freudian image of lower depths . . .

KS: I suspect that the particularly intense performance of an interiority in the bourgeois self also brings to the fore those categories of conscious and unconscious. They're foregrounded because repression makes a lot of sense to this self. So it becomes an interesting historical ethnographic question, to think about repression and unconsciousness in particular groups.

AM: On this same theme, I'm interested in what you mean by 'the new psychological depth' ascribed to the lower and excluded elements of society. How is it that they come to fill the bourgeois imaginary with dread and desire?

KS: This comes up in my book in the story of a social worker who comes into daily contact with people from the camps, and yet because of that develops an irrational dread of them in the process of being taken over by an imaginary relation to them. She objectifies their otherness, or the gap she feels between herself and them, to the point of imagining that they embody otherness and repulsion – they smell, they are violent, they are the sites of both absence or lack (of self-control, education, reason, etc.) and excess (too much eating, drinking, fighting, religion, etc). She is avoiding otherness but in the process it grows larger than life. I think it's about the need for self-control and certainty – the exclusion of contingency and the accidental.

AM: What does Kathleen Stewart mean, then, when she talks about the imaginary? How do you understand it?

KS: Well it is related both to Lacan's notion of the imaginary and to Benedict Anderson's outline of a public culture of 'imagined communities', which signals the inventiveness of culture and the inventiveness of connection. I'm playing off of the 'imaginary' in these two senses in order to produce an image of culture as a series of uncanny connections that take on a life of their own and reproduce themselves through public circulation. The idea of an imaginary allows me to think about practices of invention, creative generativity, displacement, condensation, repression as aspects of 'meaning' in culture. It's a way of imagining the excess of depth, feeling, density, desire surrounding any particular claim to meaning or experience.

AM: You seem to privilege in your work the human capacity of the imagination, and what you call its imaginings. It's not a term usually invoked in the social sciences, as it evokes, at least for me, worlds or states either unconscious or utopian . . .

KS: The imaginary is the desired . . . it's what is not real . . . what is not written as the naturalized or the necessary in a culture . . . what I'm saying is that there's more to the image of writing culture than is often developed from that concept. I'm trying to add a dimension to 'writing culture' by looking, in this case, at the dense and intense imaginary surrounding and informing story-telling. I think it's this imaginary that people identify with and find a cultural home in. Having a culture means being able to insert a shared imaginary into the real to produce a cultural real. And this of course becomes a cultural politics.

AM: As we talk, I remain confused by your use of the word desire. It sometimes echoes with a 'D' – as something essentialist, all-infusing and species-defining; while at other times it reads with a small *d*, as in the everyday desires of the people in the camps: in this case, desire as something subject to specific historical and localized discourses. Can you clarify how you mean to use the term?

KS: I guess in the context in which I'm using it – which is the effort to insert a space for it into anthropological theory – I'm using it with a capital 'D', much as I use 'Imaginary' with a capital 'I'. I want to consider questions of desire and imagination in thinking about what culture is. Desire exists universally; people have desire and in the theory of culture desire stands for something like a motivating force in culture. The question of particular desires, and modes of desire, is a different, second, question. But the question of desire itself goes beyond a sheer relativist chant that would simply assert over and over that people have different desires in different 'cultures' or places. Desire has to be theorized and culture has to be theorized in terms of desire. We need to know how something we might call *desire* works in particular places and moments and situations and what effects it has, and under what circumstances the discourse of 'desire' arises. So the search has to be in and through particularities but it has to be a search for fundamental practices and processes we can call the arena of desire.

AM: Concerning these particularities, you devote one chapter in your book to the body, used in the camps as 'a concrete performance of the self–other power relation'. I couldn't help but look at the local and linguistic cultivation of bodily symptoms – the *dizzies, nerves, smotherings* – as inscriptions of the Real, in a way, or what Freud would have seen as hysterical symptoms. In fact, you even describe these illnesses as 'a kind of remembrance' – the very language that Freud uses to define hysteria . . .

KS: I think it was implied, though I wouldn't want to use a strict Freudian frame. I am talking about a process of bodily remembrance, but that remembrance is itself a discourse – a publicly produced experience – as well as a mediating practice. The body is a medium of expression.

AM: I'd like to continue with these reflections on the body. In a lovely passage from *A Space on the Side of the Road* (p. 132), you write:

> [T]hey embed [the body] in a poetics of daily pains, eccentric markings, and monumental peculiarities that open onto the space of a social imaginary. The body is not incorporated into the self as inert substance or bodily 'self image', but retains an affecting agency all its own. They describe the body itself as an 'Other' that can be seen, felt and encountered. The body, like the hills, becomes a collection of places that remember events, haunt people, and take on a life of their own . . .

This would seem to suggest that there is, among the people of West Virginia, a lived or perhaps even a 'conscious' recognition of what we might call a split self. Your word 'collection' is a striking one in this context, suggesting as it does for me tensions between fluidity and fragmentation, or between unitary and multiple. Can you comment on these impressions of mine?

KS: A lived recognition, yes, but not a conscious one. The issue for me is tracking their precise discourses. Here, the body is narrativized. That's why they talk about the body as having particular 'places' where things happen and why they talk about the body as a thing that happens to them – because that's the mode of perception in their story-telling more generally. They're talking as if they're walking around and something happens to them, but it's happening in the body. So, you know, they say things like 'this place grabbed a hold of me and forced me down to the ground'. I think what you have to do is look at the practices that they use in narrative in general – as mediating discourse. But they don't stop and fasten onto concepts of the self in the body in that sense; they're just telling stories. I would see the 'split self', then, as an effect of expressive forms.

AM: I'd like to explore further with you the sense of a body as a permeable space, as a site where boundaries of inner and outer are transgressed . . . Among your informants, substances seem to be able to permeate the body with incredible ease, from the inside out as well as from the outside in. Is the body, then – in this cultural space called 'West Virginia', where *messes* refer as readily to kinship lines as they do to food – primarily a liminal space between two separate but equivalent dimensions? or does its 'inside' connote a privileged container of sorts – something akin to what we might call 'a space of the self'?

KS: I don't know. I think what they experience is vulnerability. They know the discourses they use and what's appropriate in particular situations and whether someone is 'good at' a certain kind of talk and whether something is a good story. I don't think they think of the self as a bounded container; I think the self is very fluid and non-binding except, perhaps, when parts of it (body parts) grow animated, become events and sort of 'turn on' you. Being hit by things that happen is what makes you a person in a place and your body is just another . . . it's the world writ small . . . it's just another place where things can happen to you. And everything for them is about place, things that happen in this place to the point that, when they explain something, they don't say 'it's because . . .'; instead, they say 'it's where . . .'

AM: In this context, specifically relating to the women and men in Appalachia, you suggest that gender ways get externalized as performative discourses, rather than internalized as identities. Can you explain what you mean? Are you implying that there aren't dominant notions of masculinity and femininity that these people carry with them?

KS: No, but it's a nervous and contradictory system, like Mick Taussig describes. I find his idea of a nervous system compelling because it expresses both the dialogic provisionality of culture 'structure' and the sense of a force field – a politics that penetrates form. In the context of your question, there is an ideology that elaborates rules of what it is to be a woman and a man and gives norms as if they should be blueprints for action. But no sooner is any such statement out of someone's mouth than someone – and more often than not the same person – will contradict it. They'll say 'it's women's job to get up and cook breakfast in the morning'. Then they'll *always* say, compulsively say, 'still yet, there's nothing worse than a man so babified he can't get up and make his own eggs if he has to'. What I'm saying is that culture isn't located in the content of explicit ideologies. Explicit statements are made in larger rhetorical contexts, and they are social performances – not reflections of some fixed inner truth or static core idea that somehow holds the secret of that culture. What's happening in West Virginia is that every ideological claim is followed by a narrative logic – a story in which the idea can be tested and where it inevitably fails as a blueprint. People are suspicious of ideology itself and do not, in their experiences, believe that codes dominate the real. What is real is the need for people to perform themselves in particular situations and to be multiply skilled. The logic of gender here, then, includes a normative order, but that order is itself structured in a dialectical relationship with its negation in stories of things that just happen, where people have to do things precisely other than the expected or normal. Western theory makes altogether too much of the normative anyway, reflecting it's own bias toward the exegetical, self-disciplined, highly bounded, self.

AM: Throughout your work – and especially in *A Space on the Side of the Road* – you often write of 'remembered things' as a 'slipping locus' or trace of culture: as being constitutive of engagement and performance. What struck me was your spelling of the word remembered, often hyphenated: re-membered, things again made members . . . perhaps of a body, or of a community . . . Could you comment on that particular spelling and usage?

KS: Re-membered, and dis-membered too. I take the metaphor from people taking apart their trucks and then re-membering them . . . putting them back together again, and this obsessive interest that people in West Virginia have in just seeing how things are put together after taking them apart. They want to mix things and mess with things, like they might try to put washing machine parts in a car just to see if it will work. I'm saying that this sort of physical 'membering' and dis-membering of things is just one expression of something that is a practice that occurs on many different planes – such as memory's function to dis-member and re-member things in narrative. In this sense, memory in narrative logic is a kind of literalized or visceral mimesis not unlike the experiments with trying out combinations of things. The concept of memory for them is important because memory moves through something again and again; it's a retelling, a re-using. Because of the constant narrativizing of things, the culture privileges not only memory in general, but also a particular kind of memory – a mimetic memory that tracks how things are put together and how they can be taken apart. In stories, memories of details just come and memory itself seems to take on a life of its own at precisely the same moment that it is tied to the image of concrete things and the following of events.

AM: Is this idea at the origins of your call for subject–object contamination?

KS: Yes, the necessity for people in the camps to contaminate themselves with their objects, if they are to make anything of them. They track things, see what they do, dismember them and remember them and keep playing with them until they seem to yield an idea.

AM: So that these pieces and parts do actually become members of the physical body in a way . . .

KS: Yes, that's interesting . . . I hadn't thought about that.

AM: Is this mode of remembering, then, among the people, somehow constitutive of 'self'?

KS: Sure . . . because the first thing I thought of when you asked me the question was how, if you ask somebody 'how are you?', they won't say 'I'm fine . . .'. They'll say, 'I was going down the road . . .' and then they tell a story about something that happened to them and everyone goes off on digressions about places on the side of the road and objects described and other like events that somehow – through one of these concrete reminders – just come to mind. But they would never abstract the self to say this is how I feel. They will dramatize an encounter, an impact, some kind of engagement, and the story will be full of embedded information about the narrator and all the other characters of the story.

AM: That would seem to lend itself also to a very different experience in conceptualization of time . . . of self as process in-narration . . .

KS: Yes . . . unfolding in time . . .

AM: . . . and space . . .

KS: . . . and that's the only way people in the camps seem to be able to imagine themselves. The self grows eccentric over time as it accrues experiences (these impacts, encounters) and embodies them. To *be* a self you have to *perform* it and people can grow obsessed with certain idiosyncratic styles or practices that get intensified in performance. As with story, so goes the life of the personality or character – one thing leads to another.

AM: Very free-associative . . .

KS: Yes. One thing leads to another, and that can mean obsessive intensification of certain states or can mean constant dispersal as they go off on one tangent after the next.

AM: I'm being reminded of how, in the introduction to your book, you immediately familiarize us and establish a degree of intimacy with the people you choose to *re-present* in your work: that is, to both 'represent' and 'present anew'. Can you say something about the apparently simple but powerful strategy of naming people from the very outset?

KS: Well, I am just mimicking the process that I myself was taken through in being told stories in West Virginia. You are immediately drawn into the particular and concrete and there's no distancing explanation of who someone is or where something is happening or what Bob Henson's beat-up old Ford actually looks like. You're expected to catch up – some day you'll see that Ford and you'll recognize it. You'll begin to wonder what Miss Henson looks like or what made her 'squirrelly' to begin with. You have to use your imagination. I'm asking my readers to do the same thing because I want to give some hint of what storytelling is like in the hills and the ways it fundamentally affects thought and feeling.

AM: Perhaps in line with Taussig's thinking, which you mentioned earlier, you define culture as 'a shifting and nervous space of desire – immanent in lost or remembered things'. Going back to some of the initial questions we addressed, does this metaphor at all reflect an understanding of the unconscious?

KS: I don't know. I am drawn to an idea of interpretative space or spaces that are almost like domains of thought. And these spaces can be generative, or have trajectories of desire. I suppose that is like certain models of the unconscious as generative. But, of course, I also think these interpretive spaces, these spaces of desire, are publicly circulating sign systems and fundamentally mediated by expressive forms like narrative. But in the spaces things do happen – the spaces are traversed by different forces and desires, they have internal structures of tension and creativity, and so on.

AM: There's a marvellous account in your book, of a man named Riley who shows up three hours late for a meeting with you and stumbles into a great story about his truck going up in flames on the way. It's as if, in the rambling fluidity of his narrative, nuclei of experience cluster around different yet coinciding selves. In my view, his story is perhaps one of the most distinctly illustrative examples of the workings of multiplicity . . .

KS: In a way I did think about Riley in those terms: of different selves, in the sense of the narrative roles . . . I talk, in fact, about Riley the narrator vs Riley the character in the narrative . . . Riley the child remembering himself walking along the creek . . . as a child. But, in addition, I'm also saying that there's something about the very structure of narrative that enables that expression, and produces these narratives . . . Something that reflects how people are aware of themselves as the ones telling the story, and telling it differently through different people . . . and they also identify with themselves in the story and imagine themselves in the story . . . So in that they do really experience themselves in these different roles. And they experience the stories, I think, from inside and outside at the same time; it's important to be able to tell a good story and be able to put yourself in another's story. I think there is a double consciousness produced in the performance of these stories. Maybe you would call it a split self.

AM: Immediately following Riley's account, there's another story of Clownie Meadows, who also replies to a simple greeting with a long and intricate rambling story. On this score, I want to share my own notes with you: 'amazing cultural assumption and form, to respond to a greeting with a flight into/emergence from narrative. In this part of the world, greetings invite a transposition of self and time, and serve as a vehicle for narrative (re)constitutions of self.' From a psychoanalytic standpoint, it would be intriguing to know the unconscious connections between a person's self experience and what the psychoanalyst Christopher Bollas calls 'psychic objects': internal representations that somehow condense mnemic traces and allow for this kind of narrative explosion . . .

KS: That's fascinating. When people are put on the spot with a question like 'how are you?' and then move into a narrative, they create a space in which they are on a par with their audience. When two people meet and stand around talking they always face in the same direction, looking out at the hills or at whatever there is to see, instead of facing each other. They establish a common world and 'lose themselves' in that object, as they stare and space out, exchanging other worlds in stories. Objects and scenes are extremely important and they establish the ground for a kind of intersubjectivity.

AM: It's almost as if they 'open' the self up from a point which allows it to genuinely expand and encompass all sorts of concerns: whether personal, ecological, generational, or historical . . .

KS: Yes, it's an expansive sense of the self which refuses to be summarized into statements like 'I am fine' or into traits that would try to define the self.

AM: I was happy to note that you do something similar in your book, with regards to the vagaries of memory, in recalling your own first 'folksy' trip to West Virginia. Wouldn't it be helpful for anthropology to have at its disposal a discourse that could somehow annotate, or at least attempt to map out, the inner spheres of such memory traces?

KS: Yes, I think it's important, and it would be exciting to see what came out, but can we? There is always the quick operationalizing move that produces precise genres for relating an ethnographer's experience – like the confession, which is really a story about the progress of overcoming initial ignorance – getting the real stuff in the end. Reflexivity is too easily reduced to an exercise people do to prove that they are conscious. It would be wonderful if we could get past that and have many more stories that could actually open up new questions about the world and modes of seeing it.

AM: This connects, I think, with another key term of yours: where you invoke a capacity for *unforgetting* . . . a capacity, I sense, beyond the reaches of the Freudian notion of lifting repressions . . . There seems to be in that invocation a fantasy of melding past and present, subject and object, in what you call a perspective at once 'both dual and haunting'. As we approach the close of this exercise, what about your own personal experience 'on the side of the road', in those spaces of alterity and desire?

KS: I think I was always aware of this space and wanted to live in it. The practice of doing fieldwork for me was like living in that space and it made me very happy.

AM: In looking back, is it at all helpful to you to frame or recollect your experience of West Virginia in terms of shifts in self states?

KS: Sure. The way I've told the story in the book is really about contingency. I tell a story about a near accident I had when I was in the field and the shift in my own thinking that experience produced, when it led me into an insider's view of the complex and multiple socialities of narrating one's experiences. That experience derailed me intellectually from the way I had learned to think in graduate school, and other experiences followed that slowly built up another habitus of thinking. And then the idea of the arresting lyric image is very important to me. I see this moment in local stories and I also have experienced it myself as a way of intensely re-membering scenes and characters and events that were always infused with the imaginary – mine and theirs – and which over the years of absence and visits have grown luminous or are forgotten and then re-emerge in a rush. They're fragments – little pieces of experiences turned into luminous signs . . .

# References

Anderson B (1983) Imagined Communities: Reflections on the Origin and Spread of Nationalism. London: Verso.

Bakhtin MM (1983) The Dialogic Imagination. Austin, TX: University of Texas Press.

Brown RH (1987) Society as Text: Essays on Rhetoric, Reason, and Reality. Chicago: University of Chicago Press.

Jameson F (1982) The Political Unconscious. Ithaca, NY: Cornell University Press.

Stewart K (1991) On the politics of cultural theory: a case for 'contaminated' cultural critique. Social Research 58(2): 395–412.

Taussig M (1992) The Nervous System. New York: Routledge.

CHAPTER 7
# Marc Augé

Marc Augé was Director of the famed Ecole des Hautes Etudes en Sciences Sociales in Paris from 1985 to 1995. Until 1970 he served for many years as Research Director for ORSTOM, the French Scientific Research Institute for Cooperative Development, on whose behalf he oversaw several missions to Africa, in particular to the Ivory Coast and Togo. It was in Africa, in fact, that Augé also conducted much of his early fieldwork

Since the mid-1980s Augé has significantly diversified his fields of observation. In this time he has often visited Latin America, and has worked closer to home to observe the multiple realities of the contemporary world from the vantage points offered by Paris, mainly, and the broader contexts of France. Looking to examine and more fully understand the dizzying proliferation of technologies and related phenomena that impact our contemporary scenes and lives, as well as our often radically new experiences of self, time and space, Professor Augé has established himself as one of the world's leading investigators of these feverish excesses of the postmodern (or, of what Augé terms *supermodernity*). Whether conceived as the disruptive and dehumanizing result of market forces in high capitalism that make marginals of us all, differentially locating us in a series of concentric circles that radiate out, at ever-increasing distances, from omnipotent centers of consumption that are nowhere and everywhere; or as a harbinger of disorienting yet wondrous transformations of consciousness heralded by rapidly changing and merging cultural forms in an era of transnationalism, it is this sensibility – and the solitudes it engenders – that are at the core of Augé's distinctive ethnographic enquiry (and mark its convergences with the concerns of today's psychoanalysis and so many of its patients). In Augé's words:

> Numerous non-localized phenomena, or phenomena dislocated in ways unfamiliar to traditional ethnological studies (I'm thinking of television, media in general, the images of advertising, the news . . .) today push our experience of spatial instability and societal change to an extreme never before imaginable. Moreover, these phenomena make for a paradox which, from an anthropological point of view, is essentially the paradox of our time: their truth is not local (media images and messages can connect anyone with the entire world), but their immediate sense (the type of

connection they facilitate) is private, and not communal. They facilitate, in short, the realization of the effects of totalization. Every individual is, or thinks s/he is, in relationship with the world as a whole. No intermediate rhetoric can today protect individuals from direct confrontation with the planet as a whole, nor – and this is to say the same thing – with the vertiginous image of solitude. (From the Italian website 'Bloom', www.bloom.it, entry no. 113 for the period 30 April–14 May 2001, my translation.)

From Professor Augé's growing number of noteworthy titles, those presently available in English include: *In the Metro* (Minnesota, 2002); *Non-Places: Introduction to an Anthropology of Supermodernity* (Verso, 1995); *The War of Dreams: Exercises in Ethno-Fiction* (Pluto Press, 1999); *A Sense for the Other: The Timeliness and Relevance of Anthropology* (Stanford, 1998); *An Anthropology of Contemporaneous Worlds* (Stanford, 1999).

The following interview with Marc Augé, which focuses on themes derived from his books *Non-Places* and *The War of Dreams*, took place in Paris at the Ecole des Hautes Etudes en Sciences Sociales on 14 June 2000.

Anthony Molino: I'd like to start with an immediate link to Freud in your work that gets lost in English translation. What you call, in your book *Non-Places*, 'supermodernity' (*le surmodernité*) might be more precisely termed 'overmodernity'. In an interview of yours to an Italian journalist you make reference, in fact, to Freud's concept of over-determination . . .

Marc Augé: That was my intention. Indeed, I was clearly thinking of the Freudian concept, which has a long history, however. For instance, I also had in my head Althusser's concept of over-determination. Althusser also makes explicit reference to Freud, even as he looked to develop Marxism in his own mechanical way. Anyway, according to some contemporary authors, the notion of modernity is out . . . we've come supposedly to the end of modernity, and can now speak of postmodernity, or something of the sort. In my opinion, what confronts us now is nothing but an evolution of the modern era. It is, however, modernity all the same – albeit overdetermined by a great number of causes. My impression is that an idea like over-determination provides a much-needed approach to the contemporary world. It facilitates understanding of the many concurrent factors that complicate our long-inherited idea of modernity in much the way that Freud used the concept to make sense of the complexity of psychic phenomena.

AM: Again in your book, *Non-Places*, in a chapter called 'The near and the elsewhere', you state: 'Anthropology deals with all forms of the other'. Among these forms you then list what you call the *internal other* and the *private other*. Most anthropologists – I'm thinking of Geertz's fundamental lesson – would not claim either as being directly observable. Is there a contradiction here?

MA: I'll try to answer by way of a detour. My initial experience in anthropology, my first fieldwork, was in Africa, where I worked from 1965 to 1970. Initially, my research was in the south of Ivory Coast, whereas I did a second stint in Togo, some years later. These are voodoo regions, where I was witness to spectacular phenomena and learned to understand conceptions of illness, the person, and relationships quite different than our own. What I personally observed were private affairs: family quarrels, witchcraft accusations, interpretations of illnesses, consultations with witchdoctors and the like . . . But these private affairs were always articulated within a symbolical framework. And that's where the difficulties come in, because in the ethnological literature these symbolic references are presented as an official system. Where one says, for example, it's the uncle who can attack the nephew by means of witchcraft, or the father who has the power to curse or put the evil eye on the son . . . The result is that all these possibilities are inscribed in the social network – but only as possibilities. Concretely, as soon as an illness or a quarrel or anger arises, any number of interpretations are possible. And as the specialists of interpretation go to work, taking into consideration, say, local circumstances at the time, or the particular symptoms of a given illness, they can only work within the set of symbolic references which allow this variety of interpretations. One cannot say just anything, and must at the same time be very precise in enunciating a diagnosis. But one needs to use certain semantical forms. You cannot say, for instance, that the father has cursed the nephew, but that you *think* that the man has caused the nephew's illness. In which case, you'd have to speak of witchcraft. Again, every interpretation is possible, but needs to be spoken in certain forms. What I would call a symbolic background necessitates a certain way of speaking.

At the same time, this initial experience of fieldwork confronted me, in effect, with a multitude of individual case histories . . . of individual stories and conflicts and tensions and crises of which one could not be aware but through certain rhetorical forms. As far as these semantic or rhetorical forms were concerned, they dealt with what we'd call the psyche, with the individual, with what in Freudian terms might be termed 'agency' (Ger. *Instanz*). It's very remarkable to see how in African systems of representation of the self, you have something which clearly approximates Freud's topography . . . For example, there is a sense of a part of a person which is permanent, stable, in charge of relationships with all the others in a community. Like the ego. There have been, among the missionaries and ethnologists, some who have explicitly tried to elaborate a comparison between local representations of the self or the person and the Freudian concepts. The missionaries spoke of the guardian angel, but the ethnologists with experience of Freudian language spoke of id, ego, and superego – terms which do function, even if illustratively or metaphorically. But what I found most interesting, in any case, was that it was not possible to speak of individual cases without referring to the symbolic sphere. Reciprocally, however, the symbolic framework only made sense and could be articulated by referencing the specifics of the individual cases.

To get back to your question, doing fieldwork and paying attention to the individualities, including some very personal aspects of people's lives, was not contradictory. These were correlated, all the more so because it's very difficult in those societies to distinguish between what is spiritual and what is material, as is similarly the case between what is collective and what is individual. It is interesting for us, I think, to see that in the contexts to which I refer the individual is always understood in terms of his relationships with others, in ways that are much more spectacular than our experience might conceive. This, I repeat, is because of the symbolic framework which connects the two dimensions. Indeed, what all the systems I've studied have in common may well be this relationship between individual concerns and the existence of a symbolic framework, which function together both as a means of interpretation and as a means of self-interpretation.

AM: I'd like to tie these themes of yours more directly to psychoanalysis. The *inner*, arguably, is already different than the private. The *inner* is already, as some people might say, a Western conception and indisputably part of psychoanalytic language. In anthropology, there persists the argument – one you yourself occasionally seem to support in *Non-Places* – that if something is not observable, then it cannot be represented and ought not to concern anthropology. How does the anthropologist Marc Augé conceive of the inner dimension, and is psychoanalysis of any help?

MA: There are two questions here. The first question is essential and rather difficult. I must say that in the first place, I had no intention of making a distinction between inner, private or whatever. I didn't have the idea or the capacity to make a distinction. I found myself confronted with a strange experience: that of an individual who, as an object of public accusations, was confessing himself in front of witchdoctors or prophets. What came out of such encounters was a remarkable concept of interiority. And here the local symbolism is very precise. It develops the idea that there is a frontier of the I, of the ego. You are either inside or outside. In fact, certain 'agencies' have the possibility, or the choice, of leaving and re-entering the person . . . of going in and going out . . .

Such agencies may enter the 'inner' world of another person and aggressively attack the other's stability. Acts of sorcery are very much represented in this physical way. When someone does not feel well, or suffers, say, from vertigo, it's often ascribed to being invaded from the outside. So this idea of inside and outside was very precise in local representations. At the same time, it was very difficult to distinguish between the private and public spheres, because all phenomena are at once both public and private.

You have, on the one hand, this idea that someone is able through possession to attack another person. On the other hand, the symbolic representation of this belief, in the external world, involves a society whose rules make possible associations with witches, whereby everyone can engage a witch friend to perform such acts of unobservable aggression. Again, such acts are also subject to very precise language when interpreted. And such interpretations, publicly enunciated, make it very difficult to speak of the inner dimension as a private domain. Indeed, one could just as easily say that, in the societies where I did my fieldwork, one can't speak of an inner person at all. And to speak of a private one is very difficult.

AM: The second part of my question had to do specifically with your relationship to psychoanalysis . . .

MA: I must confess that, at least in my early fieldwork, I had no experience at all of psychoanalysis. I had read some books by Freud, but had neither the intention to elaborate a comparison with psychoanalytic theory nor to use psychoanalysis to interpret my data. What I found at the same time was that the first ethnological books on the subject were quite discouraging, doing little else than metaphorically localizing the Freudian concepts like id, ego, superego, etc. It was easy, of course, to understand why they used such metaphors, which undoubtedly had something to say about local representation strategies. But my work was concerned with some very different things, namely, this very strong relationship between individual and collective domains. At that time, I'm sure I sensed that the stories told by patients of prophets could well be articulated in psychoanalytic language. But they were also, or primarily, making strong references to their own symbolic framework. I have since come away convinced, and have long made the point in discussions with colleagues, that ethnologists are more useful to their psychoanalyst colleagues by describing such local conceptions rather than by trying to interpret them psychoanalytically. Such attempts, in my opinion, are of little value and often appear to be prefabricated. It's as if we were dealing with ready-made deductions.

AM: From reading your work, I gather you have a degree of familiarity not only with Freud, but obviously with the more recent French excursions into psychoanalysis, as well as with the work of colleagues like Obeyesekere and Crapanzano . . .

MA: While I'm not a product of a psychological or psychoanalytic culture, I have frequented people familiar with or close to psychoanalysis. I'd say I have the same relationship to psychoanalysis as I have to architecture or medicine. There's a certain 'wild' quality to these relationships, in the way that Freud used the word. Let's just say I'm an amateur . . .

As you know, I've tried to change my fieldwork, by trying to apply types of analysis I'd attempted in Africa to more general aspects or concerns of this moment in Western culture. In so doing, I've researched themes which clearly overlap with the concerns of psychoanalysis, even though I may not have made explicit references to psychoanalysis itself. Consider how, by changing contexts of observation, I had to contend with forms of the negative, of negation. I think of non-places, for instance, with regards to places. In traditional experiences of fieldwork, the focus of the ethnologist's activity is well-defined, working as one does with local rules, symbolic frameworks, and so on . . . In such contexts, nothing new can appear. What I mean is this: if something 'new' does happen in the field – as happens very frequently! – one interprets the event in terms that are pre-given to experience, so that the novelty is dashed and is never registered as such.

Nowadays, with the experience of so many new forms of space in our societies, including African ones, I had to rethink or imagine anew just how these spaces come to play such a very important role in our lives – especially as the spaces define themselves in ways so distinctly contrary to those traditionally studied by ethnologists. In so doing, it's possible that I was doing something, or experiencing, in ways that were not very removed from psychoanalysis. But I'm not sure . . .

AM: Are you familiar with the work of the French psychoanalyst André Green?

MA: Not really . . .

AM: He writes extensively on the concept, especially in a book called *The Work of the Negative (Le travail du négatif)*. I'm thinking in particular of a paper of his, 'The intuition of the negative in *Playing and Reality*' (the latter book by British analyst D.W. Winnicott), where Green talks of the *negative hands* in prehistoric painting, and how that process may well be reflected in the work of the psyche. Moreover, he writes in that paper: 'the transitional object is what we see of this *journey of progress towards experiencing* . . . Let us remember, the transitional space is not just "in between"; it is a space where the future subject is *in transit*. . .' You can see, I'm sure, how I was led to think of your work . . .

MA: I may have read one or two articles by Green, but I cannot honestly say that I was influenced by his work. I'll need to look at his writings, for they might well be useful . . . After all, it's a conception of collective work that I'm interested in.

AM: Along these lines, you do however often adapt psychoanalytic terms and ideas to ethnographic usage. In *The War of Dreams* you talk about the Real being 'hallucinated', an idea that recalls the work of Winnicott. In *An Anthropology for Contemporaneous Worlds* you talk about fieldworkers being in a 'transference and counter-transference' situation, and refer to fieldwork itself as a 'schizoid activity' of living life and collecting data. Are these convenient metaphors, or is there a bridge you yourself are crossing or building between the two disciplines?

MA: I am uncertain whether the analytic experience can be assimilated to that of ethnology. Nonetheless, there are relations between the two. In the field the ethnologist experiences alterity in a peculiar way (one that puts to the test his or her own identity), while those who meet the ethnologist get to test the obviousness of their everyday habits: of family relations, their rules of cohabitation, the interpretations of facts, in sum the symbolic order. Things like this happen in psychoanalysis as well. And of course, in spite of himself, the ethnologist often is the agent of a sort of 'ethno-analysis', of which he is both actor and object. But an important difference between ethnology and psychoanalysis is, of course, given by the fact that in the fieldwork setting everyone is entitled to speak.

As something of an aside, I may add here that it is of course fallacious to assume that the relation between the ethnologist and his objects of study is a one-way relation. To claim as much one must either have no experience of fieldwork whatsoever, or deny having any knowledge of it. This is the reason why I have always felt uncomfortable with the reduction of any society to its 'culture', and the reduction of culture to a text. It is for such reasons that I doubt that ethnology can benefit in any way by borrowing from the language of psychoanalysis. In my view, as I've already suggested, what it can do is offer the psychoanalyst a kind of 'raw material' to treat according to its own method of enquiry: that is how, in a given local context, human relations are instituted, practiced and thought.

Finally, the incidental use of terms like 'tranference' or 'schizophrenia' is for me metaphorical or, better, literal, since psychoanalysis has defined such terms in relation to peculiar situations and with precise meanings.

AM: Let's return to your work on non-places. In this context, you take issue with Marcel Mauss's idea of seeing both culture and the individual in culture as totalities. You then go on to talk about the three figures of excess that define supermodernity . . . or what we here will call over-modernity, and refer to the excesses of time, of space, and of *the ego*.

This particular form of excess has led me to wonder whether the reason individuals are so pervasively, indeed obsessively, concerned with themselves as a totality might not be to counter a widespread but threatening experience of fragmentation . . . You know, it's as if the cult of the ego as a totality is a way of contending with multiplicity. In Italian, what in English is termed body-building becomes *culturismo*: in one word, both tourism and culture of the body, but also of the ego. Hence my question, or my perplexity: alongside a critique of totality, at the same time you note the ego as excess . . .

MA: This idea of excess, where the idea of individuality is concerned, is tied in with over-determination. I had in mind two points. Foremostly, I was thinking of the individuality of consumerism, and what distinguishes the individual of our times from its earlier expressions in history. Today we can see an individual at the supermarket, or alone in front of the television, or banking alone at a money access machine. Personally, I am much more sensitive to this aspect of individual consumerism than to any form of cultural fragmentation. In fact, I am very ill-at-ease with the concept of multi-culturalism, because it seems to me that it involves a substantive reification . . .

It seems to me that when we speak of multi-culturalism, we have in mind a reified conception of culture which serves only to disguise or define individuality through identification with a cultural collectivity. It's very contradictory when we say that there are a lot of differences in the world and ought to respect every culture, but then only pay attention to these so-called cultures through acquaintance with a single man or a woman whose identity is collapsed within an imagined collectivity. This definition of culture is but one aspect of a prevailing ideology, but does not in any way make it possible to know a real person in his or her total, human experience.

But back to the idea of today's forms of loneliness. The loneliness, or the aloneness, of the consumer is of a sort that everyone has experienced. This includes people living in those countries where there is nothing, or very little, to consume . . . It's another thing, a new form of experience, of individual excess, whose origins are modern.

AM: Along these lines you envision, at the end of *Non-Places*, what you call an anthropology of solitude . . .

MA: Yes . . .

AM: . . . and you quote Michel de Certeau, who writes in *The Practice of Everyday Life*: 'to frequent space is to repeat the gleeful and silent experience of infancy: to be other, and go over to the other, in a place.' There is, then, this call of yours for an ethnology of solitude. But there is a very sad quality to this ethnology, which reminds me in turn of a recent work by Julia Kristeva, who writes as a psychoanalyst about some of the same scenarios you discuss. She talks about 'new maladies of the soul', arguing that psychoanalysis is one of the few contemporary spaces – she talks of it as a *space* – in which life, or surprise, can still happen. Hasn't psychoanalysis, in a way, promoted an ethnology of solitude for about a century now? . . .

MA: Yes, yes. I'd no doubt accept that. Where the comparison between ethnology and psychoanalysis is concerned, what anthropology teaches me is what confronts us are not problems of identity, but problems of *alterity*. When we speak in our societies, for instance, of identity crises, it is really alterity crises that afflict us . . . That is to say, we are not able to think of the other, not only to accept the other but, literally, to conceive of the other . . . and this I associate with a condition of loneliness. When we speak of a crisis of the nation-state or of politics more broadly, the crisis always regards a form of an identity which does not perceive the means to think about, or make room, for alterity. In other words, for otherness, or difference.

AM: You talk in your book about ethno-self-analysis . . .

MA: . . . yes, that's what an ethnology of solitude would be. . . an ethnology of modern-day society. What I most appreciate about psychoanalysis is the very basis of Freud's project, his idea of freeing man from his past or from his relationship to representations of the past. Along these lines, nowadays I feel that what we have to do is liberate ourselves from a lot of social representations or images which, in providing an illusion of freedom, keep us captive. In this sense, an ethnology of solitude would have to do with the more elemental aspects of psychoanalysis . . . and could be either an individual or collective undertaking . . .

AM: In *Non-Places*, you talk at one point about palimpsests on which 'the scrambled game of identity and relations is ceaselessly rewritten'. You talk about our city's monuments, about these testaments to a history that has, for all sakes and purposes, otherwise been erased from knowledge and consciousness. You offer a marvellous image of the Paris underground, whose stops are all marked by historical sites with which people have no relationship: the subway stop as non-place. I'd like to use these considerations of yours to return us to the ego. In a way, the ego's own monumentality today becomes a response to this erasure of history. In equating, as you do, anthropological space with existential space, it seems that the ego is a monument that has to transport itself everywhere so as to make some sense of the non-places in which it exists . . .

MA: I agree, except that the problem now is that it's every day more difficult to create this monumental aspect of self. This, in my view, has to do with an acceleration of time which is, in fact, an acceleration of news. We increasingly have the feeling that history is moving faster and faster, and with it individual history. So it becomes every day more difficult to organize one's individual identity in a perspective of time, or with regards to a sense of past or future. These are, then, individual aspects of a more collective phenomenon. Today, for example, when we speak of modernity, we refer to the deaths of two kinds of myths . . . modernity as such, bridging the eighteenth and nineteenth centuries, saw the end of the myths of the past, of the myths of origins. In the twentieth century, the myths of the future also died: political ideologies, for instance . . .

AM: . . . even science fiction seems dead nowadays . . .

MA: . . . and so we have this collective loneliness, in which past and future are disjointed. And the same holds for individuals, of course. But, as we say, man is a symbolizing animal and total loneliness is unthinkable . . . which is why, finally, I remain optimistic . . . Something must happen, though I don't know what . . .

AM: When you say you're optimistic, I can't help but think – even as you discuss all the transformations of our social and private landscapes – that you never use negative or judgemental language. There's no trace in your language, say, of Durkheim's *anomie*, or of *alienation* – whether of the Marxian or French existentialist brand. There's no concrete sense that what it means to be human is somehow threatened, or being degraded . . .

MA: Yes, that's true. What you say is interesting, though I hadn't thought of it. But I do have hope . . . What comes to mind, though not directly connected with what you've said, is the thought of my mother . . . of myself . . . of my great-grandmothers . . . I knew both of my great-grandmothers, and remember them from 1940 . . . They had lost their sons in World War I, and were 90 years old in 1940 . . . that means they were 20 years old in 1870 . . . Today I have two grandsons . . . one of only some months . . . it's unlikely that I'll speak to him in 80 or 90 years, but perhaps he will speak of what I now say, about my great-grandmothers . . . In short, this brief genealogy recapitulates two centuries: we have two centuries, even more, before our very eyes . . . for an ethnologist it's an impressive time span, if you think that in referring to my great-grandmothers I speak of women who themselves told me about their parents and grandparents!

But all these individuals have led very different lives, and the world has changed immensely in just a few years, let alone two hundred . . . My mother is now 86 years old . . . and I myself was basically educated in the aftermath of the nineteenth century. And yet, my mother has adapted quite well to the fact that my own daughters raise their children very differently from the way she raised me. This is to say not only that very conservative persons may readily adapt to radically different circumstances than their own . . . it's more than that . . . What I'm thinking of is the more general human capacity to adapt – today, in a time of unprecedented change and on a scale that was previously unimaginable . . .

The real problem, perhaps, is the division of the world between those who live in supermodernity, and the rest of humankind. This new boundary is not the new world itself, nor is it some kind of demarcation between developed and underdeveloped countries . . . to the contrary, it's something that permeates all countries, albeit 'located' differently, say in Africa than in America. And, as you know, all this while the poor get poorer and the rich get richer . . . What can happen? I don't know, but beyond any facile optimism or pessimism, what I cannot imagine is what some colleagues call 'the end of history'. Perhaps history is just now beginning, in the sense that a global history is now conceivable for the first time: literally, the story of the world . . . We now know that the world is a completely interdependent place . . . everyone, every single individual, is interconnected with the whole world . . . and the history of the world, as such, has just begun: and while it may be a terrible or terrifying story, it is history nonetheless . . .

AM: With the death of modernity – better, with its being surpassed – and with the death of the grand narratives that characterized it, you seem to imply that in this new history any narrative of self will become increasingly difficult, if not altogether impossible. Not only have the connections between history and the individual, as mediated by places, become undone; even the ancestral capacity of telling a story, one's own life story, may be jeopardized. Think, for example, of the effects of the bombardment of images to which we are all subjected . . .

MA: Indeed. I especially try to analyse this problem in another book of mine, *The War of Dreams*, where I tried to describe the following situation. There are, I believe, three poles of human imagination: the individual imaginary, the collective one, and the creative. That is to say, dreams, myths, and that form of the imagination that expresses itself in works of art, in narrative or fiction. In passing let me say that it seems to me that there is always a relationship among these three poles: all three need and feed one another.

The problem we are now facing is that the images of which you speak are so pervasive as to shortcircuit these three fundamental capacities.

Bombarded by such images, a human being finds himself increasingly outside of any collective sphere; collective needs diminish, as does the need for the experience of works of art. This is a situation of tragic loneliness or narcissism, which leaves individuals swimming in a pool of artificial, prefabricated, inauthentic images. And yet, like I said before, a situation of absolute loneliness is, ultimately, unthinkable. We cannot imagine a world in which human beings live side by side without looking at or relating to one another. It is inconceivable. But we can observe and study this kind of situation, with reference to the place and the role of images within these new forms of solitude.

Let me also say here that the interrelations among these three poles (which are always bi-directional between any two), while constitutive of each, are of course also rooted in history. Colonization, for instance, has undermined the collective mythology of some peoples, and this aggression has not been without consequences for their collective psychology as well: for their dreams on the one hand, and for their artistic production on the other. Consider also those countries which experience totalitarianism. There, strong restrictions limit creativity in general, and especially the production of literary works. This is certainly a difficult experience for the psychic life of the individual author (and for deprived readers), but it is one which also affects negatively the wellspring of collective myth. Indeed, the group's psychology as well as its myths are subject to identical restrictions: for myths too wither and die, as they are victimized and emptied of meaning by prohibitions established by those who have monopolized their interpretation and fixed their meaning.

AM: You talk about how never before have the referent points for collective identification been so unstable and how, therefore, the individual production of meaning is more necessary than ever. Along these lines, your mention of dreams connects, for me, with the word *unconscious*, a term which doesn't appear in your book on non-places. And yet, in *The War of Dreams*, you seem to be suggesting quite clearly a nexus between the function, or even the structure, of the individual unconscious with what a Jungian might call the collective unconscious . . .

MA: I don't really mean to suggest that there is a nexus between the individual and the so-called 'collective' unconscious. What I just want to say is, insofar as we deal with the notion of imaginary, we have to think of the collective components of the individual the imaginary (to say it briefly, myths versus dreams). While I speak here of myths, I could just as easily speak of religion, of culture, of relationships between the sexes: all of which, according to Freud in *The Future of an Illusion*, could be called illusions, insofar as they are the production of desire. These collective representations, in the language of Durkheim, are thus material for, and perhaps give structure to, individual imagination.

AM: In this context, could you perhaps focus on the dream and critique, where necessary, anthropology's traditional understanding(s) and use of them?

MA: On the matter of dreams, I believe it is necessary to avoid two extremes: one which reduces their content to cultural items (by way of a mechanistic translation of a given symbol into the language of 'culture'); the other which totally ignores this cultural dimension – as happens in some human societies where dream life and wakeful life are conceived as continuous. I consider Devereux's work, in this domain, exemplary.

AM: You give, in *Non-Places*, a lovely definition of the individual: 'a composite steeped in otherness', you say at one point – which, as an aside, for me opens a gateway onto the possibilities of relating your work to the object relations tradition in psychoanalysis . . . But back to my question: if we have this dissociation between the individual and the collective unconscious, and given the potentially devastating effects of the imagery that bombards us all, how do you see the fate of the individual unconscious?

MA: I once noted that the day will come, perhaps, when a man will tell his last dream and everyone around him will recognize it – because they will have seen it on TV. In such an extreme situation, there will be no more unconscious. I don't want here to speak definitively on what is a very difficult matter but, clearly – as you suggest – the unconscious has to do with others, with specific others. But insofar as the category of other is undermined, perhaps the notion of unconscious is too. Of course, like I said, we cannot imagine that kind of ultimate implosion. It's unthinkable, just as unthinkable as the end of history, or the end of the world . . .

As I see things, the question today is the following: if myths – *les grand écrits* as Lyotard calls them – die, and if creative works end up becoming 'products' like all the rest, then the image will result as the compromise between myth and product. In this way, past and future acquire both the status of image. Nowadays, the majority of images belong to the realm of duplication, and no longer to that of creation. The individual imagination, then, does not confront itself with the myths and creative works but with the domain of images instead which, consequently, sends back other images. This has less to do, as Roland Barthes contends in *The Empire of Signs*, with the empty game of signs, or with the disappearance of greater or ultimate meanings like God, reason or science, than with the significant affirmation of image culture itself. (The French, you know, are all-too-accustomed to making Man, God, and ideology die from time to time.) What is certain, though, is that we are witnessing a crisis of culture that shares a common origin with the crisis of identity and alterity. At the origin of this crisis of identity and culture is the effacement of the other or, better, his being rendered an image. The other becomes image not only because we watch him on our screens, but also because a large part of the messages concerning him make him into an image: the image of a terrorist enemy, the image of a starving person receiving aid, the image of a politician or athlete, the image of the ideal family, the image of an average American or European . . .

AM: But however unthinkable that extreme situation may be, the end of history has already been postulated and here, today, you and I may well be talking about the end of the world, or at least of a certain world that until only recently was quite familiar . . .

MA: That's precisely what I'm trying to say. We have very problematic issues in our societies . . . issues we must study, for what they might reveal to us about ourselves and where we're going. We have to be vigilant . . . aware . . . I'd even go so far as to use a military term: we must be on our guard.

AM: You talk about this very strong link between the social or the collective dimension and an individual life. You write, at one point, of needing to account for a singularity of factors that go into making up a human life, and in that list of singular factors you talk about objects. I don't know if you know the work of the psychoanalyst Christopher Bollas who, from within the object relations tradition, talks about psychoanalysis as an anthropology of the subject, whose history is always being expressed through the history of that person's relationships to singular objects. He talks about transformational objects, or evocative objects . . . about how a particular place, or a painting, say, can be pregnant with individual meaning and unleash or liberate a flurry of associations . . . In this supermodern scenario that you depict for us and that we all live in, I keep thinking: what can psychoanalysis contribute to anthropology today, in the here and now? We're not talking anymore about Malinowski and his fieldwork, nor about someone like Roheim. The terms of both the anthropological and the psychoanalytic enquiries have, as we've seen, changed totally. And what I've discovered in my research – as with the case of you and André Green both talking about *the negative* – is that similar or selfsame concepts are finding place in people's work across both disciplines . . .

MA: Yes, yes, of course. While interdisciplinary work is scarce in France, we have tried here at the Social Science Institute to establish such ties between the disciplines. But we still have a lot to do. I will, however, look at Bollas's work, which ought well interest me. In closing, what I could add with respect to our subject are some reflections on memory. As we know, memory is absolutely necessary for the construction of personal and collective identity, even if what it's really about is constructing or reconstructing a story . . . But what I want to say is that we also have to forget. We could speak of the relationship between psychoanalysis and anthropology as having something to do with the relationship between memory and forgetting. Perhaps psychoanalysis, in a very classical sense, could be defined as a discipline which uses memory, or tries to use memory, in order to help a human being to forget . . . while anthropology, perhaps . . . it's difficult to phrase . . . with anthropology perhaps we should have to invert the terms . . . I don't want to make a rhetorical statement, but anthropology today – insofar as it deals with the relationship between us and the other – has to record the necessity of that relationship for our future. Perhaps ethnology can help the subject to forget the present, and its invasive plethora of images, in order to record and think of the relationship with the other as a kind of memory. I should like to think of the relationship between psychoanalysis and anthropology in terms of memory and forgetting at its very root . . . In today's context, this could prove useful.

AM: In closing, I'd like to return to my earlier question on the inner/outer boundary and just how it gets addressed – or ignored – by anthropologists. In your book *An Anthropology for Contemporaneous Worlds*, you offer an important critique of postmodernism in American Anthropology. Part of that tradition, as I've already suggested, from Geertz to Marcus to Clifford, is a refusal of the inner life in a move away from a concept of self (and thus from any sense of interiority) to a concept of identity (which can, to the contrary, be assessed from the outside). Some contemporary forms of psychoanalysis – like Bollas's, or Lacan's – maintain that understanding psychic processes is an important part of understanding the interrelationship between structure and agency. Would you agree that such a view is crucial to the kind of future you envision for anthropology?

MA: The reason why I feel uncomfortable with the continuous reference to the notion of culture, even within the context of a post-modern anthropology, is because of just how value-laden the term is within the game of identity definitions. I am, however, convinced that any anthropological approach which avoids to consider internal psychic processes risks ignoring phenomena of symbolic significance as well as the dynamism typical of instances of cultural contacts. This is even more true today, as the technological organization of the 'globalized' world impacts and weighs so heavily on the psychic life of every individual and, furthermore, on situations of social distress which are felt as collective crises (i.e. the crisis of traditional conceptions of family, of the State, of politics . . .). Let us bear in mind that individual and collective identities, as well as individual and collective cultures, get constructed through confrontation and negotiation with alterity – this being, by the way, the meaning of ritual activity. If we were to insist only on the exterior of symbolic meaning, any understanding of the complexity of the identity/alterity nexus gets necessarily limited. And by limiting such understanding, we further weaken or rupture the nexus, and thus end up threatening both forms of existence . . .

## References

Barthes R (1983) The Empire of Signs. New York: Noonday Press.
De Certeau M (2002) The Practice of Everyday Life. Berkeley, CA: University of California Press.
Freud S (1927) The Future of an Illusion. S.E. Vol. XXI.
Green A (1999) The Work of the Negative. London: Free Association Books.
Kristeva J (1995) New Maladies of the Soul. New York: Columbia University Press.
Winnicott DW (1971) Playing and Reality. London: Tavistock.

# PART III
# AFTERWORD

CHAPTER 8

# Between desire and culture: conversations between psychoanalysis and anthropology

WAUD KRACKE AND LUCIA VILLELA

## 1. Introduction  *Waud Kracke*

Two insights into the nature of humanity opened the twentieth century. One was that humans are moved by desires they are not aware of, desires they expel from consciousness because they are inadmissible, because they conflict with fundamental wishes or with the person's prized self-image: Freud's discovery of the unconscious. The other insight was the recognition that each human being is profoundly a cultural creature. We cannot be fully human except by speaking, or at least by being in language; and this we can do only by virtue of speaking a specific language. Each of us becomes human by being inculcated with the beliefs, proclivities, aspirations, values and style of a particular culture. 'Being human is becoming individual,' says Clifford Geertz (1966 [1973]: 52), and we become individual under the guidance of culture patterns, historically created systems of meaning in terms of which we give form, order, point and direction to our lives. And the cultural patterns involved are not general but specific – not just marriage but a particular set of notions about what men and women are like, how spouses should treat one another, or who should properly marry whom; not just 'religion' but belief in the wheel of karma, etc. We cannot be human without being Balinese, Navaho, American, Italian, Chinese . . . a member of *one* of thousands of cultures on earth; and being of that culture thoroughly shapes our experience of ourselves, of others and of the world.

These two insights are not incompatible, and yet they often seem to pull in completely different directions. Psychoanalysts at one time disparaged Erik Erikson and Erich Fromm for their focus on the social context of their patients; and some anthropologists still excoriate attention to diversity and inner motives as 'methodological individualism'. Yet a list of the anthropological thinkers who have been profoundly influenced by Freud go from Radcliffe-Brown (see his 1922 analysis of the Andaman greeting of tears), Meyer Fortes and Malinowski – founders of British social anthropology; Edward Sapir, Alfred Kroeber, Clyde Kluckhohn and A.I. Hallowell, ancestral figures of American anthropology; to Claude Lévi-Strauss.

The influence of psychoanalysis on Sapir, Kluckhohn and Hallowell is evident. Kroeber undertook analytic training but, so the story goes, fled from it when a patient threatened to jump out the window.[1] But Radcliffe-Brown? Yes, Radcliffe-Brown. Although his name is associated with a stern opposition to 'psychologizing' in social anthropology, a strict separation of social analysis from psychoanalysis, yet Radcliffe-Brown was influenced by Freud in many of his ideas about structural patterns in society. He drew on Freud's ideas about the expression of repressed anger or sexual desire in humour in his analysis of prescribed 'joking relationships' (between brothers-in-law, for example, in some societies) as a device for relieving the tension in structurally ambiguous relationships;[2] his view of the mother's brother in patrilineal societies as being a kind of male mother also owes much to Freud. Even more, Meyer Fortes, who came to anthropology after having studied clinical psychology. Witness his chapter on 'Tensions in the parent–child relationship' in *The Web of Kinship among the Talensi*, which opens: 'A psycho-analyst might say that the Oedipus complex is apparently openly recognized in Tale culture. He would have to add that it is built into their social organization in such a way as to enable them to control it' (Fortes, 1949: 222). This isolated acknowledgement of the Freudian concepts which underlie this chapter, and indeed the chapters leading up to it, presage his increasingly open avowal of his psychoanalytic point of view in his later articles, from his 1961 'Pietas and ancestor worship' to explicitly psychoanalytic articles in his last years (Fortes, 1961, 1966, 1977).

Lévi-Strauss also benefits from a deep influence of Freud, one he acknowledges in *Tristes Tropiques* (Lévi-Strauss, 1955: 57–8, 1961: 59). Note, for example, his very perceptive commentary on the psychoanalytic process in his article on 'Symbolic effectiveness' in *Structural Anthropology* (1949); and chapter 7 in his *Elementary Structures of Kinship* (another great chapter 7) where, as a foundation for his own doctrine of the centrality of exchange in human relatedness, he cites at length Susan Isaacs's descriptions of children struggling with turn-taking (Lévi-Strauss, 1949/1969: 85–7). At the end of that chapter (pp. 95–6) he describes an Egyptian child's fantasy. The boy, living in Alexandria, created 'imaginary countries of Tana-Gaz and Tana-pe'. Tana Gaz, in which his mother lived, was a land of sunlight and fun; Tana Pe, his father's country, was a land of rough weather where swimming is prohibited. With no comment on the evidently Oedipal nature of the Egyptian boy's fantasy, he cites it rather as an illustration of dual opposition in a child's thought.

(Playfully, I think: Lévi-Strauss loved to tweak his readers by taking a blatantly Oedipal tale, even the Oedipus story itself, and giving it a cognitive-structural twist, as Melford Spiro (1979) pointed out in his article 'Whatever happened to the id?')

On the other side, as Edwin Wallace has shown, Freud was highly influenced by the anthropology of his time. Some of his basic concepts were suggested by his readings in anthropology (Wallace, 1983: 25–7, 30). And the ideas of 'the French Freud', Jacques Lacan, were in considerable part inspired by Lévi-Strauss as well as by Saussure's structural linguistics.

The intersection of the two characterizations of man – the passion of unconscious desires on the one hand, the construction of every human's thought by his/her language and culture on the other – constitutes the field of psychoanalytic anthropology. Yet it is not so much a field as a sphere of thought, social thought rooted in introspective awareness of desire, repression and transference. It begins with Freud's own work, *Totem and Taboo* (which has been recuperated for anthropology by Robert Paul, 1976) and *Civilization and its Discontents*, and reaches its maturity on the anthropological side in Sapir and Hallowell.

Freud saw human beings as caught between language (or culture) and desire, a side of his thought that has been most developed by Jacques Lacan.[3] Language (and the culture that is encoded in every language) is what constitutes us as humans; each of us constructs ourself as a human being in a culture (Cantin, 2002). But this very constitution of ourselves in a language alienates us from our passions, our desires. We can no longer simply feel, simply desire; we are constrained to put a name to our desire, and in so doing we subject the desire to social control and to the fetters of our culture's logic.

Anthropology adds to this that we constitute ourselves as human not in Culture, but in this culture or that culture. There is not one mode of being human, but a diversity of modes. A.I. Hallowell (1954) has put it well, showing how we live in a reality constructed for us by our culture. Not only does our culture constitute for us the objects and beings that we are surrounded with (atoms and molecules, or river spirits), but our very desires: the motives that give life meaning, and the ways in which we experience and express emotions (Hallowell, 1938, 1940, 1941, 1949).

## 2. What anthropologists find in psychoanalysis
*Waud Kracke*

The anthropologists interviewed by Anthony Molino in this book come from each of the schools cited above: from British anthropology in the tradition of Radcliffe-Brown and Malinowski; from the American tradition of cultural anthropology; and from French structuralism which is the heir to Lévi-Strauss. They use analytic orientations that range from American ego psychology/self psychology to British object relations and to Lacanian or conversant with Lacan; and they employ these orientations in their own individual styles. For instance, Obeyesekere says:

> It is no accident that Weber and Freud link up in my later work . . . [A] disastrous impact on the village helped me to understand parallel consequences in the national context. This period . . . also forged the strategy that I would employ in later work: I like to argue with a major thinker in great detail and formulate my own position in the process . . . So, you see, this Oedipal model of argumentation is endemic in my work and creatively so. (See pages 47–8)

Perhaps the question we should ask, says Villela below (see p. 190ff), is not only how can anthropology help psychoanalysis, or vice versa, but which psychoanalytic and anthropological theories share enough overlap – enough of a continuum – to be able to engage in a meaningful dialogue, to be able to respect and interrogate each others' theses dialectically, in models of argumentation that are indeed creatively endemic in the author's work.

But these thinkers also have a number of questions in common. All raise a basic question of anthropology, which is also a basic question of psychoanalysis: how do we understand the other? In anthropology, the question takes the form: to what degree, and how, can we understand the desires and thought of someone of a culture very different from our own? – the question raised poignantly in Vincent Crapanzano's *Tuhami* (1980). In psychoanalysis the corresponding question is: how do we understand the unconscious of another, or for that matter our own unconscious?

Psychoanalysis has been dealing with this question for its whole existence, beginning with chapter 2 of *Interpretation of Dreams* (or even earlier with Freud's ruminations in *Studies on Hysteria* on hypnosis and the pressure technique), and continuing in Freud's paper 'Constructions in analysis' (1937) and even later in Loewald and throughout the work of Lacan. Anthropology has come more recently to such epistemological self-examination, and so can benefit greatly from psychoanalytic reflections on the encounter with the other – whether that encounter is conceived as the encounter with the absent Other (in ourselves, or in the analyst who relinquishes the position of the one who knows), or is conceived in terms of the uncovering of repressions through free association in the transference. Thus the most central contribution that psychoanalysis makes to anthropological thought is not the questions about universals that have occupied much of the literature, such as: 'Is repression universal?' 'Are all human beings motivated by sexual desire?' 'Does the Oedipus complex occur in every society?' What it *can* contribute is rather an understanding of the human element of our methodology, the method of psychoanalysis, as six of those interviewed – Crapanzano, Obeyesekere, Augé, Ewing, Williams and to some degree Rustin (e.g. 1991: 17) – emphasize and exemplify. Its methodology, and not its metapsychology, is what is most valuable. Psychoanalysis can help us to reflect on and understand our own experience *vis-à-vis* the other culture that we encounter in the field, and to listen more fully and openly to those we work with in that culture.

Vincent Crapanzano (1980) has done more than any other anthropologist to raise our awareness of the limits of what we can grasp of the discourse of our informants, and how much we can convey to them:

> What the ethnographer or the psychologist is provided with is either an immediate or a mediate verbal text and not a direct access to the mind of his informant or subject. The extent to which such texts accurately report the experience they purport to describe, the extent to which they 'realize' themselves in the experience, must necessarily remain open questions. (1980: 21)

> What we take for mutual understanding is a complicity in reading our own meanings into each other's utterances, with the illusion that those assumed meanings agree.[4]

Crapanzano also notes the role of transference in constituting the relationship between the ethnographer and his informant:

> As Tuhami's interlocutor, I became an active participant in his history, even though I rarely appear directly in his recitations . . . He was able . . . not only to create the relationship he desired but to create me, for himself, as well. I presented him with minimum resistance but, through insistence and the direction of my questions, resistance all the same. (1980: 13–14)

Indeed, what we have here is a pithy epistemological synopsis of the action of transference and of the role the analyst strives to assume, of 'neutrality' or (in Lacanian terms) 'taking the place of the Absent Other'.

Crapanzano's contributions in this area deserve a lengthy discussion; but I cannot improve on Obeyesekere's discussion of them, nor do better than refer the reader back to Crapanzano's own elaboration of the implications of his work in his interview. (See Devereux, 1967; Kracke, 1978: 135–9, 1987, 1994, 1999.)

We agree with the majority of the anthropologists interviewed that what anthropology can most benefit from in psychoanalysis, and has neglected, is its methodology. But *we* would not be so quick to dismiss psychoanalytic theory, particularly Freud's: the methodology of psychoanalysis is an integral part of a structure of which the (evolving, not static) theory is an equally integral element. One should no more precipitately dismiss Freud's ideas as 'culture bound' because they were developed in Vienna with Viennese (and English and Russian and Hungarian . . .[5]) patients than we should dismiss the concepts of culture, of symbol, of metaphor, of social structure, or of unilineal lineage system because they too are part of a system of thought developed in Europe and the United States.

The contribution is not unreciprocated. Psychoanalysis gains from this exo-cultural introspection as well. For if psychoanalysis is a kind of decentring experience, a way of achieving a deeper understanding of oneself through reflection back from another, then the experience of living in a culture very different from one's own is a further extension of this decentring. It is through seeing oneself reflected in one's informants that one gains a new perception of oneself as a creature (*creatura*, thing created) of one's own culture, and a recognition of the presuppositions of another culture as an alternate possibility of living (see Bateson, 1968). It is like psychoanalysis a self-discovery, but one extended to aspects of the self and experiences that are not easily questioned within one's own culture. It is perhaps not an accident that some of the best psychoanalytic programmes for the treatment of psychosis have been started by analysts who are also anthropologists,[6] for the anthropologist has confronted the arbitrariness of his own culture's reality, which permits him to confront the alternative reality of the psychotic's delusion – even the radical negation of cultural 'reality' at the heart of the structure of psychosis. Among those interviewed in this volume, Williams – while not the founder of the programme he discusses – shows perspicacity about some of the issues the programme faces; perhaps the weakness of the programme is precisely that, in this case, the anthropologist was not one of its organizers.

## Personal symbols, signifiers and letters on the body

Gananath Obeyesekere also has worked with phenomena which, while not constituting mental illness, may seem to some to mimic it. Indeed, the Sinhalese mystics he worked with were subject to possession states which led them to be considered *pissu*, 'mad', by those around them. In this, Obeyesekere's concept of the *personal symbol* provides a neutral term for speaking of states and symbols which are not pathological, but at the same time manifest an unconscious structure that distinctly parallels the structure of a hysterical symptom.

Freud's genius in reconceptualizing hysterical symptoms was precisely to de-pathologize them – to transform them from products of 'neurological weakness' (the dominant view in his time) into expressions of common human emotional difficulties, the manifestations of impossible love. Obeyesekere's concept of 'personal symbol' provides a way of thinking about a religious manifestation which has the same structure as a symptom, but which avoids being a symptom precisely by taking the form of a sacred symbol, or icon. In this he follows the lead of Freud (1907), who drew attention to such parallels in his article on 'Obsessive acts and religious practices', while insisting on the marked distinction between the involuntary, compulsive ritual of an obsessive neurotic and the socially prescribed but voluntarily undertaken religious rite. But Freud had no clear terminology to maintain the distinction between a symptom and a socially prescribed ritual that is deeply imbued with personal meaning. Obeyesekere's 'personal symbol' (a concept which bears a close family resemblance to the 'symbolic-interpretative elements' by which Crapanzano (1975) designated certain figures that appear in Moroccans' dreams – such as the she-demon Aisha Q'andisha – and represent the *avatars* of their inner conflicts) fills this need. The concept of 'personal symbol' enables him to talk about the matted locks of Sinhalese mystics as symbols that enable them to resolve intense emotional conflicts which entail unconscious wishes and unconscious guilt (conflicts over unresolved mourning of an ambivalently loved parent, for example) without treating them as symptoms.

Obeyesekere expresses scepticism about the value of Jacques Lacan's work; but on this point Lacan's recasting of Freud's clinical concepts works in just the same direction as Obeyesekere. One thing that is not evident on the first reading – disguised by Lacan's esoteric terminology – is that Lacan is often simply giving new names to Freud's concepts. His rewording is sometimes justified by adding clarity to Freud's concepts, naming ideas Freud had left unnamed; sometimes Lacan's recasting of Freud's ideas removes an inadvertent 'pathologizing' implicit in Freud's terminology, which many anthropologists find troubling in psychoanalytic interpretations of cultural forms.

Obeyesekere's ethnography of Sinhalese mystics, *Medusa's Hair*, and its focal symbolism of the *lingam*, the matted locks of hair that putatively cover a fleshy phallic growth from the head, provide an excellent example of how Lacan's rewording of Freud may be useful for anthropology. Freud might have regarded the matted locks, experienced as a fleshy growth, as being *like* a hysterical symptom: not as a symptom, but (like a dream) as constructed in a similar way. They are not symptoms, because they are not experienced as intrusive, as interfering with the adept's life in an unwelcome way. The matted hair may be considered a manifestation of a *letter on the body* – a concept which can well include hysterical symptoms (indeed, has its origin in Freud's discussion of hysterical symptoms) but need not be regarded as inherently pathological. The important thing, what makes it a letter in the body, is that it can be associated with various *signifiers* which embody the meanings of critical nodal points or events in the person's life history, like the 'symbolic meanings' that Freud found metaphorically expressed in the symptoms of hysterical patients.[7]

In his paper 'Obsessive acts and religious practices', Freud (1907) draws a clear distinction between a neurotic symptom and a social practice structured like one. In this essay, Freud shows the striking parallels between the obsessive rituals of a neurotic and the ritual acts required of a worshiper in a religious ritual, while making it clear that he sees the two as utterly distinct: one a debilitating act which all concerned, including the neurotic, regard as alien, sick, mysteriously imposed by some obscure force; the other a socially condoned form of behaviour which is expected, even required, of all true believers who participate in the ceremony. Again, the very controversy and misunderstanding over this stems from the fact that Freud has no neutral way to talk about such phenomena; like dreams, he can only say that they are structured in some ways like a symptom. Lacan's more abstract terms – *'signifiers'*, *'letters on the body'* – provide a clearer way of comprehending such parallels, a neutral terminology that applies equally to symptoms or social acts, without any insinuation of the latter as pathological.

Obeyesekere's concept of the *personal symbol*, 'a class of symbols that are both cultural and personal at the same time', is a step in 'abolishing the classic distinction between private and public that had till then kept psychoanalysis separate from the cultural analysis of religious symbolism'. But one can take this concept still further: psychoanalytically speaking, *any* cultural symbol may become a personal symbol: every idea that moves us, moves us because it resonates with multiple preconscious and unconscious chains of meaning in our personal lives. A cultural symbol has affective force by virtue of being a personal symbol for the individual members of the culture, or at least for those individuals for whom the symbol has some (positive or negative) personal significance. Victor Turner's analysis (1964) of the 'orectic pole' of a ritual symbol – the aspect of a symbol that evokes desire (Greek *orégein*) – depends on this. Obeyesekere recognizes this multiplicity. In his book on the matted locks of Sinhalese ascetics he gives several case histories of women who expressed their inner conflicts through such *lingams*. (Some of these conflicts, moreover, as in many of Freud's (1895) hysteric patients, were precipitated by loss of a parent or important nurturing figure.) Some of these ascetics also expressed their conflicts in different forms of religious expression – visions, trances, episodes of god-sent madness – in addition to the matted lock: different letters on their bodies, 'articulated to a larger set of personal symbols. It is necessary', Obeyesekere concludes, 'not only to identify these larger symbols, but also to show how these several symbols are manipulated by the individual for the expression of psychic conflict and for personal adjustment' (1981: 53).

These detailed case histories, like Crapanzano's (1980) *Tuhami* (which gives even fuller expression to the subject's own words), are excellent examples of one way of joining psychoanalysis and anthropology to explore human life: namely, through psychoanalytic interviewing and case histories (Kracke 1981, 1999).

### Psychoanalysis as science: a scientific epistemology of the soul

Michael Rustin (1991, 2001) affirms something I [Kracke] have always believed of psychoanalysis: at least as articulated by Freud, psychoanalysis *is* a science, in the sense of science as articulated by Bacon and recognized by the great scientific thinkers such as Darwin and Einstein. It is a science, as much as astrophysics and evolutionary biology are sciences, which differs from other sciences because of the subject matter it deals with. Every science must use methods appropriate to the field of problems it sets for itself; the methods, and the field within which they are applicable, is what define each new science. The method of psychoanalysis is a method adapted to examine most closely the processes underlying thought and experiencing, the processes outside consciousness that we are most closely in touch with when we dream, processes that make it possible to go to sleep puzzled over a problem and wake up with the answer.

The psychoanalytic consulting room, Rustin says, provides the 'laboratory conditions' for observing the unconscious. Rather than quibble over whether analysis meets the experimental conditions of other sciences, he suggests, we should 'try to find some description of what psychoanalysts actually do'. In this Kuhnian view he is accompanied by the philosopher of science Stephen Toulmin, who spent several years doing exactly that (Toulmin, 1978, 1981). Any science creates its data with its methods; and as Toulmin says, 'in the "Papers on Metapsychology", we find Freud facing the fact that he must dissociate the actual psychic processes and phenomena confronting him in the clinical situation from any particular underlying set of hypothetical physical or physiological mechanisms . . . his clinical experiences . . . demand interpretation *on their own terms*: as reflecting conflicts of motivation or intention' (Toulmin, 1978: 319).

Toulmin (1978: 319–22) goes on to point out that the worldview of psychoanalysis began to converge with that of physics during the twentieth century; but the rapprochement comes about through fundamental shifts in the way physics viewed the world: first in its understanding of complementarity (of light as a wave and simultaneously as a particle, for example), and then in the Heisenberg/Bohr principle of indeterminacy. It was physics that came closer to Freud's view, and not psychoanalytic epistemology that converged towards physics.

Psychoanalysis is at the *heart* of sciences in one sense: it deals most directly with the epistemological presuppositions with which any philosophy of science must contend. Relativity is epistemological, in that it introduces point of view – something that was irrelevant in the Newtonian universe – which undermined the Newtonian postulate of an absolute coordinate system for the universe. Biology deals with life, and so introduces a paradox which limits the efficacy of experiment: one can go only so far in experimenting before one destroys the phenomenon one set out to study. Psychoanalysis examines the very consciousness through which we perceive the world, and recognizes that consciousness is not the centre of our perception, nor of the thought process by which we anticipate events in the world (cf. Ewing, 1997: 26). In introducing the concept of the Unconscious, psychoanalysis radically undermines the basis for a positivistic view of science. Experimentation, exact logical structures, can mislead us when we ignore the motives that systematically make us scotomize, lead us to blind ourselves to alternative interpretations (Devereux, 1967).

This leads us to anthropology, because anthropology shows us that the structures in terms of which men think are arbitrary: that is, they are built up from postulates which are (reasonably) consistent within themselves, but which differ radically from the postulates and structures of thought espoused by men of other cultures. The postulates themselves are deeply preconscious, some of them are unconscious (Sapir, 1927/1949); and so the relativity of our thought is something of which we are not easily conscious – something that leads to vertigo and culture shock when we are forced, by immersion in another society, to confront it. Culture shock is the core psychic phenomenon of cultural anthropology: it is the experience of encountering the arbitrariness of our thought.

One point on which I would like to take issue with Rustin is an aspect of his 'laboratory' analogy: the idea that the clinical setting is so radically different from other settings that one cannot reliably perceive unconscious processes outside of it. Crapanzano says something like this when he restricts the notion of transference to the clinical situation of analytic treatment. While there certainly is something uniquely advantageous in the protected setting of analytic treatment for fostering the opportunity to recognize one's own repressions, and the years of meeting in this protected setting are no doubt essential for the development and resolution of a transference neurosis, still sensitivity to the manifestations of the unconscious enables one to see it in many places. Freud met a girl on a mountain path – Katarina – and was able in a single long conversation to uncover some deep contributants to her hysterical symptom, without the benefit of a clinical setting; and Hans's father was able to do a great deal, with Freud's advice and guidance, towards understanding the roots of Hans's phobia (though admittedly his 'treatment' fell short in many ways, and his reluctance to disclose the facts of conception doggedly resisted the combined efforts of Hans and Freud). While I have often stressed the difference between the anthropologist's position *vis-à-vis* the informant in the field and that of the analyst (Kracke, 1999: 268) – and heaven knows, there is, as Spiro has shown (2003), a great difference in the depth one can reach in years of analytic work with a patient – it is still possible to pick up a great deal of unconscious fantasy or response in an interview outside of a clinical setting: as Rustin recognized to his surprise. The important thing is not only the specific setting, but the way in which one listens to the other.

Rustin returns to the roots of psychoanalysis in another way – one that does not come out in his interview so much as in his writings. In arguing for the compatibility of psychoanalysis with Marxist socialism (Rustin ), he restores psychoanalysis to the revolutionary position it held in the early years of the century. As a radical critique of 'civilized sexual morality' (Freud, 1908) and other hypocrisies of nineteenth-century society, psychoanalysis contributed to, and was part of, the social upheaval that changed European culture in the early years of the twentieth century. Psychoanalysts were a core part of the Russian revolution of 1917; Lev Vygotsky and Alexandr Luria were both psychoanalytically trained members of the Moscow psychoanalytic society, until Stalin's enmity towards Trotsky led him to suppress psychoanalysis (Kracke, 2003: 65; Etkind, 1995).[8] Notwithstanding Freud's later, more pessimistic view of socialist remaking of human nature in *Civilization and its Discontents* (Freud, 1930: 112–13, 143), psychoanalysis was in the days of revolution viewed as an instrument whereby the human cupidity that obstructs the achievement of Marx's communal organization could be overcome or redirected: a relinquishing of the wish for power in property – a further step in the alliance of the brothers against the primal father.

To Rustin's Marxian concern with inequitable access to resources, Marc Augé adds that globalization intensifies these inequities and generalizes them throughout the world.

## What is a psychoanalytic anthropologist?

Like Lévi-Strauss, one does not think of Marc Augé as a psychoanalytic anthropologist, and in his interview he resists Molino's efforts to cast him as one; yet his thought – especially on the changed place of personal identity and alterity from traditional life to the modern world of globalization – is permeated with the perspectives of Freud and Devereux, even more than his occasional allusions to their work would indicate. In his analysis of mass media in *The War of Dreams* (1997/1999), for instance, he draws heavily on the Lacanian-based theories of Christian Metz (1975). The example with which he characterizes the shrinking of time perspective that technicalization has brought to the world – that for him his grandmother and great-grandmother mark his own identity, in a way that he and his parents will not mark his grandson's – is a quite psychoanalytic personal observation. The shrinking of space and time that has been brought about by the pervasive spread of technology and instantaneous transmission of information is a condition that shapes the way in which we all experience alterity (and hence our own identity) – an observation about the condition of our own psychic existence which is crucially relevant in every analyst's consulting room. I wish he had dwelled on these observations a little longer in the interview.

Augé reiterates the point that *identity* exists only in counterpart to *alterity*, and that globalization transforms both. Katherine Ewing is also concerned with issues of identity, and how in a colonial context it may often be constructed in opposition to the colonial power. But in much of her work, her concern with identity is on a much more intimate level, and deals with preconscious construction: in 'The illusion of wholeness' (Ewing, 1990a), she speaks of an awareness of context in 'shifting selves' in which 'the flux of experience is reified and made the object of self-reflection' (1990a: 263 – a concern related to Kathleen Stewart's distinction between 'performance and fixed identity', and her opposition between 'interiority' and – with echoes of McKim Marriott – 'the body as a permeable space').

What is it to be a psychoanalytic anthropologist? George Devereux (1967) made us aware of the ambiguity that inheres in such work that borders between the social and the intimate, which he formulated as 'complementarity' (borrowing back from Bohr a notion which Bohr may have got from William James[9]). In sum, all knowledge is limited by the epistemological conditions of our knowing. At the border of the individual psyche and the cultural matrix which is the fabric of the individual's life, as one deepens one's understanding of the personal desires and inner conflicts that generate personal signifiers, the linguistic regularities and cultural logic in which these signifiers are embedded lose focus (Devereux, 1967, 1978; Kracke, 1980; Villela, 1999, 2003). Our understanding can never be (as Kathleen Stewart suggests) 'decontaminated' from the interests to which our investigation is directed, nor from our involvement with the subjects, the others, with whom we participate in a collaborative work, a mutual attempt to understand one another and to impart that understanding, however imperfectly, through language to the other.

An issue that is submerged in many of these interviews, one that must be a factor in the ambivalence in anthropology towards psychoanalysis, is the difficulty – perhaps impossibility – of gaining access in anthropological interviews to the levels of unconscious motivation, to the unconscious organization of the mind that the psychoanalyst is able to attain in the psychoanalytic treatment of a patient. I am very aware in my own work (Kracke) of how the constraints of fieldwork limit even the time we have to listen to one informant, and prevent us from realizing the kind of depth that a psychoanalyst does with a patient in analysis for six, eight, ten years – a contrast beautifully demonstrated by Spiro (2003), in an article entitled 'The anthropological import of blocked dreams'.

Spiro describes some of the difficulties and differences that limitation of time brings to the anthropologist's work with informants in the field: lack of time to get the associations as well as the manifest content of dreams, or to obtain enough history as a context for the meaning of both dreams and associations. All these constraints make it difficult for an analytically trained anthropologist to get the same information as the analyst gets in his office. Spiro tells us about a 28-year-old woman he saw four times a week for two years before the treatment was interrupted because the patient had to move to another town. It was only after the last reported dream that a conflict between her consciously avowed feminism and the masochism of her first reported dream could be fully analysed.

### The importance of the concept of the unconscious in anthropology

Ewing's apparent disavowal of the unconscious – her preferred terms, 'the implicit' or 'something not articulated verbally', much better characterize the *pre*conscious than the unconscious – highlights this issue. I suspect this late renunciation of what she has so well articulated in her earlier work is an outgrowth of frustration at the limitations on reaching the unconscious in anthropological work; the abandonment of the concept of the unconscious does not do justice to her richly textured portrayals of the dynamics of relationships in a Pakistani family, or her analysis of the dreams of Pakistani Muslims in search of a Sufi *pir* (Ewing, 1990b), in which she uses free associations to infer their latent content. In her article on 'The illusion of wholeness' (Ewing, 1990a) she distinguishes between the 'contextual unconscious' and Freud's 'dynamic unconscious' (1990a: 268, 276 n.20) and uses the distinction in relating the progression of defences an informant uses when faced with painful self-representations in the course of a conversation with the ethnographer.

In the introduction to *Arguing Sainthood*, published around the time of her interview with Molino, Ewing made an excellent case for the crucial importance of Freud's concept of the unconscious, 'revolutionary ... in its decentering of the subject away from the [Cartesian] rational conscious motivated by free will' (1997: 26). Indeed, she chastens Freud for his retreat from the decentred subject in the concept of the ego, crediting Lacan, in a succinct and plausible summary of his contribution (no summary of Lacan can be said to capture his meaning in all its elusive allusiveness), with restoring Freud's decentred subject, while still upholding the social link in the 'issue of recognition' (1997: 27).

I suspect that at least part of her apparent disavowal of the unconscious (if indeed she means it literally) may be an expression of frustration at the limitation on the anthropologist's penetration into individual intrapsychic life. I am constantly frustrated by those limits even in my interviews with the Parintintin I know best, such as Jovenil and Gabriela (Kracke, 1981, 1999). Having had the experience of working with patients, she is quite aware of these limitations (Ewing, 1987).

One more limitation, which was brought home to me just last summer, is subtler but fundamental. The basis of the analyst's credibility for the patient is his (or her) desire for *savoir* – the analyst's listening to the patient with the desire to hear the patient's signifiers. This last summer I gave a presentation at the annual English-language seminar sponsored by the Ecole Freudienne du Québec, on my interviews with a Parintintin man who was living and working on a Brazilian boat along the Madeira River.

He was a man who had forgotten his native Parintintin language and assumed the identity of an Amazonian Brazilian river man. In my interviews with him, I was able to open a space where he could recover the repressed memory that had led him to renounce his Parintintin heritage: the pain of the death of his father in an epidemic which he himself survived. But this man never told me any dreams. Willy Apollon raised the question, why did he not share his dreams with me? In discussion, the reason became clear: I had, indeed, a desire for *savoir* to offer him – a desire for savoir that made it possible for him to recover his repressed memory of lying in a hammock next to his father's, both critically ill with measles, while his father was dying. But the desire for *savoir* that I held forth was for an **anthropological** *savoir*; my interest was in his unconscious insofar as it was a *Parintintin* unconscious. This is quite appropriate, indeed necessary, for anthropological work; but it did not meet his need, for his whole solution, his ego ideal, was constructed on escaping his Parintintin unconscious and *becoming Brazilian*.

## Some notes on transference, in psychoanalysis and in the field

A major contribution of psychoanalysis to anthropology, as most of those interviewed concurred, is in the psychoanalytic method. Both in understanding the dynamics of one's relationship with informants, and in having an awareness of one's own part in the network of relationships that constitute the situation of fieldwork, psychoanalytic understandings are useful. And in particular, it is useful to be aware of one's own transferences: transferences to the individuals with whom one works closely; to those individuals (often different from one's 'informants') who give one support and understanding in one's encounter with the culture (what Roberto DaMatta (1978) has referred to as 'cultural guides'); and transferences towards the culture itself (Kracke, 1987).

I cannot close this section without noting Vincent Crapanzano's important 1981 article on transference – although in doing so I anticipate the topic of the next section, contributions of anthropology to psychoanalysis. In 'Text, Transference and Indexicality', which has not been given the attention it deserves by psychoanalysts, Crapanzano (1981) compares the psychoanalytic concept of transference with the linguistic concept of 'indexicality'. Indexicality, or the 'pragmatics' of language – a concept (though not a term) going back to Malinowski's (1935) ideas about language – is that aspect of any speech act which addresses, draws attention to, or creates the immediate situation. The very meaning of such terms as 'this', 'that', 'now' or the pronoun 'I' or 'you', depends on the immediate situation of speech: what the speaker points at, the time the utterance is made, or who is talking to whom. In European languages, the choice of the formal or informal second person may reflect something about the relationship of the speaker to the person addressed, or may bring about a change in relationship – an increased closeness or a distancing. Transference, an experiencing of a (repressed) memory or fantasy as if it were present, is expressed in the person's immediate experience of the present situation: in Crapanzano's poetic phrasing, 'the past is asserted into the present in all its immediacy'. It is, then, a psychic equivalent of the linguistic phenomenon of indexicality: it is expressed not as a reference to the current situation, but as an index in it. In Crapanzano's article, this revealing parallel is developed in a discussion of Freud's treatment of Dora; its insights need still to be further disseminated in the psychoanalytic community.

In his interview, Crapanzano objects to using the concept of transference in talking about the experience of fieldwork. Since this addresses in part my (1987) article 'Encounter with other cultures', in which I argue that transference is a significant ingredient of the experience of 'culture shock', I would like to presume on my role as discussant to respond to his objections.

It is true, of course, that transference is closely associated with the analytic process. Freud first conceived the phenomenon when he noticed it in his patients' reactions (Freud, 1895), and developed it to understand his failure in treating Dora (Freud, 1905), elaborating it further in several of his 'papers on technique' (1912, 1914a, 1914b). Transference, however, is not limited to the analytic situation; it is, as Freud has presented it (1914a), a manner in which the repressed manifests itself in general, not just in psychoanalysis. It is, in Brian Bird's (1972) words, 'a universal phenomenon'. Freud talks about being in love as a manifestation of transference. Hans Loewald (1960: 27) calls transference 'virtually synonymous with object-cathexis':

> Without such transference – of the intensity of the unconscious, of the infantile ways of experiencing life which has no language and little organization ... to present-day life and contemporary objects – without such transference, ... human life becomes sterile and an empty shell. (Loewald, 1960: 30)

It is, as Freud described it in his best article on the subject, 'Remembering, repeating and working through' (1914a), the experiencing of a repressed memory fantasy as if it were present. As Crapanzano (1981: 133) put it, 'through the transference the patient attempts to assert the past in all its immediacy into the present'. It is not only the analytic patient who may experience this, but any one of us in love, or in a meaningful moment.

## 3. How can anthropology help psychoanalysis?
*Lucia Villela and Waud Kracke*

To this point we have been talking mainly of anthropological uses of psychoanalytic concepts, or the use of the psychoanalytic approach to benefit anthropology. We cannot close this Afterword without some comments on the inverse debt: contributions of anthropology to psychoanalysis.

**Symbolic effectiveness and the psychoanalytic process**
*Lucia Villela*

One of the best descriptions of the effectiveness of the psychoanalytic process, if a good description is possible, is the one given by Lévi-Strauss (1949/1958) in his article on symbols as efficient agents (*'Efficacité symbolique'*, mistranslated in English as 'The effectiveness of symbols'). In analysing the process of shamanistic cure in cases of difficult birth (which are rare and so considered a 'sickness') among the Cuna indians of Panama, Lévi-Strauss describes how the shaman 'uses specific psychological representations ... to combat equally specific physiological disturbances'. Through songs that create a specific 'psychophysiological mythology' and through actions that evoke a 'ritualized social cohesion, the shaman renders acceptable to the mind pains which the body refuses to tolerate' (pp. 186–205).

The song (which the woman already knows as part of her culture) and the shamanic ritual create a symbolic universe in which the woman's body is contextualized. As Waud Kracke suggests (personal communication), the woman's body, specifically her vulva and birth canal – is identified and described as a mythic landscape, in which a protean struggle for the soul (purba) of the woman's uterus takes place between the shaman and the goddess Muu, who presides over the development of the foetus. The song and incantations used describe how the shaman and his spiritual allies enter the symbolized birth canal and proceed along it, first in single file, then side by side in rows of three and four, signaling the relaxing of the constraining musculature and consequent widening of the birth canal.

The shaman's mystic tale offers a language in which the woman in labour can articulate her body, and her pains are named and described to her 'in a form accessible to conscious or unconscious thought' (Lévi-Strauss, 1949/1963: 195). That is, the cure consists in making explicit, through naming, an unacknowledged reaction that the body could not otherwise tolerate, a cure similar to the methods Freud (1895) used in the initial phases of treating Miss Lucy and Katarina.

This type of cure, Lévi-Strauss claims, places shamanism on the borderline between physical medicine and psychoanalysis. The process is different from medical treatment because the relationship between germ and disease is external to the patient, while the relationship between spirits gone crazy and disease is internal and symbolic. (Lacan might argue that both relationships are internal and symbolic.) It is different from psychoanalysis because the myth that establishes the symbolic relation is socially given and does not necessarily correspond to personal experience, while in the psychoanalytic cure the patient himself constructs an individual myth with elements from his own past. In the shamanic cure, the shaman speaks for the patient; in the psychoanalytic cure the patient speaks and may even 'put words in the mouth of the analyst (Lévi-Strauss, 1958: 195)'. The similarities between shamanism and psychoanalysis are also many. In both a problematic reaction takes place: and it is through the power of language and metaphor that previously unexpressed problems are formulated, and conflicts materialize in such a way that their development and eventual resolution becomes possible.

The shaman does not elicit personal information from his patient. Hence we may conclude 'that remembrance of things past' – which is often considered one of the keys of psychoanalytic therapy – 'is only *one* expression of a more fundamental method which must be defined *without considering the individual or the collective genesis of the myth*' (Lévi-Strauss, 1958: 199, emphasis ours). This article (in *Structural Anthropology*), as well as most of Lévi-Strauss' work, strongly influenced Lacan, who published a piece entitled 'The neurotic's individual myth' (Lacan, 1953/1979: 405–25).

Lévi-Strauss (1958) has also influenced the psychoanalytic interpretation of cultural artifacts in general, especially narrative and films (as Augé also has), through his specifications of the functions of myths. A myth is a narrative that imposes patterns on experiences (as seen by the shaman's song), patterns that make our daily life easier to process and easier to grasp; patterns that help us work over and over again on contradictions that refuse to go away, and that might otherwise never be expressed. A myth substitutes a system of binary opposition (mythemes) for the contradictions involved and in so doing achieves a palliative effect (Henderson, 1980; Villela, 1999, 2000, 2003). For both Lévi-Strauss and Lacan (Lacan, 1953/1979), the concretization of intersubjective relationships that takes place in analytic theory, and that we call the Oedipus complex, has the value of a myth.

Augé's *The War of Dreams* (1997/1999) shows the complexities and possible dangers that globalization and technology have introduced in this palliative function of myths, through the compression of time and space. Science-fiction films, such as Ridley Scott's *Alien* and *Blade Runner* – as well as the TV programme *The Body Snatchers*, analysed by Augé (1997/1999: 1–4) – show some of the nightmares that may invade our dreams if we do not manage to adapt these changes to the ethics of being human.

**Anthropology and psychosis, and the anthropologist as participant observer** *Waud Kracke and Lucia Villela*

The participation of Williams in the Maudsley programme for treatment of psychotics, and Williams's work in this area, bring up another striking point in the relations of anthropology to psychoanalysis: the affinity which anthropologists, or analysts with anthropological or cross-cultural experience, have had with the problematics of psychosis. One can mention L. Bryce Boyer, whose participation in Apache fieldwork with his anthropologist wife Ruth led to his becoming trained as a shaman, and whose long-time work with psychotic patients, culminated in the treatment programme of the Boyer House. T. Adeoye Lambo, the great Nigerian Yoruba psychiatrist (though not to our knowledge trained in anthropology), was keenly aware of Yoruba culture and of the African cultural context, and argued for a culturally aware treatment of mentally ill patients. In his experimental centre for the treatment of psychosis, in the Naro village cluster near the Yoruba city of Abeokuta, he made a point 'to wed the best practices of traditional and contemporary psychology', combining Yoruba healers (*nganga*) with psychiatrists (Lambo, 1978: 165). 'Our guiding premise', he says, 'was to make use of the therapeutic practices that already existed in the indigenous culture, and to recognize the power of the group in healing.' To help restore the social link for these psychotic patients, each patient lived with a family in the villages, and participate in their daily activities.[10]

In 1975, Murray Jackson, an Australian psychiatrist interested in the psychoanalytic treatment of psychoses, and trained as a psychoanalyst in England, became director of a psychiatric ward with two units at the Maudsley Hospital in London, where he started a novel experiment: the treatment, on one unit, of a selected number of psychotic patients using psychoanalytic methods as interpreted by the object relations theory of Melanie Klein and her followers (Williams and Jackson, 1994). In 1985, Paul Williams, an anthropologist with a strong early interest in Freud and experience as a psychoanalytic psychotherapist, joined the staff to do his fieldwork as a participant observer in the new Maudsley unit, an experience that later led to his training as a psychoanalyst.

Williams's task as a participant observer was to make fieldnotes, interview patients and staff and participate in staff meetings and therapeutic meetings – with the objective of finding out and describing what the patients and staff were actually doing, in a multidisciplinary programme quite different from the usual psychiatric unit, and as compared with what the staff said they were doing. One of the differences was that nurses, rather than doctors, ran the unit, and so acquired considerably more responsibilities and authority than usually given to the nursing staff in the average psychiatric unit. Williams, who has the anthropologist's as well as the analyst's gift of listening, describes his 'heart of London experience' as one which resembles severe culture shock (see Kracke, 2000). He says to Molino: 'As an ethnographer, I felt the ward could be such a mad and stressful place that all I could do for a long time was to witness the experience and record whatever I saw . . . By the end of the two years of fieldwork I had discovered that there was something in the air, permanently on the ward, that could not be talked about, but which the ward made strenuous efforts to talk about.' At the end of his fieldwork, he had come to the very analytic discovery of how important it was to open a place for speech, both for staff and for patients.

Williams is right in finding anthropology 'a complementary discipline to psychoanalysis'. Speech, and listening to the speech of the other, is central to both disciplines. Williams's role as a participant observer on the Maudsley unit was also a very psychoanalytic one. He was the object (though he doesn't use the term in his interview) of transferences of both patients and staff, 'alternately seen by the ward staff and patients as a kind of saviour or rescuer or else as a useless interloper. The staff . . . tried to get me to join up with their views and practices', but they were 'very disappointed when I had to maintain my role as a participant-observer'. He persisted in maintaining his neutrality – what Lacanians would call his role as representative of the Absent Other. By extending his role from that of participant observer to that of 'participant listener', Williams made his position central to the Maudsley enterprise.

The staff saw their task as 'a restructuring of the psychotic's internal world, using talk and relationships', and not so much as listening to find the meaning in the psychotic's inner world. They used the ideas of psychoanalysis 'in the transference and in the social setting to reconstitute an object-relating capacity in those patients: The task of reconstructing the inner world and object relationships of the patients', rather than listening to them. As Williams observes in understatement, 'this is a tremendously ambitious undertaking', and one bound to lead to frustration. Williams perceives the contradictions in this way of structuring such a task: it is bound to lead to the climate of frustration and anxiety he describes. Given his insight, and his persistence in maintaining an analytic role in the setting, it is perhaps to be regretted that his perceptions did not have a greater role in the designing of the programme.

## The '388': a programme designed by analysts and anthropologists[11]
*Lucia Villela*

A clinical programme jointly planned and implemented by psychoanalysts and anthropologists was started in Canada, in Quebec City, in 1982.

In 1976 a group of analysts, psychologists, anthropologists and sociologists banded together under the leadership of anthropologist and analyst Willy Apollon and sociologist Raymond Lemieux to found the 'Groupe Interdisciplinaire Freudienne de Recherche et d'Intervention Clinique et Culturelle', now known by its initials, GIFRIC. Danielle Bergeron (at that time a psychiatrist in training) and Lucie Cantin (a psychology student at the University of Laval) were part of that group. Throughout the following years the group evolved, increasing in numbers and differentiating into other intrinsically related but separate programmes, each with its own specialized activities: the GIFRIC research programme, which contributed to the planning and evaluation of all other programmes; the Ecole Freudienne du Québec, dedicated to the transmission of psychoanalysis in Quebec, and then expanded into an organization of 'Circles' in the US and other nations; the '388', a psychoanalytic treatment centre for psychotics, locally known by the number of its address; and the Family Center, which provides therapeutic and social services for families and children.

In February of 1982, after five years of research on clinical methods and on family structures in Quebec, GIFRIC, in collaboration with the Robert Giffard Hospital, opened a psychoanalytic treatment centre for psychotic young adults between 18 and 35 years of age. Its existence was not viewed kindly by the psychiatric community in general, whose opinion was that psychoanalysis was contraindicated for the treatment of psychoses for a number of reasons: psychoses had a biological basis and so should be treated psychiatrically, not psychoanalytically; symptoms could be more easily controlled by psychotropic drugs produced by an increasingly sophisticated psychopharmaceutical industry; Freud himself had argued that since psychotics did not develop a transference, the analyst might not be able to influence them enough to effect a cure.

There is truth in these statements. However, the rate of re-hospitalizations remained high, psychotropic drugs had dangerous side-effects and often became inefficacious with time, and though symptoms could be temporarily controlled, or at least masked, psychotics were not being cured. And besides the statement quoted above, Freud had also often said that psychoses, like all other mental illnesses were overdetermined, and that with the development of new techniques psychoses might become treatable. Lacan (Seminar 3, 1955–56) disagreed with Freud on the question of transference but warned his students that once developed transference would turn into erotomania. Apollon, Bergeron and Cantin (1990) inferred, from the result of their own clinical work, that they had found the new discoveries that made the treatment of psychoses possible.

One of the reasons most analysts shy away from the treatment of psychoses is that listening to the psychotic's delusions seems to strengthen their intensity and expand their field. But as Apollon, Bergeron and Cantin discovered in their practice, it is this very expansion that allows the analyst to discover the nature and logical basis of the delusion and of the 'mission' all psychotics are certain they have. It is only through his own speech that the psychotic is able to catch himself in contradictions that rupture his delusional certainties and provide a space in which something other than delusional speech can emerge. Furthermore, in response to the experience of being heard and to the analyst's interest in dreams, the psychotic, like other analysands, starts to dream: and because his dreams re-present his delusions in different ways, there is further rupturing of certainties and still more space is opened for the curative function of speech (a function Williams also supported in Maudsley, by his emphasis on listening to both staff and patients).

The danger of erotomania is still present, if the analyst takes the position that Lacan labels 'The One Supposed to Know'. But if the analyst's desire is focused on finding out what is the logic underlying what the psychotic knows about his delusion – and if he manages to tie that logic to the psychotic's history, and to help the psychotic see the contrast with the logic of his dreams – then analysis can proceed successfully, and the patient is better able to transform acting out into verbal actions, and better able to develop the restraints that make possible the repairing of the social link. It is in this question of building restraints and constraints – as well in the offering of practical, aesthetic and social activities – that a multidisciplinary treatment programme can provide the crucial help that enables the psychotic individual to stay out of the hospital and active in his own community.

It is important to realize how profoundly interdisciplinary this type of theory is and how much it owes to the work of anthropologists who were well versed (at times trained) in psychoanalysis and to analysts who were well versed (at times trained) in anthropology, and aware of the interdependence of the contingent and the universal. Within this diversity of perspective, they shared a structuralist philosophical orientation that included enough overlapping to facilitate the creative appreciation of differences in approaches 'endemic' in the thought of different individuals. To further describe the way the 388 was planned we'll have to examine the nature of the relation between psychoanalysis and anthropology as conceived by Willy Apollon (1997a).

Born in Haiti, trained in philosophy and anthropology at the Sorbonne, and in psychoanalysis at the Ecole Freudiénne de Paris, with internships at the Salpetrière and the Hôpital Sainte-Anne, Apollon (1997a) developed his own theories on the interaction of desire and culture in the birth of a subject, theories he articulated in epistemological terms in San Juan in 1995, in a talk entitled 'Questions posed by psychoanalysis to anthropology'. His premise was that for anthropology these questions were basically contingent, having to do with the specific and the political; for psychoanalysis they were basically universal, having to do with the ethics of being human. The unbreakable interdependence of the two disciplines was due to the fact that, for each individual subject, the ethic could be only articulated through the specificity of a given culture, a view similar to that stated by Kracke in the very first page of this Afterword. In Apollon's words (p. 110, my translation):

> We are starting from the supposition that each speaking being subjected to the ethical duty of being human cannot gain knowledge of this exigency except through his inscription in the particular way in which the history of his culture translates his sense of humanity.

Apollon further adds that mental illness – and we might add its social counterparts, such as colonization, oppression, violence – are a sign that the articulation of the universal to the specificity of a culture was damaged for a specific subject.

That poses a problem for all types of society. The defect of language, its inability to express the real, and the defects and demands of the Other make what Lacan calls 'jouissance' (the total and immediate satisfaction we assume animals have) impossible for the speaking being. Every society has a set of laws or norms regulating the relationships between its members, and except for a very few basic prohibitions the specifics of these laws and norms are arbitrary. Since these laws and norms limit human gratification, every society has a twofold problem: on the one hand, a society must veil as best it can the fact that its norms are arbitrary, in order to keep its credibility (and here is where many conflicts between psychoanalysis and anthropology take place, Apollon, 1997a: 115); on the other hand, each society must in some way compensate its subjects for giving up the gratifications forbidden by societal laws (including the 'jouissance' we assume possible). The inability to do so creates a climate of such negativity that it results in the loss of credibility of the tenets necessary for the stability and cohesion – and eventually the survival – of that society.

Taking into consideration this view of the intrinsic tie between the contingent and the universal, if the transmission of ethics is to take place – and that's Apollon's definition of mental health – then no psychoanalytic act can ignore the importance either of the unconscious or of the social link, or the significance of the Other in the birth of a subject and the management of desire. Furthermore, the importance of the psychoanalytic act cannot but increase as its problematic is made more complex by the globalization that, based on the interests of G7 nations, has created strategies of domination that have imperilled the status and the political logic of 'non-northern' nations. Apollon's very labelling of the imperilled cultures as non-Northern (rather than non-Western) is itself a commentary on how naming may support or distort the culture, history – and even the geography of nations – through domination strategies. It is also important to know that Apollon's theory implies that words like neuroses, psychoses and perversion refer to specific structures of the mind, which of themselves are not necessarily pathological. Whether or not they become so depends on how well a specific culture transmits or fails to transmit the universal ethic of being human to a specific individual.

It was on the basis of the postulates and inferences made above that the 388 was planned. Affiliated though it was at that time with the Robert Giffard Hospital, the 388 was a free-standing project, subsidized by the state government and located in its own large old English house – a house chosen after research by analysts, anthropologists and their interdisciplinary teams found that the site was easily reachable by transportation, and situated in a community diversified enough socially to be willing to have a treatment and residence centre in its area and to allow its residents and day users to participate in community activities.

The space provided by three floors and a finished basement was used to both unify and diversify the different functions provided. The 388 has 'usagers' (as patients are called, a word that does not have the pejorative connotation of 'users' in English) who live in the community and come for help and therapy during the day or evening. But when in crisis, these 'usagers' reside in the premises for short periods of time (generally between a few days and two or three weeks). The third floor, with seven bedrooms, was to be used only by patients in crisis (previous experience had indicated that out of 60–80 patients only seven or less were likely to be in crisis at the same time); the second floor was to be taken by analytic, psychiatric and consulting offices; the first and social floor was for the daily use of all 'usagers'; the space in the finished basement was used for art ateliers, writing workshops and other aesthetic activities, and a ceramic workshop was housed in the garage.

Most hospital and mental health facilities consider psychotics basically unable to take responsibility for themselves – let alone cooperate in psychoanalytic therapy – and aim mostly at the control of symptoms that might cause the patients to become dangerous to themselves or to society. At the 388 the aim is not to change the structure of psychosis – which cannot be changed any more than that of neuroses or perversions – but to change the position of the psychotic within his or her own structure, through psychoanalysis and the restoring and repairing of the social links destroyed by recurrent psychotic breaks. More specifically, one of the staff's main objectives is:

> To provide a treatment that is both global and individualized, based on a psychoanalytic approach that is Lacanian and ethnoanalytic in its orientation, conducted by a multidisciplinary team on rigorous multidisciplinary principles such as those developed by GIFRIC in Quebec since 1974. (Apollon, Bergeron and Cantin, 1990: 24, my translation)

This combination of psychoanalysis and repairing of the social link – which should not be confused with what is called 'psychosocial interventions' in halfway houses and behavioural programmes – kept the 'usagers' out of the hospital and active in their communities, and was cost effective enough to guarantee the 388 government funding for about 20 years. (At this time it costs the state about 110,000 Canadian dollars a year for the hospitalizations of the 84 patients in the 388 programme, as compared with $875,000 a year for previous hospitalizations of the same patients before they joined the programme. And 47 per cent of these usagers have been returned to the status of taxpayers.)

A number of the problems described by Paul Williams as existent in the Maudsley unit were also part of life at the 388, such as the emotional difficulties faced by the members of a staff daily involved in the care of psychotic patients. Maybe a comparison between the 388 and the Maudsley unit can highlight both the similarities and differences between a medical setting (one of the hardest challenges Jackson and Williams had to face) and a free-standing multidisciplinary programme planned by psychoanalysts conversant with anthropology and anthropologists conversant with psychoanalysis.

Both programmes were new departures, supported by their governments but criticized by the general psychiatric community. Both used highly trained personnel, and their originators were highly creative and competent people well versed in their respective theories. Both programmes also lasted for a considerable number of years. They differed greatly, though, in the theories and techniques used and in the outcome of their differences with the supporting government agencies. The Maudsley special unit was operative for 13 years, ending only with the retirement of its original creator. The 388 has now been going for 22 years, but in 2002 it also had to face such an opposition from the staff at the Robert Giffard Hospital that its existence was temporarily threatened. It managed to survive but only after a political fight in which the programme had the support of patients, their families and their communities, an opposition that led the state government to appoint an independent commission to evaluate the 388. The evaluative report was highly positive and resulted in arrangements to continue funding through a general hospital rather than a psychiatric one.

In this case, historical events confirmed the necessity of a cooperation between anthropology and psychoanalysis for a successful but controversial clinical programme to survive. These events also confirm Apollon's claims about the importance of credibility in the survival of a group – a credibility based on the liaison between ethics and politics, between the contingent and the universal – and a credibility without which the 388 might not have survived. The results might have been different if the 388 had not been planned by an interdisciplinary and multidisciplinary staff that had been working on this project at GIFRIC for a number of years, since 1974. These years of interdisciplinary work thus influenced that staff's very survival, as well their clinical research and clinical planning.

The basic team that accomplishes the work of treatment in the 388 is composed of four individuals: the 'intervenant' (case manager plus psychotherapist is the closest we can get in English to the meaning of this function), the psychiatrist, the social worker and the patient. The 'intervenant', for whom we do not have an adequate English word, is the patient's main resource within and outside the 388. If a patient feels uneasy about shopping, or about finding an apartment to rent, his 'intervenant' will accompany him in these endeavours, both to facilitate the re-establishment of social links and to listen to what the patient has to say about these activities and about his source of discomfort with them. The psychiatrist prescribes psychotropic drugs and other medicines if needed, and coordinates the patient's needs for physical care with other physicians and physical therapists. The social worker provides linkage with the family and with governmental and social institutions. The fourth member of the team responsible for the planning of a specific programme is the patient himself.

The analyst is not part of the team and only enters the scene later, after the patient is admitted, thus avoiding contamination of the psychoanalytic process itself, and of its necessary confidentiality, by the practicalities of daily life and of the negotiations involved in developing an individual programme.

Other members of the staff present daily in the centre are: a half-time anthropologist or ethnoanalyst, a research worker, three analytic clinicians (two of whom are psychiatrists), a supervisor of meal preparation, one secretary, one nightwatchman, one person responsible for maintenance and upkeep. The 388 is open 24 hours a day, seven days a week, with a reduced staff during the night and on weekends.

The prospective 'usager' himself or herself must ask for admission, and requests by members of the family or other sources are met by a counter-request to have the patient call for an interview. This admission procedure may or may not of itself be a selective factor influencing the type of patients admitted: on this question one can only speculate. But most patients if not all have had two to three previous hospitalizations, and most patients – even those whose families or referring sources do not believe them capable of taking the initiative – do in fact call for appointments upon learning of this rule.

Once a request is made, an intervenant is appointed to welcome the patient, an intervenant who will then go on working with the patient if he or she is admitted. The intervenant conducts the patient on a tour of the building, answers his or her questions, and describes the programme and available services and activities, as well as the rules that regulate patterns of behaviour within the 388 – that is, that regulate the ethical choices available in the centre. These rules and regulations are also given in writing to the patient, and are often used later, after admission, as a basis for the negotiation of specific problems that may come up.

The patient then meets with the two members of the admission committee, a psychoanalyst and a psychiatrist, and information is obtained as to the patient's family structure and the patient's history. Further interviews on family history and family structure will be done later, individually, with the patient and other family members, by an ethnoanalyst.

I would like to conclude by describing two areas in which the collaboration of anthropological theory and psychoanalytical theory can be clearly seen in the setting up of the 388: (1) how studies of the structures of kinship and the family were used to inform the planning of the treatment programme, and (2) how both questions of social rules and the ethics of desire were used in order to establish a system of constraints and restraints that was in harmony with the goals of opening a place for speech.

In the years that preceded the opening of the 388, an interdisciplinary team of mostly anthropologists and analysts at GIFRIC started a study of the elementary structures of the families in Quebec, using transformations of and additions to Lévi-Strauss's (1949/1969) 'elementary structures of kinship'. (In his study Apollon also mentions Augé, 1975.) After the opening of the 388, the study was extended to the families of the patients. As these interviews progressed, it was noticed that certain specific structures generally appeared in the family of psychotics (Apollon, 1990, 1997b, 1999).

Apollon was interested in finding out what specific structures support the passing on of the paternal metaphor, which for Lacan is the basis of the child's ascension to subjectivity and to the symbolic order – that is, to the acceptance of the ethics of being human in the special way that a society and culture have of passing these ethics to the child. The paternal metaphor includes a paternal function (the cut that separates the child from the mother) and the 'Nom(non)-du-Père' (which supports the symbolic and its laws). The name of the father is passed on by the mother and made efficient by her good faith. But even when the mother's desire is to be the object of the father's desire, and his name is passed in good faith – even then certain relationships in the maternal matriline (the mother, her mother and her mother's mother), and in the paternal matriline may invalidate her word.

In the 'normal' structure the marriage of father and mother is part of a 'contract' that involves three women and one man: the child's mother, his mother's mother, the father's mother, and the father. This structure supports the Name-of-the-Father and the coexistence of the paternal and maternal clan. However, women from the mother's matriline may start rumours against the paternal mother and her matriline. Or the women in the matriline of the father's mother may start rumours that impute bad faith to the mother's word. In both these cases, pathology may result.

In the first case, the authority of the father may be destroyed, for the rumour started against his mother's lineage could harm his reputation as a representative of the symbolic and could invalidate the mother's word. This may lead to perversion (Apollon, 1999: 97–127). In the second case, the sense ('sens') itself of the symbolic may be destroyed, and even the possibility of coexistence between the maternal and paternal clans could be destroyed, thus invalidating any limits, which immediately brings up, for Apollon, the question of psychoses.

As for the question of constraints, the intake process, jointly established by anthropologists and analysts, illustrates how the psychotic patient is treated and expected to behave as a subject. In the words of Willy Apollon (1990: 355, my translation):

> Treating psychosis requires reconsideration of the civic status of the psychotic as a subject in today's society – as a responsible citizen who can establish social links, negotiate his place and satisfactions in life, and assume responsibility for his limitations and his sorrows, like all other

citizens. That is the reason why psychoanalysis entered the field of treatment of psychoses, not with a promise of cure – which has never been given either in the treatment of neuroses or perversions – but as a way of putting to work the very position of the subject, within the structure of his own unconscious.

In the 388 there are no locked doors, no physical restraints, and each patient participates in the formulation of his own programme and schedule. The 388 has two types of patients, those who reside there, generally because they are in crisis, when round the clock care is needed; and those who come for treatment during the day or the evening. How often the second group comes is decided by each individual in collaboration with the intervenant/therapist or the full team, but when the programme is decided upon it must be followed or renegotiated. Many programmes involve groups and activities, whether social, artistic or technical, and the usual social norms of the regional society must be respected.

Williams vividly describes in his report on the Maudsley unit how upsetting it was for the staff to withstand the aggressivity and hostility of patients, and the same is true in the 388. However, in spite of many norms and rules, actual cases of violence or vandalism by patients are very rare. In more than twenty years only ten cases – all of them involving the destruction of physical objects rather than physical violence towards others – were serious enough to warrant the only imposed consequence, the ending of the patient's connection with the 388. A way is left open for readmission, should the patient again ask for treatment and go through a second admission process. Readmission is not always asked for; of those asked, only two have been refused.

The opening up of a space for speech, the unusual experience of being listened to and asked to give opinions, the psychoanalytic sessions which are treated with total confidentiality, seem to enable patients to rely on language in order to deal with their rage and problems: this, in spite of the flaws they know language has and of the many uncertainties it will introduce in their lives.

## Coda *Waud Kracke and Lucia Villela*

Let us return to the question posed at the outset of this discussion of treatment programmes. Why are anthropologists so drawn to psychosis? Perhaps it is because what psychosis puts into question is culture itself. This is evident in Williams's description of the anxiety provoked in health workers at Maudsley when confronted by psychotic patients and, indeed, in the very goal of trying to *change* the inner world of the psychotic. In psychoanalytic treatment of the neurotic, we are content to promote the neurotic finding an *understanding* of the core of the neurosis; we leave it to the patient to reach such an understanding (helped, perhaps, by the questions we pose to him), and to decide on his own in what way to change – or not to. The enduring success of the programme at the 388 is based on extending this fundamental principle of psychoanalysis to the psychotic: opening a space for the psychotic to speak, to articulate his delusion and provoking the psychotic himself or herself to come to his or her understanding of it (not evading crises on the way), then allowing the psychotic to come to his or her own integration. To permit this process to unfold, however, we must confront the participants in it with a challenge to their own cultural centring. The psychotic's delusion calls into question that culturally constituted consensual world that we call 'reality', and shows it for the conventional fiction that it is.

The seven anthropologists interviewed by Anthony Molino in this volume have opened some hitherto unexplored avenues of collaboration between anthropology and psychoanalysis, and given fresh perspectives on some of the old questions.

Psychoanalysis is discovering the profound linkage between symbols, culture and language in structuring the psyche. All of the contributions to this volume come together in this, but take it in diverse ways: looking for communication, or for the holes in language that make communication necessarily incomplete; constructing symbolic ways to articulate our fragmented pains, or performances to avoid being caught in an identity; facing fear of the other (psychotic, spirit, alien) or seeking community with him. In this volume we have seven different perspectives, coming from multiple schools of psychoanalysis – Freudian, Object relations, Lacanian – which direct themselves to diverse problems (psychosis, religious stigmata, marginalization, globalization, encounters with the other . . .) but with several common concerns: concern with identities and alterity, coherence and fragmentation, symbolization as efficacy or as complicity in covering mutual misperception.

Susanne Langer said half a century ago that each epoch is marked by key questions that cluster around certain generative ideas – certain (generally unconscious) motive concepts. The end of an epoch is heralded by the exhaustion of its motive concepts, signalled by the fragmentation of theories into questions which can be answered in contradictory but equally persuasive ways that do not rule each other out. Perhaps we are at the limiting edge of an epoch, entering a new horizon, to face yet undivined questions, stemming from new motive concepts that are still in formation, yet to be discovered. The age of symbolization, which Langer saw looming on the horizon in 1942, may be about to end. Or to be transformed in ways that we cannot yet imagine.

## Notes

1. Kroeber's underlying ambivalence towards Freud is evident in his 1920 review of Freud's *Totem and Taboo*, which (despite his later, more considered 1939 re-review) has set the anthropological view of that work for the rest of the century. Robert Paul (1976) has refuted Kroeber's dismissal of Freud's myth of the murder of the primal father ('just-so story' as Freud characterized it), pointing out that Freud's tale of prehistory metaphorically presented the major task human evolution had to perform in establishing human society: to transform a social order based on dominance hierarchy into one based on rules. Lévi-Strauss's discussion of the evolution of rules (1949/1969: 3–51, the first four chapters of *Elementary Structures*) unabashedly adapts Freud's argument point for point, but puts it in more abstract terms more palatable to anthropological sensibilities. Anthropologists cannot tolerate a mythic form of expression in their discipline!
2. Meyer Fortes confirmed this supposition on my part in a personal conversation.
3. Lucie Cantin (2002) has an excellent explication of Lacan's point of view on language.
4. I found this last sentence written in my handwriting of years ago on a slip of paper tucked into *Tuhami*. I have not so far located it in the book; perhaps it is something from 'Saints, Jnun and dreams' that I found apposite as I read *Tuhami*, perhaps it is my own reworking of something Crapanzano wrote – although the marks of his fluency are in it, so I believe it is his.
5. The Russian Wolf Man led Freud (1918: 104) to reflections on the difficulty of 'feeling one's way into the patient's mind'. Ferenczi's patients, of course, were mainly Hungarian, prompting Freud's (1900: 99n) observation that 'every tongue has its own dream language'. Later, Akiro Kosawa, the founder of Japanese psychoanalysis, was analysed by one of Freud's circle.
6. See the last section of this Afterword.
7. *Studies on Hysteria* (Freud, 1895: 152). Lacan's terms *signifier* and *letter in the body* relate to Freud's understanding of the structure of such symptoms, but generalize it to a level above pathology. They highlight Freud's view that hysterical symptoms are not special stigmata, but rather manifestations of human processes we all share. Lacan's terms embrace symptoms, religious rituals which 'write' on the body, and all of those processes we share as humans that link an outward manifestation (a fantasy, an act, a bodily mark or feature or malfunction) with those unconscious principles that govern our lives.
8. Due to the strong support given to psychoanalysis by Trotsky, whose brother suffered from psychosis.
9. In a 1962 interview with Thomas Kuhn and Aage Peterson, Bohr indicated that his concept of indeterminacy – the electron's position will be changed by the photon used to observe it – was inspired by reading William James's (1950) observation that the act of introspection modifies the thought processes being observed (Holton, 1970: 1034–5).
10. In 1982, the anthropologically trained analyst Willy Apollon, along with his colleagues psychiatrist Danielle Bergeron and psychologist Lucie Cantin, founded the

successful '388' treatment programme in Quebec (Apollon, Bergeron and Cantin, 1990), which from its very inception was jointly designed by anthropologists and analysts. A key part of the 388 programme is to create conditions in which the psychotic can re-establish a social link. Anthropological research is thus a central part of this programme, which will be described in detail in the last part of this section.
11. Information on this programme was gathered from visits to the site and interviews with staff and patients, as well as from published information. We are especially grateful for the help received from Benoit Belanger, 'intervenant' at the 388 and analyst in private practice, and from Denis Morin, ethnoanalyst and researcher at the 388 and analyst in private practice.

# References

Apollon W (1990) Conclusion. In: Apollon, Bergeron and Cantin, Traiter les psychoses. Quebec: GIFRIC, pp. 355–57.
Apollon W (1997a) Questions de la psychanalyse à l'anthropologie. In: L'Universel, perspectives psychanalytiques. Quebec: Collection le Savoir Analytique, pp. 109–18.
Apollon W (1997b) Problematique.../ de la recherche sur les discours et les structures familiales. Savoir 3: 217–37.
Apollon W (1999) Psychoses: L'offre de l'analyste. Quebec: GIFRIC.
Apollon W, Cloutier B (1990) L'ethnoanalyse et la famille. In: W Apollon, D Bergeron, L Cantin (eds), Traiter les psychoses. Quebec: GIFRIC.
Apollon W, Bergeron D, Cantin L (1990) Traiter la psychose. Quebec: GIFRIC.
Apollon W, Bergeron D, Cantin L (2002) After Lacan (ed. R Hughes, K Malone). Albany, NY: SUNY Press.
Augé, M (1975) Les domaines de la parenté. Paris: Maspero.
Augé, M (1997/1999) The War of Dreams: Studies in Ethno-fiction. London: Pluto Press, 1999 (original French: Editions du Seuil).
Bateson MC (1968) Insight in a bicultural context. Philippine Studies 16: 605–21.
Bird B (1972) Notes on transference: universal phenomenon and hardest part of analysis. Journal of the American Psychoanalytic Association 20: 267–300.
Cantin L (2002) The trauma of language. In: W Apollon, D Bergeron, L Cantin (eds), After Lacan, (ed. R Hughes, K Malone). Albany, NY: SUNY Press, pp. 35–47.
Crapanzano V (1975) Saints, Jnun and dreams: an essay on Moroccan ethnopsychology. Psychiatry 38: 145–59. Reprinted in: V Crapanzano, Hermes' Dilemma and Hamlet's Desire: On the Epistemology of Interpretation. Cambridge, MA: Harvard University Press, 1992, pp. 239–259.
Crapanzano V (1980) Tuhami: Portrait of a Moroccan. Chicago: University of Chicago Press.
Crapanzano V (1981) Text, transference and indexicality. Ethos 9: 122–148. Reprinted in: V Crapanzano, Hermes' Dilemma and Hamlet's Desire: On the Epistemology of Interpretation. Cambridge, MA: Harvard University Press, 1992, pp. 115–135.

DaMatta R (1978) O ofício de etnólogo, ou como ter 'anthropological blues'. Boletín do Museu Nacional de Antropologia 27 (May).
Devereux G (1967) From Anxiety to Method in the Behavioral Sciences. The Hague: Mouton.
Devereux G (1978) The argument. In: Ethnopsychoanalysis. Berkeley, CA: University of California Press, Ch. 1, pp. 1–18.
Etkind A (1995) Russia until 1989. In P Kutter (ed.), Psychoanalysis International, vol. 2 (America, Asia, Australia and Further European countries), pp. 333–44. Stuttgart: Frommann-Holzboorg.
Ewing KP (1987) Clinical psychoanalysis as an ethnographic tool. Ethos 15: 16–39.
Ewing KP (1990a) The illusion of wholeness: culture, self and the experience of inconsistency. Ethos 18: 251–78.
Ewing KP (1990b) The dream of spiritual initiation and the organization of self representations among Pakistani Sufis. American Ethnologist 17: 56–74.
Ewing KP (1997) Arguing Sainthood: Modernity, Psychoanalysis and Islam. Durham, NC: Duke University Press.
Fortes M (1949) Tensions in the parent–child relationship. In: The Web of Kinship among the Tallensi. Oxford: Oxford University Press, Ch. 8, pp. 222–35.
Fortes M (1961) Pietas and ancestor worship. Reprinted in: Time and Social Structure and Other Essays. London: Prometheus Books, 1990.
Fortes M (1966) Totem and taboo. Proceedings of the Royal Anthropological Institute: 5–22.
Fortes M (1977) Custom and conscience in anthropological perspective. International Review of Psychoanalysis 4: 127–54.
Freud S (1895) Studies on Hysteria. Standard Edition of the Complete Psychological Works of Sigmund Freud, vol. 2. London: Hogarth.
Freud S (1900) The interpretation of dreams. S.E. vols. 4–5.
Freud S (1905) Fragment of an Analysis of a Case of Hysteria (The Case of Dora). S.E. vol. 7, pp. 3–122.
Freud S (1907) Obsessive actions and religious practices. S.E. vol. 9, pp. 117–27.
Freud S (1908) 'Civilized' sexual morality and modern nervousness. S.E. vol. 9, pp. 179–204.
Freud S (1912) The dynamics of the transference. S.E. vol. 12, pp. 99–108.
Freud S (1913–14) Totem and Taboo. S.E. vol. 13.
Freud S (1914a) Remembering, repeating and working through (Further recommendations on the technique of psychoanalysis II). S.E. vol. 12, pp. 145–56.
Freud S (1914b) Observations on transference love (Further recommendations on the technique of psychoanalysis III). S.E. vol. 12, pp. 159–71.
Freud S (1918) From the history of an infantile neurosis. S.E. vol. 10, pp. 7–122.
Freud S (1930) Civilization and Its Discontents. S.E. vol. 21, pp. 64–145.
Freud S (1937) Constructions in Analysis. S.E. vol. 23, pp. 255–69.
Geertz C (1966) The impact of the concept of culture on the concept of man. In: C. Geertz (ed), The Interpretation of Culture. New York: Basic Books, 1978, pp. 33–54.
Hallowell AI (1938) Fear and anxiety as cultural and individual variables in a primitive society. In: Hallowell (1955), ch. 13.
Hallowell AI (1940) Aggression in Saulteaux society. In: Hallowell (1955), ch. 15.

Hallowell AI (1941) The social function of anxiety in a primitive society. In: Hallowell (1955), ch. 14.
Hallowell AI (1949) Psychosexual adjustment, personality and the good life in a nonliterate culture. In: Hallowell (1955), ch. 16.
Hallowell AI (1954) The self in its behavioral environment. In: Hallowell (1955), ch. 4.
Hallowell AI (1955) Culture and Experience. Philadelphia, PA: University of Pennsylvania Press (reprinted New York: Shocken, 1967, and Westview Press, 1995).
Henderson B (1980) 'The Searchers': an American dilemma. In B Nichols (ed.), Movies and Methods, vol. 2. Berkeley: University of California Press.
Holton G (1970) The Roots of Complementarity (The Making of Modern Science: Biographical Studies). Daedalus: Journal of the American Academy of Arts and Sciences, Fall.
James W (1950) The stream of thought. In: Principles of Psychology, vol. 1. New York: Dover.
Kracke W (1978) Force and Persuasion: Leadership in an Amazonian Society. Chicago: University of Chicago Press.
Kracke W (1980) The complementarity of social and psychological regularities. Ethos 8: 273–85.
Kracke W (1981) Amazonian interviews: dreams of a bereaved father. Annual of Psychoanalysis 8: 249–67.
Kracke W (1984) Commentary: Malinowski and the Sphynx. (Discussion of Spiro, 1984). In: J Gedo, G Pollock (eds), Psychoanalysis: The Vital Issues, Vol. 1, pp. 201–12.
Kracke W (1987) Encounter with other cultures. Ethos 15: 58–81.
Kracke W (1994) The savage self: introspection, emphathy and anthropology. In: M Suarez-Orozco, G Spindler, L Spindler (eds), The Making of Psychological Anthropology II. New York: Harcourt-Brace, 1994, pp. 195–222.
Kracke W (1999) A language of dreaming: dreams of an Amazonian insomniac. International Journal of Psychoanalysis 80: 257–71.
Kracke W (2000) Culture shock. In: The International Encyclopedia of the Behavioral Sciences. London: Elsevier.
Kracke W (2003) Psychoanalysis and anthropology. Encyclopedia of Medical Anthropology. New Haven, CT: Human Relations Area Files, Yale University Press, pp. 58–68.
Kroeber A (1920) Totem and Taboo: an ethnographic psychoanalysis. American Anthropologist 22: 48–55. Reprinted in: W Lessa, E Vogt (eds), Reader in Comparative Religion: An Anthropological Approach. New York: HarperCollins, 1979.
Kroeber A (1939) Totem and Taboo in retrospect. In: W Lessa, E Vogt (eds), Reader in Comparative Religion: An Anthropological Approach. New York: HarperCollins, 1979.
Lacan J (1949/1977) The mirror stage as a formative of the function of the I. In: A Sheridan (tr.), Ecrits: A Selection. New York: Norton, pp. 1–7.
Lacan J (1953) Le mythe individuel du névrosé, ou Poésie et Vérité dans la névrose. Centre de Documentation Universitaire, Paris.

Lacan J (1953/1979) The neurotic's individual myth. Psychoanalytic Quarterly 48 (1979): 366–404.
Lacan J (1953–54) Seminar 1: Freud's Papers on Technique. New York: Norton, 1988.
Lacan J (1955–56) Seminar 3: The Psychoses. New York: Norton, 1993.
Lacan J (1959–60) Seminar 7: The Ethics of Psychoanalysis. New York: Norton, 1992.
Lambo TA (1978) Psychotherapy in Africa. Human Nature (March).
Langer S (1942) Philosophy in a New Key. Cambridge, MA: Harvard University Press.
Lévi-Strauss C (1949) L'efficacité symbolique. In: Revue de'Histoire des Religions 135(1): 5–27; reissued in Antropologie Structurale. Paris: Plon, 1958.
Lévi-Strauss C (1949/1969) Elementary Structures of Kinship, tr. JH Bell, R von Sturmer; ed. R Needham. Boston, MA: Beacon Press.
Lévi-Strauss C (1955) Tristes Tropiques. Paris: Plon (French).
Lévi-Strauss C (1949/1963) The effectiveness of symbols. Translation of L'efficacité symbolique. In: Symbolic Anthropology, tr. C Jacobson, BG Scheopf. New York: Basic Books, pp. 186–205.
Lévi-Strauss C (1961) Tristes Tropiques, tr. J Russell. New York: Athenaeum, 1970.
Loewald H (1960) On the therapeutic action of psychoanalysis. International Journal of Psychoanalysis 41: 16–33. Reprinted in: Papers in Psychoanalysis. New Haven, CT: Yale University Press, 1980, pp. 221–56; and in G Fogel (ed.), The Work of Hans Loewald. Northvale, NJ: Jason Aronson, 1991, pp. 13–60.
Malinowski B (1935) An ethnographic theory of language. In: Coral Gardens and their Magic, vol. 2: The Language of Magic and Gardening. Bloomington, IN: Indiana University Press, 1965, pp. 3–74.
Metz C (1975) The Imaginary Signifier: Psychoanalysis and the Cinema. Bloomington, IN: Indiana University Press.
Obeyesekere G (1981) Medusa's Hair: An Essay in Personal Symbols and Religious Experience. Chicago: University of Chicago Press.
Obeyesekere G (1990) The Work of Culture. Chicago: University of Chicago Press.
Paul RA (1976) Did the primal crime take place? Ethos 4: 311–52.
Paul RA (1996) Moses and Civilization. New Haven, CT: Yale University Press.
Radcliffe-Brown AR (1922) The Andaman Islanders. Cambridge: Cambridge University Press. Reissued: Glencoe, IL: The Free Press, 1964.
Radcliffe-Brown AR (1940) On joking relationships. Africa 13: 195–210. Reprinted in: Structure and Function in Primitive Society, Glencoe, IL: The Free Press, 1952, pp. 90–116.
Rustin M (1991) The Good Society and the Inner World. London: Verso.
Rustin M (2001) Reason and Unreason: Psychoanalysis, Science and Politics. Middletown, CT: Wesleyan University Press.
Sapir E (1927/1949) The unconscious patterning of behavior in society. In: ES Dummer (ed.), The Unconscious: A Symposium. New York: Knopf, pp. 114–42. Reprinted in: DG Mandelbaum (ed.), The Selected Writings of Edward Sapir. Berkeley, CA: University of California Press, 1949, pp. 544–59.
Sapir E (1934/1949) The emergence of the concept of personality in a study of cultures. Journal of Social Psychology 5: 408–15. Reprinted in: DG

Mandelbaum (ed.), The Selected Writings of Edward Sapir. Berkeley, CA: University of California Press, 1949, pp. 590–97.
Spiro M (1979) Whatever happened to the id? American Anthropologist 81: 5–13.
Spiro M (1982) Oedipus in the Trobriands. Chicago: University of Chicago Press.
Spiro M (1984) Psychoanalysis and cultural relativism: The Trobriand case. In: J Gedo, G Pollock (eds), Psychoanalysis: The Vital Issues, vol. 1, pp. 165–82.
Spiro M (2003) The anthropological import of blocked access to dream associations. In: J Mageo (ed.), Dreaming and the Self. Albany, NY: SUNY Press.
Toulmin S (1978) Psychoanalysis, physics and the mind–body problem. Annual of Psychoanalysis 6: 315–51.
Toulmin S (1981) On knowing our own minds. Annual of Psychoanalysis 9: 207–21.
Toulmin S (1991) The archaeology of the emotions. Annual of Psychoanalysis 19: 51–7.
Turner V (1964) Symbols in Ndembu ritual. In: The Forest of Symbols. Ithaca, NY: Cornell University Press, pp. 19–47.
Villela L (1999) From film as case study to film as myth: psychoanalytic perspectives on cinema and culture. Annual of Psychoanalysis 26/27: 315–30.
Villela L (2000) Executors of an ancient pact. In: K Malone, S Friendlander (eds), The Subject of Lacan. Albany, NY: SUNY Press, pp. 345–60.
Villela L (2003) Western perspective on a film from the East: 'Not One Less'. Psychoanalytic Review 90: 125–39.
Vitebsky P (1993) Dialogues with the Dead. Cambridge: Cambridge University Press.
Wallace ER IV (1983) Freud and Anthropology: A History and Reappraisal. New York: International Universities Press.
Williams P, Jackson M (1994) Unimaginable Storms: A Search for Meaning in Psychosis. London: Karnac.

# Index

n after a page number refers to a numbered note on that page

adaptational psychodynamics (Kardiner), 10
agency, 54
  equation with the subject, 95
aggression: as universal trait, 106
alterity, 38, 171
  identity and, 186
  problems of, 164
Althusser L, 157
anthropology
  and the affective spheres, 14
  anti-psychology bias in, 83
  crisis in, 28
  early history of, 3–19 *passim*
  Marxist approaches, 15n
  orthodox scientific model, 105
  and participant observation, 192–4
  postmodern, 135
  psychoanalysis and, 101–2, 175–209
  psychoanalytic, 49, 185–7
  and psychosis, 192–4
  relationship with psychoanalysis, 20–42
  resistance in, 70–1
  'touchy–feely', 78
  the unconscious and, 51–2
Apollon W, 194, 196–7, 201–2, 204–5n
*Arguing Sainthood* (Ewing), xii, 17n, 80, 84, 96–7, 187–8
Augé M, xii, xiii, 36–8 *passim*, 156–71
  biographical details, 156–7
awareness: development of, 60

Bakhtin M, 143
basic personality structure (Kardiner), 10
being there, 87–8
Benedict R, 16n
Benveniste E, 94–5
Bhaskar R, 117
binary oppositions, 105–6
Bion WR, 129–30
  container-contained, 128
  personality types, 110–11
Boas F, 5, 16n
bodily remembrance, 148
body: as permeable space, 149
Bohr N, 204n
Bollas C, 27–8, 33, 34, 138, 169
Boyer LB, 192
Buddhism, 60
*Buddhism Transformed* (Obeyesekere), 51
bureaucratic self (the), 144

Cantin L, 204n
capitalism
  globalizing nature of, 13
  individualism and, 53
  *see also* globalization
Cardinal M, 58
case study: as an imprisoning genre, 78
catastrophic change, 129–32
  Bion on, 129–30
Chodorow N, 38n, 39n, 41n, 114
*Civilization and its Discontents* (Freud), 177
clinical ethnography, 29, 114
collective subjectivity view, 7–8
collective unconscious (the), 167–8
colonization, 167

Comaroff J & J, 32–5 *passim*
complementarity (Devereux), 186
conceptual strings, 108
consulting room: as laboratory, 118–20 *passim*
consumerism: individuality of, 163
container-contained (Bion), 128
'contamination' (Stewart), 26
  of theorizing, 139
counter-transference
  conceptualizing, 68–9
  in fieldwork, 94
  recognition in anthropology, 108
*Crafting Selves* (Kondo), 93
Crapanzano V, xi, xiii, 4, 14, 37, 57–8, 63–79, 91–2, 179, 189–90
  biographical details, 63
creativity: and totalitarianism, 167
*Cruelty, Violence and Murder* (Williams), 132–3
*Cult of the Goddess Pattini, The*, 49–50
culture, 175, 180
  constitutive aspect of, 177
  crisis of, 169
  defined, 85–6
  and desire, 148
  discomfort with notion, 170
  as mode of questioning, 139–40
  shock, 184, 189, 193

decentred processes, 90
defences, 96
depth models: hostility to, 141
desire, 175
  and culture, 148
  Herdt and Stoller on, 30–1
  nature of, 145, 147–8
  social control of, 177
  theory of, 60
Devereux G, 49, 56, 186
*Devil and Commodity Fetishism, The* (Taussig), 32–3
dialogue, 73–4
'diary disease', 39n
dis-membering, 150–1
'dissemination' (Bollas), 27, 39n
dreams, 166–7
  Moroccan dream theory, 70
  Tuhami's, 76

drive theory: culturalist rejection of, 9
dualism: subject-object, 142
DuBois C, 10, 11
Durkheim E, 16n
  collective subjectivity view, 7–8

ego: idea of the cohesive, 87
ego psychology, 53, 56–7
Ellenberger H, 16n
Elliott A, 17n, 38n
empathy: courage for, 78
empiricism: critique of, 16n
  *see also* positivism
Erikson E, 49
erotomania: danger of, 195
ethnographic authoritarianism, 57–8
ethnography, 25, 26,
  under erasure, 70
  and frame of reference, 132–3
  Herdt and Stoller on, 30
  and narcissism, 20
  person-centred, 39, 114
  postmodern turn in, 26
  *sine qua non* of, 47
  subject-object relations of, 140
  transference and, 179
  *see also* clinical ethnography, ethnographic authoritarianism
ethno-self-analysis (Augé), 164
Ewing K, xii, xiii, 3–4, 17n, 20–1, 28–9, 37, 80–97,
  biography, 80–1
experience
  denial of, 78
  non-unitary, 110
  primacy of, 60

fantasy, 17n, 38n
fashioning (Stewart), 146
feminism, 76
fieldwork, 52, 92–3, 161–2
  Augé on, 158–9
  constraints of, 186
  counter/transferences in, 94, 107–8
  Crapanzano on, 64, 67, 75
  encounters with, 120–2
  ethics of, 75
  Ewing on, 81

Obeyesekere on, 47–48
positivist ideology of, 29
reflection on, 67
Rustin on, 133–4
Stewart on, 141
Williams on, 99–101
Fischer M, 26–8 *passim*
Fortes M, 176
forgetting, 170
foundationalism: psychoanalytic, 72
Freud S, 53, 57, 101, 117
  anthropological critique of,
    5–12 *passim*
  -bashing, 12
  conjuncture with Weber, 54
  deep influence of, 176–7
  on the father, 58
  on hysteria, 204n
  influenced by anthropology, 177
  Malinowski's encounter with, 6
  retreat from decentred subject, 187–8
  on transference, 190
  and treatment of psychosis, 195
  *see also* psychoanalysis

Geertz C, 4, 15n, 21–2, 67, 85, 129
  critique of, 29, 54
  on objectivity, 92
genre: routinization of, 77
GIFRIC, 194
globalization, 185, 197
  of capitalism, 13
Green A, 161

Hallowell AI, 177
Herdt G, 29–31, 39–40n
hermeneutics, 51
  loop, 145
*Hermes' Dilemma and Hamlet's Desire*
  (Crapanzano), xii
history: memory and forgetting in, 5
Hopkins J, 108
hysterical symptoms, 180–1, 204n

I Ching, 73
identity, 38, 142
  and alterity, 186
  crisis of, 169
  ideology and fixed, 95

preconscious construction of, 186
  as a process, 94
images: role of, 166–7, 168
imaginary, the, 147, 167
imagination: poles of human, 166–7
implicit, the (*vis-à-vis* the unconscious)
  (Ewing), 89
indexicality, 189
individuality: vs individualism, 53
infant observation, 126–8 *passim*
  development of, 119
inner (the), 159–60
inner/outer boundary, 39n
innovation, 77
interiority: critique of, 144–5
interpretivism: Geertz's, 29
interview
  analytically inspired, 39n
  anthropological (Ewing), 84
  *genre* of the, x
  leading questions, 67
  open-ended questions, 84
  the psychoanalytic, 30
*Intimate Communications* (Herdt and
  Stoller), 29, 39–40n
Islam, 80

Jackson M, 130, 193
Jacobs M, 47
Jones E, 55
Jones M, 110

Kardiner A, 6, 9–11
knowledge generation (Latour), 117
*Knowledge and Passion* (Rosaldo), 22–3
Kohut H, 82
Kondo D, 93
Kovel J, 103–4
Kracke WH, viii, 175–94, 202–9
Kristeva J, 96, 137–8, 164
Kroeber AL, 6, 176, 204n
Kuhn TS, 117

Lacan J, 12, 14, 17n, 64–5, 87, 177,
  187–8, 191, 204n
  rewording of Freud, 181
  on transference, 68–9
  and treatment of psychosis, 195
Lambo TA, 192–3

language, 64–5
  pragmatics of, 189
Latour B, 117
Lemieux R, 194
letter on the body, 181–3
Lévi-Strauss C, 176–7, 190–2, 204n
libido theory
  Kardiners's revision of, 9, 10
  Malinowski on, 8–9
liminality, 130
Linton R, 10
*Local Knowledge* (Geertz), 129
Loewald H, 190
loneliness
  collective, 165
  of the consumer, 163

'Madman and the migrant, The' (Comaroffs), 32–5 *passim*
madness: *see* psychosis
magic: as response to oppression, 33
Malinowski B, 6–9, 134
  encounter with Freud, 6
  on libido theory, 8–9
  psychoanalytic critique of, 8
Marcus G, 23–4
Maudsley Hospital study (Williams), 98–101 *passim*, 108–9, 115, 124–5, 19–4 *passim*, 202
  and 388 project, 198–9, 202
Mead M, 9, 16n, 134
meaning: Weber on, 54
medical intervention, 75
*Medusa's Hair* (Obeyesekere), xi, 50, 54, 181
memory, 151, 154. 170
  *see also* bodily remembrance
methodological objectivism, 49
methodology: human element of, 179
Miller E, xiv
modal personality type (DuBois), 11
modernity
  end of, 157
  presumption of, 91
  surpassing of, 166
  *see also* supermodernity
Molino A, vii, 20–42
Moroccan dream theory, 70
motivational structure, 87, 88

Multiple Personality Disorder:
  emergence of, 103
multiple selves, 142
multiplicity
  experience of, 91
  *see also* Multiple Personality Disorder
myth, 192

narrativity, 137
negative capability (Keats), 78, 131
neutral observation, 126
*Non-Places* (Augé), 157, 162–3, 168
  and ego, 164
*Nurturing Doubt* (Miller), xiv

O: receptivity to (Bion), 130
Obeyesekere G, xi, xiii, 37, 41n, 45–62, 91–2, 180
  biographical details, 45–6
  lifework of, 47–8
object relations: phylogenetic evolution of, 102
'Obsessive acts and religious practices' (Freud), 182
Oedipus complex/story, 46
  Lévi-Strauss on, 176–7
  Malinowski on, 8
  in *Totem and Taboo*, 7
other (the): as image, 169
over-determination, 157, 163

paranoia, 112
Parsons T, 54
participant observation, 192–4
patient's narrative, 58
Pattini cult, 46, 49–50
Paul R, 204n
performativity, 137
personal symbol (Obeyesekere), 180–2 *passim*
personality
  basic personality structure, 10
  modal personality type, 11
  Multiple Personality Disorder, 103
psychotic vs non-psychotic, 110–12
play, 88
poetics of the everyday, 33, 35
positivism
  critique of, 39n

# Index

in fieldwork, 29
in psychoanalytic anthropology, 49
the unconscious and, 26–7
*see also* empiricism
postmodernism
  anthropological critique of, 66
  anthropology and, 135
  critique of, 170
  in ethnography, 26
  *see also* supermodernity
power, 87
pre-symbolic mentation, 112–13
primary process, 110
psyche: need for model of, 13
psychoanalysis, 132
  anthropological view of, 12
  and anthropology, 101–2, 175–209
  as anthropology of the subject, 169
  case histories in, 97
  and context of observation, 123
  crisis of identity, 25–6
  criticism of, 129
  'culturist', 9
  diffusion of, 119
  early history of, 3–19 *passim*
  an ethnography, 135
  as form of poetry, 34
  French model, 88
  as ideology, 6
  the interview in, 30
  methodology of, 179–80
  revolutionary position of, 185
  as science, 117, 128, 183–5
  similarities with shamanism, 191
  and social theory, 38
  sociology of, 133–4
  symbolic effectiveness in, 190–2
  universalizing claims of, 106
  *see also* Freud S, psychoanalytic anthropology
'Psychoanalysis and anthropology' (Jones), 55
psychoanalytic interview: and ethnographic practice, 30
psychoanalytic anthropology, 49
  defined, 185–7
psychohistory, 49
psychosis, 98, 109–14 *passim*, 124–5
  anthropology and, 192–4

erotomania, 195
treatment of, 180,
'388' programme, 194–202,
  204–5n *see also* GIFRIC
*see also* psychotic anxiety
psychotic anxiety: universality of, 110, 113
public/private dichotomy, 96

Radcliffe-Brown AR, 176
Rapoport R, 110
rationality: as myth, 55–6
reflexivity, 39n
  real, 93
  *see also* self-reflexivity
relativity, 184
re-membering, 150–1
repression, 146
resistance: in anthropology, 70–1
*Retelling a Life* (Schafer), 138
Ricoeur P, 20, 51
Rivers WHR, 55
Roland A, 3
Rosaldo M, 22–3
routinization: avoiding, 77
Rustin M, xiii, 14, 16n, 38, 116–36, 183
  biographical details, 116

Sapir E, 9
Sartre J-P, 95
Schafer R, 138
Schiller H, 37
science, 117
  psychoanalysis as, 117, 128, 183–5
scientism, 106
self (the), 110, 111
  African models of, 158–9
  different meanings of, 103
  expansive sense of, 153–4
  as experiencing centre, 142
  political model of, 142–3
  postmodern, 143
  Sartre's notion, 95
  unitary model of, 103
  *see also* multiple selves
'Self in a world of urgency, The' (Wikan), 65–6
self-consciousness, 70
self-psychology, 82

self-reflexivity, 93
  see also reflexivity
sexuality: 103
  see also libido theory
'shadow dialogues', 3–19 *passim*, 68
shamanism, 190–1
Shumar W, viii, 3–19
social exclusion, 120–2
social science: totalizing, 65
solitude, 163–4
space
  new forms of, 161
  shrinking of, 186
*Space on the Side of the Road, A* (Stewart), 137, 143, 150–5 *passim*
Spiro ME, 47, 187
Sri Lanka, 48
Stewart K, xiii, 26, 35–8 *passim*, 137–55
  biographical details, 137–8
Stocking G, 7–9 *passim*
Stoller RJ, 29–31, 39–40n
stories, 94
storytelling, 137
structuralism, 85
*Structure of Scientific Revolutions, The* (Kuhn), 117
subject (the)
  bureaucratic, 144
  decentred, 143
  reification of, 95
  social construction of, 139
  split, 143
  universal, 143–4
*Subject to Ourselves* (Elliott), 17n, 38n
subjectivity:
  anthropology's withdrawal from, 30
  fieldworker's own, 134
  as performance, 142
supermodernity, 156, 162–3
symbolism
  cultural symbols, 182
  public vs private, 54
symbolic effectiveness, 190–2
  see also personal symbol
symbolization
  age of, 203–4
  capacity for, 112–13
Taussig M, 32–3, 150

Taylor C, 60–1
'Text transference and indexicality' (Crapanzano), 189
theory
  contaminated theorizing, 139
  and experience, 78
third, the (Crapanzano), 79
time
  acceleration of, 165
  shrinking of, 186
*Totem and Taboo* (Freud), 177, 204n
  Oedipal story in, 7
Toulmin S, 183
transference, 188–90
  conceptualizing, 68–9
  and ethnography, 179
  in fieldwork, 94, 107–8, 188–90
  Lacan on, 68–9
  one's own, 188–9
  towards culture, 189
transitional space, 161
trans-subjective relations (Bakhtin), 139
trauma–affect model, 102
Trobriand society, 7–8
*Tuhami* (Crapanzano), xi, 39n, 57–8, 74–7, 178
Turner V, 15n, 130, 182

unconscious (the), 106–7, 118, 141, 184
  anthropology and, 51–2, 187–8
  Bollas's model of, 27–8
  collective, 167–8
  fate of the individual, 168–9
  infinite sets of, 106
  inhabited by *beings*, 55
  the political, 141
  positivist view of, 26–7
  reifying of, 89–90, 95–6
unforgetting, 154
*Unimaginable Storms* (Williams), 98, 114–15

Villela L, vii–ix, 190–209
*Vital Impacts* (Stewart), 138
Waddell M, 131
*War of Dreams, The* (Augé), 36–7, 162, 166, 185–6, 192

Weber M, 54
Whiting JWM, 52
Wikan U, 65–6
Will D, 117
Williams AH, 132–3
Williams MH, 131
Williams P, xii, xiii, 14, 37, 98–115, 124, 193–4, 202
  biographical details, 98

Winnicott DW, 58–60 *passim*, 87
  on presence, 87–8
Wittgenstein L, 130–1
*Words to Say It, The* (Cardinal), 58
*Work of Culture, The* (Obeyesekere), xi–xii, 49–52 *passim*
*Works and Lives* (Geertz), 21–2

Žižek S, 14–15,